QUEST FOR BETTER BETTER PREACHING

QUEST
FOR BETTER
PREACHING

Resources for Renewal in the Pulpit

Edward F. Markquart

AUGSBURG Publishing House • Minneapolis

QUEST FOR BETTER PREACHING
Resources for Renewal in the Pulpit

Scripture quotations unless otherwise noted are from the Revised Standard Version of the Bible, copyright 1946, 1952, and 1971 by the Division of Christian Education of the National Council of Churches.

Library of Congress Cataloging-in-Publication Data

Markquart, Edward F., 1940-
  QUEST FOR BETTER PREACHING.

  Bibliography: p.
  1. Preaching. I. Title.
BV4211.2.M274   1985   251   85-13500
ISBN 0-8066-2170-2

Manufactured in the U.S.A.   APH 10-5349

      2   3   4   5   6   7   8   9   0   1   2   3   4   5   6   7   8   9

To the members of Grace Lutheran Church in Des Moines, Washington. They are indeed the people of God in whom Jesus lives. I have appreciated their love for my family, their love for each other, their willingness to listen to the gospel, their fight against world hunger and social injustices, their opening their homes and hearts to refugees, and their commitment to evangelism. My life has been blessed to have lived and moved among them.

Given the text,
Given the people I know and love,
Given the world in which I live,
The important question is:

"Lord, what is your message for this
Sunday in this time and place? What
do you want me to say? Give me the power,
the words, and the courage to say it."

Contents

Preface

This book would not have been pos-
sible without the help of many good friends. Especially, I am grateful
to: Eilleen Jobe, my faithful transcriber and typist; Dr. Roland Mar-
tinson, Dr. Douglas Anderson, and Dr. Charles Mays who, as theologians, read and critiqued the manuscript; Carolynn Spies, Darlene
Malmo, and David Head who, as concerned and perceptive laity, also
carefully edited these pages; my wife, Janet, who read each chapter
several times. Based on suggestions from the above people, the manuscript was rewritten. Then I asked a cluster of pastors to read and
critique the text. I belong to the Renton, Washington, text-study group
(about 25 clergy), and they were more than pleased to criticize my
work, line by line and comma by comma. Based on our discussion and
their comments, the book was again modified. None of these people
are responsible for the contents of this book, but I am grateful for their
friendship, time, and assistance during this project.

Acknowledgments

Quotations from *As One without Authority* by Fred B. Craddock are copyright © 1979 by Abingdon Press and are used by permission.

Quotations from *Between Two Worlds* by John R. W. Stott are copyright © by John Stott, published in 1982 by Wm. B. Eerdmans, originally published under the title *I Believe in Preaching* by Hodder & Stoughton Ltd. in 1982, and are reprinted by permission of both publishers.

Quotations from *The Bible in the Pulpit* by Leander E. Keck are copyright © 1978 by Leander E. Keck and are used by permission of the publisher, Abingdon Press.

Quotations from *Creative Preaching* by Elizabeth Achtemeier are copyright © 1980 by Abingdon Press and are used by permission.

Quotations from *Design for Preaching* by H. Grady Davis are copyright © 1958 by Fortress Press and are used by permission.

Quotations from *Early Christian Rhetoric* by Amos N. Wilder, Harvard University Press, 1974, are reprinted by permission.

Quotations from *Encounter with Spurgeon* by Helmut Thielicke are copyright © 1963 by Fortress Press and are used by permission.

Quotations from *Lectures on Preaching* by Phillips Brooks, Baker Book House, 1969, are used by permission.

Quotations from volumes of *Luther's Works* published by Fortress Press are used by permission.

Quotations from *Overhearing the Gospel* by Fred B. Craddock are copyright © 1978 by Fred B. Craddock and are used by permission of the publisher, Abingdon Press.

Quotations from *Power from the Pulpit,* copyright © 1977 by Concordia Publishing House, are used by permission.

Quotations from *Preaching for the People* by Lowell O. Erdahl are copyright © 1976 by Abingdon Press and are used by permission.

Epigraph:
Luther on Preaching

Whoever . . . does not know or preach the gospel is not only no priest or bishop, but he is a kind of [plague] to the church.

> *Luther's Works,* vol. 36 (Philadelphia: Fortress, 1959), p. 116

I did not invent this Word of God and this office. It is God's Word, God's work, his office. There we two [i.e., God and I] are one in the cause. . . . It is our confidence, no matter how much the world may boast, that God has qualified us to be ministers, and, secondly, that it is not only pleasing to the heart of God but also that we shall not preach in vain and that this ministry will lift to heaven some few who receive the Word.

> *Luther's Works,* vol. 51 (Philadelphia: Fortress, 1959), p. 223

The office of preaching is an arduous task. . . . I have often said that, if I could come down with a good conscience, I would rather be stretched upon a wheel and carry stones than preach one sermon. For anyone who is in this office will always be plagued; and therefore I have often said that the damned devil and not a good man should be a preacher. But we're stuck with it now. . . . If I had known I would not have let myself be drawn into it with twenty-four horses.

> *Luther's Works,* vol. 51, p. 222

Preach one thing: the wisdom of the cross!

> *Luther's Works,* vol. 51, p. 14

1

"Why Can't We Have Better Preaching?"

In his preface to Thielicke's book, John Doberstein asked the question, "Why can't we have better preaching in the church? We don't hear laity asking for more liturgy, more form, more organization, more discussion groups. People are asking for better preaching."[1] William D. Thompson, editor of the Abingdon Preacher's Library, states that the "lay parish committees seeking pastoral leadership consistently ranked preaching as the most desirable skill."[2] My own survey of American Lutheran Church pastors in the North Pacific District shows that these clergy also rank preaching as the most important pastoral skill.[3]

Reuel Howe, in his research on the opinions and values of the laity, concluded that "the majority of congregations tend to rate their pastors highly in their overall ministry, but *much less* highly on their sermons."[4] Congregations believe that we are better pastors than preachers. This is good. This is the way it ought to be. We are shepherds of the flock who love and care for our people. We don't need to be like Buttrick and Scherer to be faithful shepherds of the flock.

But then another question emerges: What can we pastors do to become better preachers? Knowing that preaching is one of the many important facets of ministry, we dare to ask the *personal* question: Specifically, what can be done to improve *my* preaching? Can we have better preaching in the congregation I serve? That's what this book is all about. Paul Scherer, in his homiletics textbook, *For We Have This Treasure,* says it well:

> The only thing in God's economy that can ever take the place of preaching is better preaching. And every man is capable of that. Not of good preaching. Good preaching may be quite beyond us. But better preaching. That is beyond none of us.[5]

All of us can become *better* preachers of the gospel!

READ BOOKS ON PREACHING

One goal of this book is to improve the quality of your preaching (and mine) by listening to the wisdom of contemporary preachers and professors of homiletics and putting some of their insights into practice. Recently I was trying to find ways to renew my own preaching and so I began reading in the area of homiletics. I wrote to the Lutheran seminaries in the country, requesting their reading lists for preaching. A total of 28 books was recommended by these seminaries. I read these books and found 23 of them to be especially helpful. I read each of these books three times and, during the last time through, typed out the most valuable insights, quotations, and stories. In other words, I was trying to cull out "the best from the very best." To use an analogy, I went diamond mining. Every book was like a diamond mine, and I went searching for gems of homiletical brilliance. Some books had 10 diamonds; others had 50. What I attempted to do was to gather as many homiletical diamonds as possible into one collection. Knowing that pastors are busy people and may not have the time to read the most recent literature in homiletics, I have read these books and organized their contents into a teachable whole, bringing their best insights into one compendium on preaching.

This is not to suggest that you should avoid reading these books. Many of them are classics; you can purchase 10 outstanding books on preaching and have a glorious summer reading them. In fact, I encourage you to do so. From my perspective, the following are the most outstanding books which should be required reading in every seminary.

Achtemeier, Elizabeth. *Creative Preaching.* Nashville: Abingdon, 1980.

Brooks, Phillips. *Lectures on Preaching.* Grand Rapids: Baker, 1969.

Craddock, Fred B. *As One without Authority.* Nashville: Abingdon, 1971.

Craddock, Fred B. *Overhearing the Gospel.* Nashville: Abingdon, 1978.

Davis, H. Grady. *Design for Preaching.* Philadelphia: Fortress, 1958 (chaps. 1, 9-15).

Gonzalez, Justo L. and Catherine. *Liberation Preaching.* Nashville: Abingdon, 1980.

Meuser, Fred W. *Luther the Preacher.* Minneapolis: Augsburg, 1983.

Mitchell, Henry M. *The Recovery of Preaching.* New York: Harper and Row, 1977.

Stott, John R. W. *Between Two Worlds.* Grand Rapids: Eerdmans, 1982.

Steimle, Edmund A., Niedenthal, Morris J., and Rice, Charles L. *Preaching the Story.* Philadelphia: Fortress, 1980.

In my opinion, the following 13 books on the reading lists for seminary courses in homiletics are also worth studying:

Buechner, Frederick. *Telling the Truth.* New York: Harper and Row, 1977.

Erdahl, Lowell O. *Preaching for the People.* Nashville: Abingdon, 1976.

Fant, Clyde E. *Preaching for Today.* New York: Harper and Row, 1975.

Farmer, H. H. *The Servant of the Word.* Philadelphia: Fortress, 1942.

Harms, Paul. *Power from the Pulpit.* St. Louis: Concordia, 1980.

Halvorson, Arndt L. *Authentic Preaching.* Minneapolis: Augsburg, 1982.

Howe, Ruel L. *Partners in Preaching.* New York: Seabury, 1967.

Jensen, Richard A. *Telling the Story.* Minneapolis: Augsburg, 1982.

Keck, Leander E. *The Bible in the Pulpit.* Nashville: Abingdon, 1980.

Scherer, Paul E. *For We Have This Treasure.* Grand Rapids: Baker, 1979.

Stuempfle, Herman G. Jr. *Preaching Law and Gospel.* Philadelphia: Fortress, 1978.

Thielicke, Helmut. *The Trouble with the Church.* Grand Rapids: Baker, 1965.

Wilder, Amos N. *Early Christian Rhetoric.* Cambridge: Harvard University, 1971.

Every one of these books is worth your investment of time. If I personally had to choose only one on preaching, it would be Thielicke's *Encounter with Spurgeon* (Grand Rapids: Baker, 1977), and I would read it over and over again. Thielicke's Spurgeon is better than Spurgeon's Spurgeon; that is, Spurgeon's lectures can be laborious reading. But Thielicke has lifted out the very best of Spurgeon's wisdom and humor and fashioned these into one solidly condensed text on preaching.

I approached this preaching literature from the perspective of a working parish pastor, whose thought processes are governed by the needs of the congregation. This book is what one parish pastor learned from these giants of faith. I am a parish pastor who visits the sick, prepares sermons, marries and buries, teaches confirmation, goes on youth retreats, arranges for speakers, counsels individuals and families, telephones new visitors, converses with the unchurched, and helps people to know Jesus Christ more fully during all of these encounters. From this perspective as a working parish pastor, I sat at the feet of these preachers, prophets, and poets. If I were a theological professor, seminary student, or church official, I would have heard differently. My ears are those of a parish pastor and intuitively I test everything I read against the realities of parish life. That doesn't make my listening any more or less valuable, but it is a specific way of hearing and applying what you read.

Quest for Better Preaching contains an unusually large number of quotations, and these quotations are one of the keys to this book. This text is a compendium of contemporary homiletical wisdom. Read the quotations slowly. For example, six different authors write eloquently about the preacher's struggle with egotism, and all six quotations are listed on one page. That is not the time to skim, but to slow down. These quotations are the gems of wisdom which have been fashioned in the creative imaginations of these artists. As Phillips Brooks advises, let their wisdom "sift through, not trickle over, the deep soil of the preacher's mind and heart. . . ."[6] The earlier chapters of this book are especially loaded with quotations and insights from these homiletical sages. As the book progresses, more of my own perceptions will be presented.

2

Criticisms of Preaching

BORING BANALITIES

Boring!" That word is to be found in every book on preaching and is the universal reaction to sermons through the centuries. There seems to be one word persistently and consistently used to describe much preaching: boring! That doesn't mean that all preachers are "dull, duller and dullest."[1] It doesn't mean Anthony Trollope is correct when he said that "there is, perhaps, no greater hardship at present afflicted on mankind in civilized and free countries than the necessity of listening to sermons."[2] It does mean that the most consistent criticism leveled against our preaching is that it bores, that "it doesn't touch my life where I am living, and therefore I do not listen."

Craddock says that "boredom is a form of evil!"[3] One of Søren Kierkegaard's characters was perhaps more correct when he said, "Boredom is the root of all evil."[4] Many Christians today have accepted boredom as "one of the crosses" that come with Sunday morning worship. "Boredom works against the faith by provoking contrary thoughts or lulling people to sleep or draping the whole occasion with a pall of indifference and unimportance."[5] A preacher may have many powerful ideas left unheard because of a boring form.

William A. Hughes, a Roman Catholic bishop, quoting research among Catholics, indicates that "the vast majority of Catholic people are unhappy with the quality of Sunday preaching."[6] Walter J. Burghardt, a patristics scholar and known as a "preacher's preacher" among Catholics, says: "Our homilies are rarely heretical. They fail rather because they are stale and flat, vapid and insipid, dreadfully dry and boringly barren."[7]

Thielicke says that "boresomeness paralyzes people, but it does not make them angry. And finally even the demons fall asleep. . . . Not a single person [who left the church in discouragement] was offended or upset; nobody protested. It was only boredom that emptied the pews."[8] With a powerful uppercut to the jaw, Thielicke clobbers many of his German clergymen: ". . . the man who bores others must also be boring himself. And the man who bores himself is not really living in what he so boringly hands out."[9]

Harms contends that "a moment's reflection reveals that most preaching is unrelieved dullness . . ."[10] and Luther remarks that some sermons are so boring that they would not have lured a dog from behind a warm stove.[11]

A small child, wearied by a preacher's boring sermon, appealed, "Mother, pay the man and let us go home."[12]

W. D. Davies, the New Testament scholar, when asked for his estimate of the effectiveness of preaching today, said: "Preaching is like churchbells. It is a familiar sound which is welcomed so long as it doesn't wake us from sleep or interrupt some important activity."[13]

And Dorothy Sayers complains about the "insipidity" of much preaching:

> Not Herod, not Caiaphas, not Pilate, not Judas ever contrived to fasten upon Jesus Christ the reproach of insipidity. That final indignity was left for pious hands to inflict. To make of history something that could neither startle, nor shock, nor terrify, nor excite, nor inspire a living soul is to crucify the Son of God afresh and put Him to shame. . . .[14]

Clyde E. Fant has several pages which describe the history of boring banalities coming from the pulpit. I found these pages to be both comforting and entertaining, as he put into perspective the long history of pulpit boredom. He insists that the "poor reviews" of the pulpit began as early as 2 Cor. 10:9-10 when Paul reported the opinions of others about his own preaching: "His bodily presence is weak and his speech of no account." Such criticisms have continued throughout history. The following are a few gems:

> During the Middle Ages the sermon was attacked as mechanical, dull and usually nothing more than a poor plagiarism of earlier works. In the sixteenth century preaching was the butt of ridicule by the laity who found it to be incredibly boring and who passed the time away by sleeping, chattering or playing simple games. One woman who had been rebuked in the midst of a sermon for gossiping with her neighbor promptly jumped and said, angrily, "Indeed, sir, I know the one who has been doing the most babbling! For I do but whisper a word with my neighbor, and thou has babbled there all this hour."[15]

> In 1670, John Eachard complained bitterly in his tract, "The Grounds and Contempt of the Clergy Inquired Into," about the unintelligible, unnatural and uncommunicative speech in the pulpit. . . . [And] John Caird declared that "the pattern sermon of the Georgian era seems to have been constructed almost expressly to steer clear of all possible ways of getting human beings to listen to it."[16]

We preachers need to remember C. S. Lewis' advice: "To interest is the first duty of art."[17]

After his lengthy description of the history of monotonous monologs (called sermons), Fant then asks: "Where are all the great preachers today?" The answer? "Where they have always been—few and far between."[18] "There is a tendency to romanticize the past and be overly pessimistic about the present. . . . We need to lay to rest once and for all the unrealistic 'golden age' myth, and we need to know that pulpit criticism was not born in our generation."[19]

CONTEMPORARY CRITICISMS OF PREACHING: ELEVEN DEADLY SINS

It is helpful to listen to contemporary critiques of the American pulpit. Reuel Howe, at his Institute for Advanced Pastoral Studies, has systematically examined lay criticism of preaching. I will use his basic outline and supplement it with insights from other scholars, including Luther.

When Howe recites his litany of criticisms, the tendency for us parish pastors is not to take him seriously or to assume he is talking about someone else. Most of us pastors think we are fairly decent preachers. We are who we are; and there is little need to improve. In a survey of American Lutheran Church pastors in the Pacific Northwest, I found that the vast majority rated themselves as "good" or "very good" preachers. Only a few rated themselves "excellent," only a few "fair," and almost none rated themselves "poor." The category with the most number of votes was "very good."[20] If these survey statistics are accurate, and most preachers rate their sermons as "very good," there may be a tendency *not* to take Howe's critique seriously or to think he is describing someone else.

There is another fact to face: Howe demonstrates that laity rate their pastors much more highly on overall ministry than on preaching. I do not know precisely what this means, but I am sure we need to listen to honest criticism of our preaching because we receive so little honest feedback from our parishioners.

1. Most preaching is too abstract and academic, too theoretical and theological. Farmer, the patron saint of many preachers, wrote that "abstractness in some ways is the greatest curse of all our preaching. I speak as a great sinner in this respect." He asks the question why abstractions are such a curse. The answer is not that people will misunderstand or be bored, but "that God comes at people not through abstractions at all, but through persons and through the concrete situations of day to day personal life."[21]

This same thought is expressed by H. Grady Davis when he writes:

We preachers forget that the Gospel itself is for the most part a simple narrative of persons, places, happenings, and conversation. It is not verbal exposition of general ideas. Nine-tenths of our preaching is verbal exposition and argument, but not one-tenth of the Gospel is exposition. Its ideas are mainly in the form of a story.[22]

Davis is correct in his assessment: preaching tends to be an exposition of ideas, arguments, generalizations, assertions, abstractions, whereas the Bible is primarily story. And he goes on to say, "We overestimate the power of assertion, and we underestimate the power of narrative to communicate meaning and influence the lives of our people."[23] Perhaps Davis points us in the right direction: if the Gospels themselves are at least 90% narrative, perhaps our sermons need to be 90% narrative rather than 90% ideas, points, truths, abstractions, and generalizations.

Reflecting on the same theme, Steimle says that the "use of abstractions is risky business." Such words as "creation, incarnation, redemption, forgiveness, resurrection [are] words from which the blood of action has been drained." Even such words as "sin and grace and gospel" have become abstractions because of their overuse.[24]

Thielicke entitles a chapter "Abstract Man: The Wrong Man to Address." He says that preachers may talk abstractly and eloquently about human nature, human existence, and our existential situation but "no longer gear into real life as men live it and only make men say, 'There is nothing there for me' or 'This never touched me at all.' "[25] Thielicke has heard some preachers pompously intone from the pulpit: "God is not an idea but reality." He calls this an "intellectual fraud because here one reduces God to an abstraction while seeming to assert just the opposite."[26] Preaching is then often reduced to theological problem-solving of sterile, "intra-professional" issues that the laity couldn't care less about. Such preaching is "pinpoint boring."[27]

In the preaching of ideas and abstractions, the minister often takes a parable or miracle and squeezes out the points to be made during the sermon. Much like squeezing out the juice from an orange, the preacher squeezes the juice out from a parable, miracle, or narrative and that intellectual juice now forms the basis for the sermon. Jensen says that 90% of the sermons he hears and has preached are essentially informational, "a collection of truths."[28] Halvorson warns against sermons that are a "collection of definitions."[29]

Reuel Howe observes that laymen often feel sermons are more like theological essays—unrelated to the issues of everyday life:

> Another comment from laymen states that sermons are too formal and impersonal. The lack of personal urgency in preaching conveys

the impression that the minister is not dealing with life and death issues. . . . They sense that there ought to be a difference between a lecture and a sermon. . . . Apparently, there is a longing on the part of the layman for a preacher to give an honest, intelligent, passionate, personal presentation of Christian conviction rather than the coldly rational, dispassionate presentation of objective truth.[30]

Lowell Erdahl also understands the problem of sermons sounding like theological lectures:

What I often hear is a religious sounding lecture, a kind of oral theological essay. It then seems what I need to be a Christian is to agree with your ideas—as if believing the idea of justification by grace through faith is the same thing as being justified by faith. Having faith in God is not the same thing as holding an idea about God. A lecture about food is not a steak dinner. Nor is a lecture about the Gospel the same as a proclamation of the Gospel . . . . I don't want lectures instead of sermons. When I am hungry, I want a meal, not a menu or a page from a cookbook.[31]

Several authors had variations on this Kierkegaardian theme: When a person is hungry he wants a meal, not a menu; when someone is starving she wants rice, not a recipe.[32] The sick need medicine, not a lecture on medicine. Brooks writes:

Much of our preaching is like delivering lectures upon medicine to sick people. The lecture is true. . . . The lecture is interesting. . . . But still the fact remains that the lecture is not the medicine and that to give medicine, not to deliver lectures, is the preacher's duty.[33]

Spurgeon, in the same vein, said that preachers are to lead "people to paradise, [not] merely give them a lecture about paradise."[34]

There is a subtle but distinct difference between explaining and proclaiming, between religious lectures which explain grace and biblical sermons which proclaim grace. The primary difference between explanation and proclamation is that the former uses more religious abstractions and the latter uses more stories, analogies, and images that illustrate God's grace. When stories of God's grace are told, grace is often recreated in the hearer's mind and heart. "The purpose of a lecture is to explain a subject. The purpose of a sermon is to transform a life."[35] (In Chapters 8 and 9, we will examine the power of stories, analogies, and images to transform and shape human beings.)

In working with the unchurched, I hear one comment over and over again: "I am trying to find a place where someone speaks to my needs, through the Bible, in language I can understand." That is what would bring the unchurched to a worship service in the first place: they want to be strengthened in faith toward God and in love toward one another, because down deep they sense they are not right with God and their fellow human beings. They want a meal, not a menu; they want food, not a philosophical essay; they want rice, not a recipe.

Luther was also aware of the tendency for pastors to want to sound theologically erudite:

> Cursed be every preacher who aims at lofty topics in the church, looking for his own glory and selfishly desiring to please one individual or another. When I preach here, I adapt myself to the circumstances of the common people. I don't look at the doctors and the masters, of whom scarcely forty are present, but at the hundred or the thousand young people and children. It is to them that I devote myself. . . . Take pains to be simple and direct.[36]

> Today Master Morlin pleased me very much when he preached. He instructed the common people about the duties of wives and maidservants. . . . The people can take this home with them, but nobody understands a sermon which is turgid, deep, removed from life.[37]

> Osiander should refrain from erudite preaching. . . . We preach publicly for the sake of the plain people. Christ could have taught in a profound way but he wished to deliver his message with the utmost simplicity in order that the common people might understand. Good God, there are sixteen-year-old girls, women, old men and farmers in church, and they don't understand lofty matters. If one can present fitting and familiar comparisons, as Link can do in a masterful fashion, the people will understand and

remember. Accordingly, he's the best preacher who can preach in a plain, childlike, popular and simple way. I prefer to preach in an easy and comprehensible fashion, but when it comes to academic disputations, watch me in the university. There I'll make it sharp enough for anyone. . . . Someday I will have to write a book against artful preachers.[38]

I don't think of Dr. Pomeranium, Jonas or Philip in my sermon. They know more about it than I do. So I don't preach to them. I just preach to Hansie or Betsy.[39]

And although I know full well and hear every day that many people think little of me and say that I only write little pamphlets and sermons in German for the uneducated laity, I do not let that stop me. Would to God that in my lifetime I had, to my fullest ability, helped one layman to be better! I would be quite satisfied. . . . I will not be ashamed in the slightest to preach to the uneducated layman and write for him in German. . . . As far as I am concerned, it is quite enough, really more than enough, that some laymen—and those the most distinguished—are humble enough to read my sermons.[40]

In my preaching, I take pains to treat a verse of Scripture, to stick to it, and so to instruct the people that they can say, "that's what the sermon was all about" . . . When Christ preached, he proceeded quickly to a parable and spoke about sheep, shepherds, wolves, vineyards, fig trees, seeds, fields, plowing. The poor lay people were able to comprehend these things.[41]

Although Luther's lectures are highly sophisticated and complicated (e.g., *Lectures on Galatians*) and although his *Postils* are comprehensive expositions intended for pastors to enable them to understand the text, it seems that the sermons which are given to the laity are direct, simple, and clear explanations of Scripture.[42] That is not to say that Luther's sermons for laity are shallow, childlike, or devoid of theology—far from it! But there is a simplicity, directness, and clarity to his thought. His sermons are often laced with humor and use everyday examples of happenings in the home, congregation, city, or nation. They are easy to understand.

It is interesting that Luther considered Link to be the best preacher;

Link, the one who masterfully used "fitting and familiar comparisons" that people could understand and remember.

To the problem of preaching over people's heads, Spurgeon wittily commented: "Christ said, 'Feed my sheep. . . . Feed my lambs.' Some preachers, however, put the food so high that neither lambs nor sheep can reach it. They seem to have read the text, 'Feed my giraffes.' "[43]

Pastors are not only accused of using abstractions but of using vague religious generalizations. For example, we tell our people of the need to be "witnesses in the world" in their homes, offices, and schools. Often we say no more than that: Simply be witnesses in your world. It is vague and nonspecific. Craddock tells a delightful story about a layperson who was tired of his pastor's vague generalizations. One day the preacher got lost while driving his car through a big city, and he asked the layman for directions. The layman reached into the backseat of the car, pulled out a globe and said: "Here, maybe this will help you find your way."[44]

Abstractions, generalizations, religious lectures—these often are the curse of preaching.

Farmer, Davis, Steimle, Thielicke, Jensen, Howe, Erdahl, and others *all* point out the foolishness and fallacy of preaching "idea" sermons, especially if 90% of the content of the Gospels comes to us in narrative form and especially if God changes us by means of story, analogy, illustration, vivid imagery, and concrete experiences more than by means of abstract ideas and points. As Brooks emphasized, the gospel is most eloquently and powerfully communicated not in dogmatic form but in personal life.[45]

2. Sermons contain too many ideas which are too complex and come at the listener too fast. Not only are sermons perceived as too abstract, they are also accused of having too many abstractions. If you have a three-point sermon, each with three subpoints, you then have a nine-point sermon. Or the simple three-point outline may be three different sermonettes. Fant writes:

> The preacher is like a juggler of colored balls. His ideas are the balls, and a total concentration is required to keep all of them up in the air at the same time. A few years of this kind of

preoccupied preaching and the whole congregation could get up and silently tiptoe out without his ever missing them.[46]

Luther tells about Pomeranus (Bugenhagen) and his tendency to have too many points.

> Pomeranus preaches . . . whatever comes to mind. Dr. Jonas is accustomed to say, "One shouldn't hail every soldier one meets." And it is true. Pomeranus often takes along everyone he meets with him. Only a fool thinks he should say everything that occurs to him. A preacher should see to it that he sticks to the subject and performs his task in such a way that people understand what he says. Preachers who try to say everything that occurs to them remind me of the maidservant who is on her way to market. When she meets another maid, she stops to chat with her for a while. Then she meets another maid and talks with her. She does the same with a third and a fourth and so gets to market very slowly. That is what preachers do who wander too far from their subject.[47]

That is why Davis and every other author talk about the importance of designing a sermon around one major theme, trunk, magnetic field, or thread. Every author emphasized the need for a central theme because most sermons tend to be far too complex. Sermons usually need to have one fundamental assertion/theme/truth/message which is reinforced by story, illustration, anecdote, parable, and quotation—all serving to visualize that one fundamental motif. As many preachers were taught: "Better to drive home one point than to leave three stranded on base." Spurgeon wrote, "One tenpenny nail driven home and clenched will be more useful than a score of tin-tacks loosely fixed, to be pulled out again in an hour."[48]

Craddock teaches that a sermon should experience the restraint of a single idea. He calls this a "homiletical magnet" that draws certain material to itself, but repels other materials. More than anything else, this central message helps the unity and movement of a sermon.[49]

Pastors are aware of the appeal of children's sermons which usually have one dominant idea, use vivid images or objects, tells a story, employ ordinary language, relate to everyday life, and are easily remembered. Those same characteristics need to be found in "adult" sermons.

It must be very difficult for us preachers to design and confine ourselves to one central theme because all 23 authors tried to convince us to do so.

Thielicke talks about the problem of preachers saying too much and overwhelming people with their numerous religious insights.

> Why are you always setting forth your multitudes of truths and blinding us as with a thousand-watt lamp? We are moles who have just crawled out of the ground and we can stand the light of only a small candle, we can bear only a very small truth. . . . But you descend upon us with the floodlight of all the truths of the centuries. You serve up everything at once. Please, just one candle, one single candle![50]

Howe reports that laity want simple sermons with deep truths.[51] And Harms reminds us that what is wanted is simplicity, not poverty of thought or feeling![52] And Thielicke? He wants just one candle.

3. There is too little concern for people's needs. Mitchell, more than the other authors, clearly spells out the importance of addressing people in their needs. It is time to read slowly.

> As simple and as obvious as this may sound, the fact is that most preaching in all cultures today ignores peoples' deepest human needs.[53]

> Preaching must speak to the human condition. However clever an idea, if it does not speak to real need, it is useless.[54]

> Recently, I asked a seminar of preachers what their deepest needs were, as persons rather than as preachers. We wrote ten needs on the board. Then I turned around and asked point blank how many of them had preached a sermon on how many of these topics. The startling response was that one preacher had preached one sermon on perhaps the most pervasive problem of the bunch.[55]

> Since I have been working on this material, and thinking more about real needs, I have found myself disciplined to preach on utterly new topics, so far as my experience was concerned . . . ,

e.g., Why the youth of today are lazy . . ., Why children trained up in the way they should go still don't always follow it. My experience is that the minute one announces the intent to offer a word from God's Word on nitty-gritty issues like the ones I mentioned, the attentive ear of the audience is guaranteed.[56]

Paul Harms understands the importance of the preacher embodying the needs of his hearers:

> The purpose of this analysis of the hearer is to stimulate the pastor's concern so that he gets his whole being wrapped around the hearer and his needs. As the preacher embodies the hearer's needs, his message becomes empowered as it struggles and agonizes to serve the hearer. The more specific he can be about the hearer, the greater will the possibility be that he speaks to the hearer. . . .[57]

Intuitively, listeners tune in on the preacher who is addressing their needs. This doesn't mean that a preacher tells the people what they want to hear, but that he addresses their struggles and victories in language which they can understand. William D. Thompson, editor of the Abingdon Preacher's Library, writes:

> Hearers answer that question [What is good preaching?] instinctively, tuning in the preacher who meets their needs, whether in the pulpit of their neighborhood or on the broadcast.[58]

John Stott, who has been preaching for more than 25 years, has written numerous books on preaching, and has traveled around the world giving lectures on preaching, was "ashamed" to admit that during this entire time he had never given a sermon on divorce, "a burning contemporary issue [on which] many people are wanting help. . . ."[59]

Preachers, because of the long-term intimate relationship with the people in our parishes, begin to know their genuine needs; and because we love our people, we address those needs in our preaching. Elizabeth Achtemeier writes:

We know our people not because we analyze them but because to the depths of our being we love and care for them. . . . Perhaps it rises first of all out of living with the people for so long that one comes to know deeply their terrible, terrible need. Each individual in every congregation is undergoing some form of suffering. . . . When Jesus saw the crowds, he had compassion for them. . . .[60]

Phillips Brooks encourages us to be open in two directions: both towards God and human need:

The real preparation of the preacher's personality for his transmissive work comes by the opening of his life on both sides: towards the truth of God and towards the needs of man. . . . The preacher's instinct is that which feels instantly how Christ and human need belong together, neither thinks Christ too far off for the needs, nor the need too insignificant for Christ.[61]

He [the preacher] must receive truth as one who is to teach it. He cannot, he must not study as if the truth he sought were purely for his own culture or enrichment. . . . [He has] a desire to find the human side of every truth, the point at which every speculation touches humanity. . . . Some men receive truth abstractly. They follow it into its developments. They fathom its depths. But they never think of sending it abroad. . . . Other men necessarily think in relation to other men, and their first impulse with every new truth is to give it its full range of power. Their love for truth is always complemented by a love for man. . . . So the student preparing to be a preacher cannot learn truth as the mere student of theology for its own sake might do. He always feels it reaching out through him to the people to whom he is someday to carry it. He cannot get rid of this consciousness. It influences all his understanding.[62]

Spurgeon suggests that the preacher uses material in which people have a vested interest: "I never did hear of a person going to sleep while a will was being read in which he expected a legacy; neither have I heard of a prisoner going to sleep while the judge was summing up and his life was hanging in jeopardy. Self-interest quickens attention. Preach upon practical themes, pressing, present personal matters, and you will secure an earnest hearing."[63]

A criticism of contemporary preaching is that it often is more concerned about "religious truths" than "God's truth for us in our needs." As Farmer advises, when preaching about suffering don't fill your mind with theological lectures about theodicy, but fill your heart with love and concern for a friend who has cancer and is dying in a hospital bed.[64]

4. There is too much theological jargon and biblical talk. Before I began doing research on homiletics, I was unaware of a new code word, "language of Zion," which is mentioned in several of the books on preaching. "Language of Zion" describes the phenomenon of using biblical and theological language from the pulpit, rather than the language of the people. It has already been pointed out that most of the laity do not have "gut associations" with such words as salvation, redemption, incarnation, gospel, and theology of the cross. Ninety-eight percent of our laity don't use these words in their everyday lives. This becomes a problem for many of us clergy because we all have our favorite words: gospel, cross, grace, liberation, which may electrify our emotions but have little impact on the average parishioner. I still remember one of our interns using the word *salvific* in one of his first sermons. As one layman said to Reuel Howe, "If I used that much jargon with my customers, I would lose them."[65] Just as Jesus used the secular language of his time (as did the biblical writers), we need to use the living language of our people. (Jesus used Aramaic rather than Hebrew, and Luther in his sermons used common German rather than Latin.)

Jesuit theologian Karl Rahner, in his book *The Renewal of Preaching* writes: "Many leave the Church because the language flowing from the pulpit has no meaning for them; it has no connection with their own life and simply bypasses many threatening and unavoidable issues. . . ."[66]

The problem is not only the overuse of biblical language but the use of theological and philosophical language. "Existence," "meaninglessness," and "despair" do not resonate in the inner lives of our people unless they have first been illustrated by a story, anecdote, or parable from everyday life.

    5. *Too much time is spent describing the past and telling about the "land of Zion."* As we tend to use the language of Zion, we also may spend too much time talking about the "land of Zion." H. Grady Davis refers to a published sermon on his desk which devoted four and one-half pages to examining the motives for Judas' betrayal of Jesus, but focused on the present only during the last paragraphs.[67] Davis, especially, is aware of this homiletical tendency to focus on the past:

> Biblical scenes and incidents may hold us too long in the past. The historical and textual introduction necessary in the study may have too large a place in the content of the sermon. . . . The preacher may be so interested in the antique world or in the methods of research that he never gets beyond them, never gets down to the here and now. Mistakes such as these may keep him speaking in the past tense until finally the backward look becomes his habitual attitude.[68]

Davis allows his imagination to go to work visualizing Jesus giving his first sermon at Nazareth. He has Jesus, like a biblical bloodhound, preaching his exegetical insights:

> If, in the synagogue at Nazareth, Jesus had preached as many of his followers do, he would have talked first about Isaiah, or about his book, about the situation at the time when Isaiah spoke, about the office of prophecy. After that, he would have argued about the faithfulness of God's covenant with Israel, about the un-changeable truth of God's Word. Then he would have asked what meaning Isaiah's words had for people in the synagogue that day, their permanent or contemporary value. Thus he might have reached the Gospel God anointed him to preach and to the an-nouncement that the Gospel is now fulfilled. He would have been speaking in the past tense. . . . Perhaps the scribes taught as too many preach today, in the past tense. . . . Jesus, however, began

very differently. He spoke in the present tense. The first word he spoke was *"today."*[69]

Perhaps a primary difference between Jesus and the scribes was that the scribes were always talking in the past tense, about the Bible and the land of Zion.

Most sermons are divided into two poles: past and present, what the text said and what the text says, what it meant and what it means. Obviously, we need electrical energy vacillating between both poles, but Howe is suggesting that the laity complain that they hear too much "past tense" preaching. The most serious consequence is that God is often not addressing our present situations because the sermon is so habitually looking back. It is a safe way to preach, to keep God active in past centuries or past decades. Or perhaps, as Fant suggests, Jerusalem is more familiar territory to the preacher than the avenues of his own hometown.[70]

6. There are too few illustrations and these are often too literary and not helpful.[71] The laity would like illustrations drawn from everyday life (the way Jesus did it) rather than from theological books. In Reuel Howe's study of clergy and their resources for preaching, he discovered that clergy were primarily using exegetical studies, theological books, and seminary notes as resources. Obviously, it is good to be using these and using them exceptionally well, but by themselves these resources are much too narrow.[72]

The laity's dislike of literary illustrations is interesting. Some of the authors tell us to "read, read, read" as a means of vitalizing our preaching, and I certainly concur with that. But I also know theological professors who "read, read, read" and are often poor preachers, precisely because of the kind of illustrations they often give: literary or theological and not out of the "gut situations" of human life.

Literary illustrations can be used effectively and powerfully. There are many good stories in literature. Of course, a preacher reads, reads, and reads—novels, plays, newspapers, social justice books, poetry. The key is to find illustrations that the laity themselves have experienced firsthand, that grow out of their everyday lives. Literary examples of that type can often be helpful. But laity complain of those literary illustrations that are imposed on their lives rather than grow out of them.

Of course, Jesus in his parables is the model of the gifted preacher, storyteller, illustrator. He found ways imaginatively to communicate the truth of God's kingdom by referring to what was most common and familiar: sheep, shepherds, fish, nets, boats, wheat, weeds, soil, flowers, children, parents, lost, found, treasurers, enemies, friends, blind, sick, temple, synagogue, Pharisees, money, marriage, lust, greed. Illustration after illustration was drawn out of the common lives of the people. He didn't spend time giving the exegetical history of a text, or doing a map study of old Jerusalem (back to the land and language of Zion). He illustrated his understanding of God by using the objects, images, and relationships nearest to the common lives of the people.

The point is that laity want more illustrations, illustrations that use *familiar* objects, relationships, images—in other words, the stuff of their lives. Remember Luther's insistence on using "fitting and familiar comparisons."

7. In preaching, there is too much bad news and not enough good news, too much diagnosis and not enough prognosis, too much "what's wrong with the world" and not enough "this is what we can do to make it better."[73]

Niedenthal tells of the time a layperson questioned a professor of preaching: "Why do I hear so much bad news from preachers? I thought they were supposed to preach good news." Since the professor didn't know the layman, he assumed that the layman "wanted a neat and simple Gospel which did not disturb him . . . , a Gospel which did not impinge directly on the tensions and crises of our common and public life . . . , a Gospel that nurtured a serene inner piety."[74] But the professor was wrong. This layman was working with social needs, part of a lay school of theology, very much involved in the mission of the church. But he was tired of hearing bad news from the pulpit, tired of hearing "all this analysis which leads to paralysis." Niedenthal goes on to say:

Many people, lay and clerical alike, are tired of hearing that they have to be more involved in the affairs of the community, that they have to do their duties as parent, citizen, teacher and church member. They are tired of hearing that they have to be more totally committed to Christ and other people, whatever that means. They are tired of feeling a failure because they don't have an Atlas complex, which would enable them to shoulder the burdens of the world. People are tired of hearing all these admonitions.[75]

Most laity don't have an Atlas complex which enables them to shoulder the burdens of the world. Similarly, Harms writes:

The hearers are Christians, not a spiritual Olympic squad, capable of running three-minute spiritual miles and eight-second one-hundred-meter dashes. . . . Many, if not most, are bruised reeds.[76]

Buechner tells us that the poets and novelists have a keener eye for the tragedies of life than most of us.[77] I think he is right, and we preachers at times tend to emulate the poets and their fascination with "the shadow side" of our lives. In some ways, we are like Albert Camus who, in his book *Exile and the Kingdom,* is gifted in describing the "exile" but not nearly as gifted in describing "the kingdom."

Sometimes we preachers ask ourselves: "Why does it seem easier to preach the law than the gospel? Why is our creative energy aimed at "exile" and "bondage" more than at "kingdom" and "freedom?" Why is it easier to tell what's wrong with the world than to describe visions of hope and renewal?" Or, as the laity sometimes ask, "Why is there so much bad news preaching when Jesus came preaching the good news?" Stuempfle and Davis are most helpful in explaining why it is easier to preach exile than kingdom. Stuempfle writes perceptively:

But why is it, in the preparation of the sermon, that the articulation of the Gospel often seems the hardest part? Is it because in a fallen world images of sin and brokenness always seem closer at hand than the images of grace? Is it because we as preachers find some strange corner of our egos more satisfied by exposing darkness than by announcing light?[78]

Similarly, Davis understands why we preachers have this tendency to preach negation:

> The vision of good is never so clear as the palpable actualities of evil. . . . It is easier to preach negation. Examples of failure and falsehood, harbingers of judgment, omens of doom, are many and near at hand. Examples of nobility, courage, goodness, faith, though they exist, are all compounded with human dross.
>
> Further, the prophet's images of retribution are abundant and concrete, while those of promised salvation are less sure, and they are the more questionable the more concrete they become.
>
> Preaching is thus foredoomed, perhaps, to be more explicit in its account of evil than it can be in its description of good.[79]

It seems to me we preachers need to put more of our creative energies into "imaging" Easter, resurrection, kingdom, freedom, and all the "re" words: restoration, reconciliation, renewal, rebirth, refashion, re-mold. (The "re" words presuppose a fallen world in need of restoration.) This does not mean we need to reduce the gospel to the power of positive thinking. The need is simply to put more of our poetic energies into describing the good news. Mitchell suggests that we are to "flesh out the positive side of the same idea, to a two-thirds majority of the sermon. The preacher is not always willing, especially when it turns out that some of the most clever negatives have very little counterpart."[80] When I first read the above sentence by Mitchell, I thought: "Impossible! Two-thirds of a sermon towards illustrating, picturing, imaging gospel? Can't do it." Then I remembered the powerful Greek verb *euangelizomai*, preaching the good news. There is no equivalent Greek verb which means "preaching the bad news."

But even Buechner seems more capable of describing the tragedy of human condition ("He looks into the mirror all in a lather, what he sees is at least eight parts chicken, phony, and slob") than he does of describing the comedy and fairy tale. Even so, I hear Buechner trying to image, picture, and illustrate not only the tragedy of sin, but also the comedy of being loved even though I am a slob, and the fairy tale of actually being transformed by the power of that love.

Lowell Erdahl emphasizes the importance of preaching to the possibilities of people. He quotes Scherer:

> "When you look into the faces of your congregation, leave your disappointments at home and turn your imagination loose in this amazing world. Speak to their other and better selves." My goal in the pulpit will be to help my hearers to be more fully human— to be more nearly the persons they were born to be. . . . People are not just problems. They are possibilities waiting for fulfillment. . . . If we forget that fact, we may become so preoccupied with problems that our problem-centered preaching creates more problems than it solves. Preaching to the possibilities of people involves more than belief in human native ability. Confidence in the positive potential of people is founded in trust in the presence of God.[81]

I like Scherer's line: "Speak to their other and better selves."

Reuel Howe's studies similarly show that the laity tire of all that preaching of bad news and would appreciate hearing more of the gospel.

8. Sermons are often too predictable and passionless. Craddock and Fant both have sections describing the "fairly high degree of predictability of sermons" (three-point outline with opening and closing): "the whole occasion has the dead air of familiarity."

> Most preaching lacks impact because of its absolute predictability. It begins the same; it ends the same; its volume level is the same. It is always flat; or it is always excited. Its order of arrangement is always the same, or nearly so. Its topics vary but not much. Preachers change churches and churches change preachers in an effort to get some kind of variety into the preaching and worship experience.[82]

Overhearing the Gospel by Craddock is directed at this problem of overfamiliarity. His book is a study of Kierkegaard and the state church in Denmark in which the gospel had become "a piece of information. Passion was replaced with descriptions of passion," where people have no need, where religion is but one of many activities, such as square dancing. "The biggest obstacle to faith in Christendom is the illusion of participation where none exists. . . ."[83] Communication of the gospel is an act of passion, and Craddock suggests that the loss of passion may be at the heart of the problem of American preaching.

Clyde Reid in *The Empty Pew* suggests a similar idea when he writes that preaching "does not lead to change in persons."[84] Preaching is the same old thing, Sunday after Sunday, and most preachers don't expect much change in anyone or anything. Kierkegaard compares preachers to swimming coaches, who shout instructions to their swimmers, but don't actually think anyone will jump in: "In fact, if one were to plunge in and start towards the deep, the coach would be frightened and threatened."[85]

No one expects too much change from the preaching event. Rather, it is a Sunday morning exercise we all go through, like a weekly visit to the supermarket—necessary, important, and one of the essential, pleasant rituals of life, like reading the Sunday paper.

On the same theme, laity notice the "lack of courage" in their pastors. I wasn't sure what this meant until I once heard a sermon at Holden Village. In preparation for Sunday's sermon, during the text-study group, the pastor asked the laity present (who were from many congregations) what the difference was between a prophet and a preacher. The answer, as reported in the sermon: "Preachers tell people what they want to hear; prophets tell people what they need to hear, even if it hurts and causes rejection of the pastor." During the discussion, the preacher challenged the laity about their perception of their pastors. The laity in that group discussion were persistent: their pastors lacked courage and were afraid to tell people what they need to hear.

Preachers often tell people what they want to hear; we don't expect much change. Pastors, like the laity, are primarily committed to our cultural creeds of family, career, and standard of living. The sermon is a nice Sunday pattern we repeat again and again, which helps retain our moral values, traditions, and sense of middle-class mystery. Kierkegaard's Christendom is here!

9. *Much preaching is moralistic.* It is striking that although only a few of the laity complain about moralistic preaching, almost every single author does. As laity vehemently complain about "abstractions," the professors vehemently complain about "moralizing."

Moralizing is premature preoccupation with questions of personal behavior. Keck most thoroughly addressed this issue:

> The renewal of Biblical preaching requires us to find an alternative to moralizing. It is hard to conceive of any mode of preaching more deadly to the hearer or more inimical to the Bible itself than the prevailing pattern of drawing lessons for today from a text that has been briefly explained.[86]

Keck observes that the Bible itself does not draw "little lessons for life" from the texts; therefore, "moralizing 'application' of the text is a markedly unbiblical way of preaching the Bible."

C. H. Dodd, in *The Apostolic Preaching,* said that early Christians would not recognize the gospel in much of what is heard from our pulpits because preaching in the New Testament church did not center on moral instructions or exhortations on how to be better people. "While the church was concerned to hand on the teaching of the Lord, it was not by this it made converts. It was by *kerygma* [proclamation], says Paul, not by *didache* [moral instruction], that it pleased God to save men."[87]

The central thrust of the Bible is not the wise sayings for wise living in the book of Proverbs, or Romans 12–15, or 1 Corinthians 13, or other favorite passages of moral discourse. By narrowly emphasizing the call to a moralistic life, the preacher often ignores the "Bible's own overarching concerns, such as the election of Israel, God's commitment to establishing justice on earth (most moralizing sermons are oriented to individuals), the meaning of Christ as the fulfillment of the Old Testament, the kingdom of God. . . ."[88] These themes become valuable to the moralistic preacher only if they serve the primary objective of such sermons: to improve moral behavior. "Frequently, moralizing either treats the Bible as a basis of advice as if it were reducible to the book of Proverbs or to a collection of exemplary hero stories or it treats the Bible as the warrant for a rather narrow and often parochial morality." When the moralistic preacher goes to work, he then often "idealizes the past in a way that the Bible usually does not." The preacher needs those moral heroes of the early church where "faith was pure, love pervasive, prayers effective, courage dauntless, and the presence of the Spirit warmed every heart."[89]

One of the many problems with moralistic preaching is the distortion of the "Bible's own understanding of moral obligation."[90] A phrase by Stuempfle is helpful: "The Christian can no more fail to exhibit a good life than a rock lying in the sun can fail to grow warm."[91] Such moralistic preaching detaches the branch from the vine, the warmth of the rock from the sun, the effect from the cause. The foundation of biblical morality is Paul's famous phrase, "faith active in love" (Gal. 5:6), a love which grows out of a relationship of trust. Davis says it well when he suggests that moralistic preaching is premature:

> There is danger that the proclamation of the Gospel may be displaced—danger that we shall not preach at all, but only teach, exhort, and persuade. . . . That is to say, the mere instruction, exhortation, admonition, persuasion which form so large a portion of our contemporary pulpit speaking, is largely fruitless because it is premature.[92]

Moralistic preaching is often fruitless because it doesn't address first things first. Good works are a consequence of grace and not its cause.

In an environment which demands immediate relevance, a preacher may not thoroughly deal with the text but quickly use it as a launching pad, a cause for moral action. "The results tend to be either a distressing trivialization of the Bible into reasonable advice for the individual or a shrill demanding of absolutes for the church and society."[93] Or, as Paul Scherer quips, such preaching consists of "helpful hints for hurtful habits."[94]

One night at vespers at Holden, a sermon was given. The young preacher had been instructed at the seminary to give concrete directions, suggestions, and exhortations at the close of his sermon. So the young pastor told us to go and clean our closets of excessive clothing and give it to Goodwill. Of course, no one did. And I thought of a line from Steimle: " . . . The dreary procession of musts, oughts and shoulds bounce off their hides like hailstones on concrete."[95]

H. Grady Davis approached the problem of moralistic preaching in a slightly different way, and I found his chapter on "Modes in Preaching" most helpful. He speaks of three "modes" of preaching: indicative, subjunctive, and imperative.[96] There is the indicative mode, direct statements of fact: is, was. The subjunctive mode: *if* you do these things, *then*. . . . And the imperative mode: do this, do that, or we *ought* to do this and *should* do that. Preachers have their favorite personal modes of preaching.

Davis then takes the positive indicative statement, "Jesus is Lord," and converts it satirically into the two other modes. The subjunctive: "If Jesus is your Lord, then you will be blessed." "If you believe with all your heart that Jesus Christ is Lord, it will be greatly to your advantage." Such preaching appeals to enlightened self-interest, the pragmatist and moral idealist. In the imperative mode, the mood changes: "We ought to believe with our whole hearts that Jesus Christ is Lord, and we ought to confess and accept him as our Lord." The sermon then becomes a series of "oughts" and "shoulds," not necessarily calling for moralistic behavior, but that "we ought to believe with our whole hearts; we ought to be gracious people; we ought to be committed to Christ."

The indicative mode of preaching is clear: God made Jesus Christ both Lord and God. Keeping this statement in the indicative, Davis preaches a powerful sermon which includes these lines:

> God has made him Lord. God did it alone and unassisted, without consulting any man. Pilate, Herod, the Roman emperor did not make Jesus Lord. The Jewish Sanhedrin and people did not make him Lord. Peter and the disciples and the church did not make him Lord. . . . God made him Lord. [Note the parallelism and repetition which aid the ear in listening; we will return to this later.]

> He [God] did not consult the Congress in Washington, the Parliament in London or the Kremlin in Moscow. He did not wait until the Bureau of Scientific Research approved his plan as feasible. He did not stop to ask what all the professors in universities and theological schools would think if he made Jesus Lord. He

just made him Lord, and then sent his messenger to announce what he had done.[97]

Davis' sermon is a good illustration of indicative preaching.

Moralistic preaching may be the result of an exaggerated desire to be relevant.

In comparing the constructive criticisms by professors and laity, it seems that the laity are more critical of *form* and the professors of *content*. Professors seem to be the guardians of *biblical truth* and laity of *human need*. The best of both need to be retained.

10. Preachers don't take quality study time. Keck and Thielicke are most pointed in their concern for the loss of quality preparation time. Keck claims that "preaching has lost its centrality in most mainline white protestant churches."

> Today it is administration which gets the lion's share of one's energy. What is left is apportioned to counseling and routine pastoral care, "board sitting" on community agencies; *sundry matters have displaced Sunday matters.* The proliferation of tasks has squeezed virtually to the vanishing point blocks of time free from interruption, time essential for sermon preparation and especially for long-range reading and reflection.[98]

You can't say it more succinctly than that. His words are a description of my own pastoral life, trying to carve out quality time for reading, preparation of sermons and classes, and especially long-range reading and reflection. Brooks talks about the need for long-range reading in which one grows as a person, reading not exclusively focused on preparation for next Sunday's sermon. He says that you can tell the difference "between a sermon that has been crammed and a sermon which has been thought through long before."[99] It is out of the breadth of reading (and pastoral concern and ministry) that a pastor matures as a person, and it is from this greater depth and breadth, that a pastor speaks. Unfortunately, doing it the American way, we pastors often join the rat race and get busy doing parish activities, and fail to discipline our lives to have the quality of time needed for long-range reading and reflection.

In the opening sentences of *The Trouble with the Church,* Thielicke states:

> [I am] appalled at what has happened in the church of Luther and Calvin to the very thing which its fathers regard as the source and spring of the Christian faith and life, namely, preaching. In the hectic bustle of ecclesiastical routine, it appears to be relegated more and more to the margin of things. The big city pastor must spend his evenings sitting in meetings of esoteric church organizations where he is always seeing the same faces. During the day, he is chewed up by instructional classes, occasional services, pastoral calls, and the Moloch of his bureaucracy. All this pulverizes him. . . . Here there is nothing but a busyness that distracts and dissipates a man's mind. [100]

In another place he refers to the pastor's temptation to

> . . . throw oneself into the hectic business of "running" a congregation, the busyness that sucks up all one's energies and creates the illusion that one is consuming oneself in the service of the kingdom of God. [101]

Thielicke greatly admires Spurgeon and writes of him:

> He did not allow himself to become swamped with externals and consumed with busyness. Instead he immersed himself in the quietness of prayer and meditation, receptively filling his mind and soul. . . . [102]

Similarly, Reuel Howe, at his Institute, found pastors embarrassed because of the little time they spent in sermon preparation, due to the pressure of other duties:

> How much time do you spend on your sermons? The response . . . is often one of embarrassment, because the amount of time that they spend in preparation is so little. The reasons for this are mainly two: 1) the pressure of other duties makes it difficult for ministers to stake out and hold time for study; 2) their frus-

trations in preaching increase their ambivalence about it, and therefore, their likelihood to procrastinate.[103]

Stott says that "many [pastors] are essentially administrators, whose symbols of ministry are the office rather than the study, and the telephone, rather than the Bible."[104]

Caught up in the busyness of the American way, we pastors far too often allow church activities to absorb more and more of our time. What a struggle this is for most of us!

11. Preaching too often consists of "Saturday night notions."[105] Far too often, we preachers try to prepare Sunday's sermon on Saturday night. Reuel Howe, in his conversations with hundreds of clergy at his Institute, discovered that many pastors cannot produce anything until late Saturday night or Sunday morning when the pressure is really on. They are often exhausted and depressed by Sunday morning, are often disgusted with themselves for procrastinating, are often washed out by Sunday afternoon and perhaps are totally lethargic on Monday morning. He suggests that such preachers are like bakers "who have mixed the ingredients for bread, worked it into the shape of a loaf, but are forced to deliver the bread before it is baked because the customers have arrived and demand immediate delivery. Under these circumstances, the homiletical loaf is either unbaked or half baked." Howe suggests that a cause for these Saturday Night Notions is frustration and ambivalence towards preaching; therefore we procrastinate.[106]

Brooks is devastating in his impatience towards clergy who prepare sermons on Saturday nights. He calls Saturday night preparation "the crowning disgrace of a man's ministry." It is dishonest. It is giving only the last flicker of energy from the week to our most important task. He says that a doctor couldn't give his patients such shoddy care, nor could a lawyer neglect the needs of his clients with such poor preparation.[107] One devastating consequence of doing study on Friday to preach for Sunday is that the "material comes across the man, but it has not come through the man. It has never been wrought in his experience."[108] His fundamental criticism is that such pastors "aren't doing their best." "The first necessity for the preacher and the hodcarrier is the same. Be faithful and do your best for every congregation and every occasion." [109] Brooks suggests to young pastors that they learn the proper work habits early in their ministry because "the way in which [work habits] form themselves in the earliest years of his ministry tend to rule him with almost despotic power to the end." [110]

Farmer refers to the need for "absorbing" the manuscript, otherwise the sermon will remain an "it" and not become an "I-Thou" communication. [111] Harms points to the need for a coalescence between the inner form of the sermon and the inner form of the preacher. [112] What Harms and Farmer suggest is very difficult if a person is finishing his sermon on Sunday morning during the preaching itself. Mitchell states clearly: "Preachers simply must stop the practice of sitting at a desk and pleading for power to be breathed into human homework completed as recently as 11:30 P.M., Saturday." [113] Or, as someone else has said, "There is no reason the Holy Spirit cannot inspire on Thursday morning as well as Saturday evening."

SUMMARY

To review, the eleven deadly sins of preaching lead to sermons that have:

1. too much abstraction;
2. too many complexities;
3. too little connecting of the Scriptures to human need;
4. too much language of Zion;
5. too much reference to the land of Zion;
6. too few illustrations from everyday life;
7. too much bad news;
8. too much predictability and lack of passion;
9. too many moralisms;
10. too little careful preparation;
11. too many Saturday night notions.

Knowing that the history of the church has included a history of "let's eat the preacher for Sunday lunch," it is wise for us to allow these criticisms to "sift through our hearts" and not merely "trickle over our minds." The tendency is to dismiss these criticisms, to think that this critique is describing the other preacher—you know, the dull one down the street—and not myself. Surveys have told us that most pastors evaluate their own preaching as "good" or "very good"; consequently there is a natural tendency to discard these suggestions, ignore them, and get on to other and more important things. How foolish if this is our attitude!

Besides, most of us preachers receive very little honest feedback about our sermons. We have the typical pleasant handshake and "Nice to see you today" or an occasional "Good sermon, pastor." Rarely, if ever, do we receive thoughtful, analytical feedback about our sermons. Two-thirds of the regulars seldom or never say anything to a preacher about the sermon.[114] Howe says that most laity are aware that we tend to take criticisms of our preaching as personal rejection, and so they will be most cautious of saying anything too negative. They know how fragile our egos are, even to the slightest suggestion for improvement.[115] And that is unfortunate. Consequently, we receive very little honest feedback.

Almost every other occupation has some form of review, some form of constructive suggestions for improvement. My preaching needs it, and I assume yours does as well. We need to be less personally sensitive about our preaching and more open to constructive, helpful analysis by our laity who faithfully listen to us week after week and year after year.

3

The Preacher as Person

Between the Word and the world is the figure of the preacher."[1] Arndt Halvorson says that a sermon is "shaped as much by the interior world of the preacher's mind and imagination as it is by the text."[2] Phillips Brooks teaches that a sermon consists of two elements, truth and personality, and it is a "defect" in one or both of the elements that causes every sermon to fall short.[3] For better or worse we all know that the pastor is at the heart of the preaching event.

What qualities are desirable and necessary in a preacher? Fant warns us that "the traditional listing of personal characteristics needed by a minister generally becomes superficial and usually winds up sounding like a Boy Scout oath: 'brave, clean, reverent.' "[4]

Luther lists the necessary attributes:

A good preacher should have these properties and virtues: First, he should be able to teach in a right and orderly way. Second, he should have a good wit. Third, he should be able to speak well. Fourth, he should have a good voice. Fifth, a good memory. Sixth, he should know when to stop. Seventh, he should make sure of his material and be diligent. Eighth, he should stake body and blood, goods and honor on it. Ninth, he must suffer himself to be vexed and flayed by everyone.

Luther also lists qualities that the world enjoys in the preacher:

> As the world would have him, six things are necessary to the preacher: 1. He must have a fine accent. 2. He must be learned. 3. He must be eloquent. 4. He must be a handsome person, whom the girls and young women will like. 5. He must take no money but have money to give. 6. He must tell people what they like to hear.[5]

Brooks, Mitchell, Achtemeier, Davis, Thielicke, Craddock, Halvorson, Fant, Erdahl, Buechner, Harms, Steimle—all had perceptions about desirable characteristics of preachers. The following is a collation of their insights.

WHAT A PREACHER NEEDS

Piety

The authors wrote more paragraphs and pages about the pastor's personal faith than any other factor:

> I must not dwell upon the first of all the necessary qualities, and yet there is not a moment's doubt that it does stand first of all. It is a personal piety, a deep possession in one's own soul of the faith and hope and resolution which he is to offer his fellowmen for their new life. Nothing but fire kindles fire. To know in one's whole nature what it is to live by Christ; to be His, not our own . . . .[6]

Achtemeier was most eloquent in her statements about a pastor's personal faith. As mentioned in Chapter 1, I ask you to read these quotations slowly. They are gems.

> But if you set in the midst of all that a preacher who truly knows God, who loves him with a burning love, and who woos a congregation into sharing such knowledge and passion, the hungry come. . . .[7]

> When once asked the basis of Charles Spurgeon's success as a preacher, his brother replied: "I think it lies in the fact that he loves Jesus of Nazareth, and Jesus of Nazareth loves him." Or, as Augustine put it, "What I live by, I impart."[8]

The Gospel cannot be lived out by one who has it only as secondhand information, nor can it be communicated by the preacher
who has inherited it simply by hearsay—little snippets gathered
here and there from the latest books and theologians. . . . Such
secondhand experiences of the Gospel result in scissors-and-paste
sermons, ideas developed around the thoughts of another and
strung together in an outline. They may make logical sense but
they will seldom reveal the living God, because the preacher who
speaks them has no sense of that God and communicates no
experience of having lived in him and loved him. Our people
want credible witnesses.[9]

It is not surprising therefore that the final issue of this daily
disciplined dialogue with the Word of God is love for him—
swelling, passionate, heart-filling love which takes over our personalities.[10]

It has often been noted of pulpitmasters that they lead lives of
continual and constant prayer. The reason is that they already
know the God to whom they pray, and they turn to him as the
One from whom they literally live and breathe, seeking even
deeper faith, greater knowledge, surer guidance and sustenance.
They know that, apart from God, they can do nothing.[11]

Arndt Halvorson also writes about the interior life of prayer:

Prayer is, above all, the practice of the presence of God. To pray
is to be open to God. Sadly, the devotional life of the preacher
is the first fatality of being busy. Without prayer, we become
pretenders, phonies, and no amount of human warmth, intellectual honesty or moral earnestness will hide the truth.[12]

Of all the authors studied, Walter Burghardt seems to have the
deepest sensitivities to the inner life of piety of a pastor. Dr. Burghardt
is one of the most eloquent experts on preaching in the Roman Catholic
church. Of the 10 renowned essayists at the First National Ecumenical
Scriptural-Theological Symposium on Preaching at Emory University,
sponsored by the Word of God Institute, Dr. Burghardt seemed to
have the finest contribution. In a few pages, he wove words and wisdom

together that stressed the importance of a preacher knowing and loving God. Again, it is time to read carefully:

> Sheer study is not enough. To preach effectively . . . it is not enough to know *about* God; I must know God. . . . I urge on all preachers a burning, humbling question: For all you know about God, do you really know God?
>
> [Quoting Ignatius:] All I say is I knew God, nameless and un-fathomable, silent and yet near, bestowing himself upon me in Trinity. I knew God beyond all concrete imaginings. I knew him clearly in such nearness and grace as is impossible to confound or mistake. . . .
>
> Can you say that, like Ignatius, you have truly encountered the living and true God? Can you say that you know God Himself, not simply human words that describe him? If you cannot, I dare not conclude that you are an unproductive preacher. . . .
>
> I do say that if you know only a theology of God, not the God of theology, you will not be the preacher our world desperately needs. . . .
>
> Our people are hungry for preachers who, like Magdalene, have seen the risen Lord. My darkest moments in homiletics are not when my theology is porous. My darkest moments are when I have ceased to pray—when the familiar phrases fall trippingly from my pen and tongue but it is all rote, prepackaged, with the life-giving juices dried up. My preaching is least effective when I experience nothing—neither God's presence nor His absence. [13]

Milo Brekke, Merton Strommen, and Dorothy Williams did a survey of pastoral effectiveness and then published their conclusions in *Ten Faces of Ministry*. The most important characteristic that the laity wanted in their pastors and that pastors wanted in their colleagues was deep, genuine faith. [14] The following is a list of descriptive sentences that the laity wanted to be found incarnated in their pastors (the highest possible rating was 4.0):

3.77 Believes the Gospel he or she preaches.

3.57 Receives Holy Communion regularly.

3.54 Acknowledges sin before God.

3.35 Uses Scripture for nourishment.

3.30 Spends time in personal prayer.

Other qualities which revealed the pastor's inner piety were:

3.48 Sets a Christian example.

3.48 Knows the Bible well.

3.40 Wants others to know Christ.

3.36 Believes in the resurrection.

3.34 Sees own need for spiritual growth.[15]

Compared to the hundreds of other factors, the above are all rated extremely highly. These laity want a pastor who lives in God and in whom God lives. In the past, such a person would be called "a man of God."

On the other side of the coin, the authors were critical of preachers who didn't have a passion for God. The first chapter of Thielicke's book, *The Trouble with the Church,* is entitled, "Our Credibility." He writes there about the loss of pastoral piety:

> In order to form a judgment concerning his credibility, we would have to know whether he lives, whether he really exists in the house of dogmas he proclaims. This means that what a preacher says in the pulpit must have a relationship to what fills the rest of his existence. Sure [he] is a nice, pleasant, affable fellow. But I ask you, when does anything about Christ come out in his ordinary human conversation? When is his name uttered quite naturally when he is talking to me about the weather or about my son . . .? If not, I am inclined to accept the conclusion that he himself is not living in the house of his own preaching but has settled down somewhere besides it, and that therefore the center of gravity of his life lies elsewhere.[16]

Thielicke compares the inner life of a pharmacist and a pastor:

> When we meet a druggist, we do not necessarily note whether he loves or hates, whether he dispenses pills with delight or whether he is eating out his heart in envy and care. The sales talk goes on its routine way. But with the preacher, it soon comes out whether he has come to terms with himself or not. And the

thoughts that bicker and grumble in his heart become voices that shout from the rooftops. What the druggist thinks does not undermine the words with which he recommends this or that cough medicine; but the preacher, by the state of his soul, can belie the words which are committed to him, no matter how well chosen and well disposed they are as he utters them. [17]

Similarly, another author comments: "People will no more accept our Christian message if our life contradicts it than they would take a cold cure recommended by a salesman who coughs and sneezes between each sentence." [18] Thielicke is critical of clergy when he asks, "Why aren't people going to church as much nowadays?" Because of TV? Work? Recreation? Prosperity? Scientific progress? He goes on to suggest that the real problem lies within the "spiritual condition" of the pastor and "his unconvincing Christian existence." The "diagnosticians of the spirit of the times . . . seem to me to be like a doctor who discovers a wart or infected tonsil, but overlooks the rampant carcinoma." [19] The rampant carcinoma is the "unconvincing Christian existence" in the lives of the pastors. They (we) don't live in the house of their (our) doctrine. The center of gravity is not Christ but located elsewhere.

John Stott tells the story about David Hume, the 18th century British deistic philosopher who rejected Christianity. A friend once met him hurrying along a London street and asked him where he was going. "To hear Whitefield preach," was the reply. "But surely you don't believe what Whitefield preaches, do you?" his friend asked in astonishment. "No, I don't," answered Hume, "but he does." [20]

Spurgeon has many pages and chapters that emphasize the importance of the vitality of a pastor's spiritual life and faith. He described Luther's faith and preaching graphically:

Nobody doubted that he [Luther] believed what he spoke. He spoke with thunder for there was lightning in his faith. The man preached all over, for his entire nature believed. You felt, "Well, he may be mad, or he may be altogether mistaken, but he assuredly believes what he says. He is the incarnation of faith. His heart is running over at his lips."

Spurgeon went on to say:

> There is no rhetoric like that of the heart and no school for learning it but the foot of the cross.

> Know Jesus. Sit at his feet. Consider his nature, his work, his suffering, his glory. Rejoice in his presence. Commune with him from day to day.

> There is something about the very tone of the man who has been with Jesus which has more power to touch the heart than the most perfect oratory.[21]

What is the most needed quality in a preacher? A deep personal faith, a love of Christ, a life of prayer.

Passion

Brooks, Achtemeier, Thielicke, Burghardt, and Stott wrote at length about this concern for the preacher's inner life. Another person was Fred Craddock. It is interesting to me that Craddock's first book, *As One without Authority,* written in 1971, was about form. He tried to help us pastors with "induction," "movement," "unity," "text," and "structure." But there seems to be a shift in Craddock between 1971 and 1978, because in 1978, his second book, *Overhearing the Gospel,* is concerned about the pastor's lack of or loss of passion. This book is a study in the life and preaching of Søren Kierkegaard and his critique of passionless pastors and passionless Christians in Denmark. When I read his two books, I had the feeling that Craddock didn't deal with the fundamental problem of preaching in his first book. As 20th century, affluent American pastors, his second book about passion may be the one with which we need to deal. He writes:

> The act of communicating the Gospel is, by its very nature, an act of passion.

> SK [Søren Kierkegaard] punctuated his descriptions of those who would be communicators of the Christian faith with such words as intensity, discipline, passion, pathos.

> But the Gospel had become, SK lamented, a piece of information. Passion was replaced by descriptions of passion. The net effect

for the Church, said SK, would be compared to reading a cookbook to a man who was hungry.

SK regarded it as a common fault of the pulpit in his day that there was very much standing on the legs and proving God's existence and very little thanking him upon the knees.

SK is saying that the way to understand and communicate the Christian faith is through discipline and participation in the faith. This is not an option for the communicator. . . . If the speaker is not in his speaking, if his absence is evidenced by the overage of cliches, quotations and secondary resources, the hearer feels deceived and deprived.

The distance may have developed unconsciously as an old habit took the place of conviction. The words and phrases are all there, and the appearance of teaching and preaching so approximates the real thing that the illusion is complete in its deception. The speaker steps up to the platform as before, unaware as was Samson, that he had been shorn of his strength, unable to name the date or the hour when the glory of God had departed.[22]

What is passion? Craddock uses such words as "intensity," "discipline," and "pathos." The word *passion* comes from the Latin word *passio* and the Greek *pascho*. It means suffering, an intensity of love born out of shared suffering, empathy, identification with those who are hurting as a result of injustice, abuse, or the nastiness of life.

The opposite of passion is lukewarmness. Harms cleverly speaks about conduct unbecoming to a pastor:

Do we need the reminder that a pastor's life and behavior had not best negate his sermon with "conduct unbecoming a pastor"? . . . I speak not of flagrant immorality. . . . I speak rather of a more subtle response, a lack-luster diffidence. . . . The church is able to rise above the grand assault of immorality. . . . It is lukewarmness that kills. . . .[23]

The British theologian William Sangster, author of numerous textbooks on preaching, writes about the time he was on a panel, interviewing candidates for the ministry in the Methodist church. A nervous young man presented himself and said that he was not the kind of person who would set the Thames River on fire. To which Dr. Sangster responded: "I'm not interested to know if you could set the Thames on fire. What I want to know is this: if I picked you up by the scruff of your neck and dropped you in the Thames, would it sizzle?"[24]

Other authors echo the same theme. Spurgeon: "Give us more of the speech which comes of a burning heart, as lava comes of a volcanic overflow."[25] Paul Scherer: "If you ever want to set anybody on fire, you have to burn a little yourself."[26] Phillips Brooks: "Nothing but fire kindles fire."[27] John Stott: "Truth and eloquence, reason and passion, light and fire."[28] Martyn Lloyd-Jones: "Logic on fire."[29]

Helmut Thielicke fell in love with Spurgeon's lectures on preaching and advised his readers to sell all their books on homiletics and feast on Spurgeon alone. He advises us to let Spurgeon be our Socrates to help us find our way. And for Spurgeon, what was the most important quality for effective preaching? Earnestness!

> What in a Christian minister is the most essential quality for winning souls for Christ? I should reply earnestness . . . , an intense zeal, a consuming passion for souls, and an eager enthusiasm in the cause of God. . . .
>
> We preachers must always be earnest in reference to our pulpit work. . . . To go into the pulpit with the listless air of those gentlemen who loll about . . . is most censurable. . . .
>
> It is not in the order of nature that rivers should run uphill, and it does not often happen that zeal rises from the pew to the pulpit. . . .
>
> A burning heart will soon find for itself a flaming tongue.[30]

Many students of the Bible have come to appreciate the apostle Paul's passionate language (e.g., Gal. 1:9, "If anyone is preaching to you a gospel contrary to that which you received, let him be accursed"). But in my years of study of the book of Acts, I had failed to focus on two words which were used to describe his preaching in Ephesus: "For three years I did not cease night or day to admonish every one *with tears.*"[31] This is not to suggest that preachers are to weep in the pulpit and whip up crocodile tears for dramatic effect, but these two little words, "with tears," reveal that Paul was a passionate preacher. Paul describes passionate preaching when he advises Timothy how to speak: "Preach the word, [that is:] be urgent in season and out of season, convince, rebuke, and exhort, be unfailing in patience and in teaching" (2 Tim. 4:2).

Authentic humanness

Halvorson entitles his book *Authentic Preaching,* and one of his first subchapters is labeled "Authentic Personhood." The skills of exegesis, interpretation, theology, and relevance are "strangely impotent," he writes, "if they are not employed by an authentic person."[32]

Billy Graham conducted a rally in Tacoma, Washington, and a newspaper headline announced: "Billy Graham's Appeal: A Changeless Authenticity." In that same article, the dean of Seattle's Episcopalian cathedral said of Graham, "His appeal has to do with the personality of the figure of Billy Graham himself; it's somehow congruent with what he says. He's authentic in some way . . . and all of us are impressed with the authentic." Another said of him: "He has retained a firm hold of who he is. He hasn't read his own press clippings."[33]

Several authors say it slightly differently, but all of them want us preachers to share fully in the struggle of being human. People want their preachers to be authentic human beings, who experience all the same feelings and struggles as the laity, who do not hide behind the role of "Reverend So-and-So" or "detached religious professionalism." Again, it's time to read slowly:

> Such an experience [Ralph Waldo] Emerson had that snowy day he went to church and was sorely tempted never to go again. "The snow storm was real [so he wrote]; the preacher merely spectral, and the eye felt the sad contrast in looking at him and then out of the window behind him, into the beautiful meteor of the snow. He had no word intimating that he had laughed or wept, was married or in love, had been commended or cheated, or chagrined. If he had ever lived or acted, we were none the wiser for it. The capital secret of his profession, namely, to convert life into truth, he had not learned."[Scherer].[34]

The less you are like a parson, the more likely you are to be heard; and if you are known to be a minister, the more you show yourself to be a human being. . . [Spurgeon].[35]

"That preacher knows what it is like to be me." That feeling can be evoked only by the preacher who does not forget what it is to be human, who knows that faith is forever in tandem with doubt. . . . To be a preacher . . . is to be radically human and to be unafraid to say so. . . . Being human serves the Gospel. The more we feel free to be ourselves, to be with people, to be free to make mistakes and to fail, to celebrate small victories and to cry when the tears well up, the more we are likely to serve the Word of God [Rice].[36]

The preacher must always try to feel what it is like to live inside the skins of the people he is preaching to, to hear the truth as they hear it. . . . He listens out of the same emptiness that they do, for the truth to fill him and make him true [Buechner].[37]

We do our best preaching out of our weakness and our awareness of our sins and our sinful inclinations. Weakness and sin are not synonymous terms. Our sin is the result of coddling of our weakness. Our sin is a direct action we take to cover up our weakness [Halvorson].[38]

First of all, no one needs to become human. He is already human. He simply needs to be honest, to avoid playing dishonest games with himself and others which deceive him into believing otherwise. . . . Naturalness means not adding to or subtracting from your personality. It means being neither more nor less than you are. Some men try to be more than they are; they want to appear holier or more profound or more dynamic. Others are scared to death to seem to be as much as they are; they do not want to be regarded as zealous or devout. . . . By imitating others, you create a Frankenstein. . . . Mary Shelly wrote about a similar attempt. Dr. Frankenstein pieced together the parts from a number of cadavers to make a man, then he created a monster. But no more so than the preacher whose personality is a composite of the different pieces of others, some long dead and nearly decomposed. Then when that monster roars and stalks about, he should not be surprised when children will not play at his feet [Fant].[39]

But let him take heart. He is called not to be an actor or a magician in the pulpit; he is called to be himself. He is called to tell the truth as he experienced it. He is called to be human . . . and that is calling enough for any man. If he does not make real to them the human experience of what it is to cry into the storm and receive no answer, to be sick at heart and find no healing, then he becomes the only one there who seems not to have had that experience because most surely under their bonnets and shawls and jackets, under their afros and ponytails, all the others there have had it whether they talk of it or not. As much as anything else, it is their experience of the absence of God that has brought them there in search for his presence, and if the preacher does not speak of that and to that, then he becomes like the captain of a ship who is the only one aboard who either does not know that the waves are twenty feet high or will not face up to it [Buechner].[40]

The laity do not want their preachers to be *religious* phonies who "speak too smoothly about God," pretending to be more virtuous, healthy, and holy than the people in the pews. They do not want us to be *human* phonies, who speak too smoothly of our own struggles, pretending we do not share fully in the agonies and ecstacies of living. They want us to be who we are, authentic human beings in whom sin and grace live.

Humor

One way of being human is to laugh at ourselves and chuckle at our human foibles and frivolities. Nearly all the authors I read discussed the role of humor in the pulpit. They encouraged the use of humor but were cautious that no one is "laughed at." It has always amazed me that Luther, when listing 10 desirable attributes of a preacher, lists "a good sense of humor" as second in importance.[41] I have to admit that I myself am attracted to preaching where there is laughter. Oswald Hoffman, the radio preacher on *The Lutheran Hour,* is an absolute master of wit and on occasion has the listener belly-laughing during half of his sermon; but after the laughter, inevitably comes that powerful penetration of words and insight. Or as another has said, "After the mirthquake, the still small voice."[42] Spurgeon had the gift of humor and he used it to show the truth in such a way his readers didn't become defensive. For example, rather than simply saying that we preachers "talk over people's heads," he suggests: "Jesus said: Feed my lambs. He didn't say: Feed my giraffes!" And our response is to laugh at ourselves and our temptation to want to sound intelligent and learned in the pulpit. Humor has a way of breaking through our defenses and making us more open to the truth. Humor helps us not to take ourselves too seriously. I enjoy the joke: "Why can angels fly so high?" "Because they take themselves so lightly."

In *Encounter with Spurgeon* Thielicke asks: Why was Spurgeon such a popular preacher? Why did 6000 people come out to listen to him every Sunday—and 24,000 one particular Sunday? Thielicke accounts for Spurgeon's popularity by referring to his deep spirituality. Spurgeon drank continuously from the spring of living water. Thielicke adds, however, that the effectiveness of Spurgeon's preaching is "determined by two characteristics: its cheerfulness and its worldliness."

> This cheerfulness is something like a manifestation of grace itself. . . . When Spurgeon was cheerful and humorous in the pulpit, he was putting himself into his preaching. He was entering into the sermon with his whole being. . . . Should we not see that lines of laughter about the eyes are just as much marks of faith as are the lines of care and seriousness? . . . A church is in a bad way when it banishes laughter from the sanctuary and leaves it to the cabaret, the night club and the toastmasters. . . . [Humor] accomplishes the relaxation of ministerial stiffness.[43]

Elton Trueblood, in his book *The Humor of Christ* tells the story of how he discovered the humor of Christ quite by accident. While reading devotions at the family table, his four-year-old began to laugh when he heard the words of Jesus about specks and logs in people's eyes. Dr. Trueblood then lists 30 humorous passages in the Synoptics and challenges "the conventionalized picture of a Christ who never laughed."[44] According to John Stott, Dr. Trueblood attempts to show that the "commonest form of humor was irony ('a holding up to public view of either vice or folly') and not sarcasm (which is cruel and wounds its victims)."[45]

Most pastors don't have the skill and wit of Spurgeon and Hoffman, but I sense that many pastors know how to use humor in the pulpit, poking fun at human nature, themselves, and the world around them. Stott talks about the importance of humor:

> pricking the bubbles of human pomposity, . . . poking fun at human eccentricities which bear witness to our fallenness, . . . so we preachers ought to use satire more skillfully and more frequently, ensuring always that in laughing at others, we are also laughing at ourselves within the solidarity of human pomp and folly.[46]

Humor was appropriate in Jesus' preaching and can be appropriate in ours. Each person, as in everything else, will have a distinctive style and way of using laughter.

Selfless, caring love

Of course, we would expect these to be a desirable cluster of virtues in a preacher. This begins to sound like the Boy Scout list, "brave, clean, obedient." But Fant talks about these qualities in a way that is especially helpful to clergy. He knows the preacher's temptations:

> The pastor needs to be a selfless person. . . . The hireling runs away from the needs of the flock because he is a hireling, that is, because he is in it strictly for himself and what he can get out of it. The faithful servant is paid—but he cares about his duties, and he loves the flock and he risks himself for them. . . . He is perceived as genuinely caring for them.[47]

> The preacher must be committed to the same selfless service as his Lord. If he is perceived as persuing ministry for gain, either monetary or professional; if he seems to care for nothing more than ladder-climbing and status-seeking; if he says only that which will please the galleries; if he prays loudly for "results" to build his reputation—then he may be assured, whatever his own inflated self-image, that his credibility is undermined by his obvious personal interests.[48]

When an audience suspects that a preacher has something personal to gain from his persuasive efforts—more money, a larger pulpit, denominational status, popular acclaim—he is regarded as a manipulator. However, even if the end which the preacher seeks is good, he is still a manipulator if he uses deceitful means to accomplish it.[49]

How we preachers struggle with impure motives! Perhaps that struggle will end at the parousia.

Gift for preaching

Mitchell tells us that black preachers ask of one another, "Can he tell a story?" Luther talks about the preacher's gifts of teaching, wit, speaking ability, voice, memory, courage. Brooks writes about the "born preacher."

> I speak of only one thing more. I do not know how to give it a name, but I do think that in every man who preaches there should be something of that quality which we recognize in a high degree in some men of whom we say, when we see him in the pulpit, that is a "born preacher." Call it enthusiasm; call it eloquence; call it magnetism. . . . Something of this quality there must be in every man who really preaches. He who wholly lacks it cannot be a preacher.[50]

As in all vocations, there is a gift, a God-given ability to do certain kinds of work, including preaching. That's what this book and other preaching books are all about: they try to help us develop our God-given gifts, no matter how meager or abundant they may be.

ONE QUALITY NOT NEEDED IN A PREACHER: EGOTISM

What are those qualities which are not wanted in a preacher? Almost all the authors mentioned one persistent and stubborn problem that affects most of us public communicators: *egotism*, defined as "excessive love and thought of self." Among preachers, the danger is to use the gifts and calling of God to gain the admiration and respect of others, rather than using God's gifts for his service and glory.

Egotism is not to be confused with ego strength, self-acceptance, or self-respect. To stand in front of a congregation takes ego strength. As one of my colleagues in my text-study group said, "I don't appreciate a shriveling violet in the pulpit."

Knowing the value of genuine self-respect, we still need to listen to the wisdom of the sages as they warn us about the preacher's occupational hazard of egotism.

> I want to try to estimate with you some of the dangers to a man's own character which come from being a preacher. The first of these dangers, beyond all doubt, is self-conceit. . . . He finds out that the Old Adam is too strong for the young Melanchthon.[51]

> The ego, not voice or gestures, remain the teller's greatest obstacle in the path of effective communication of the story of faith.[52]

> Most of us are too aware of those in our balconies observing our performances, whom we wish to please or impress: family, former teachers, peers. How large an obstacle is the ego, especially in the path of communication.[53]

> The principal stumbling block for all clergy is our own pride. . . . And so in our pride, we preach ourselves and not Jesus Christ as Lord.[54]

> We are like those tiresome people who so genuinely admire the sunset but when they speak of it, you know at once, in addition, they admire themselves admiring the sunset.[55]

> The Prayer of the Cock captures perfectly the unreality of the mood: "I am your servant . . . only do not forget, Lord, I make the sun rise."[56]

> SK . . . So that at bottom, instead of benefiting him, I want to be admired.[57]

The insight that I enjoyed most was from Erdahl:

> I must often confess to being self-saving and self-serving in my preaching. I try to preach good sermons which will reward me with approval and appreciation, and in doing so, I'm sometimes more of a performer than a proclaimer. I see that I should stop trying to preach good sermons and concentrate on sharing an honest message which speaks to vital business in both my life and yours. I am grateful to hear that you sometimes find that happening, and I pray that my attention may be called away from myself to the message.[58]

I appreciate that quotation from Erdahl because he is so honest about a struggle that all of us clergy have, of being "self-serving and self-saving." He fully admitted his struggle with egotism. At that moment, Erdahl was sharing his full humanity, and we preachers understand all too well what he is writing about. To recall Carl Rogers: "What is most personal, is most universal."[59]

Erdahl is particularly helpful because of the spirit of his confession. As Halvorson said, "We do our best preaching out of our weakness. . . . Sin is trying to cover up our weakness."[60] Evil penetrates every part of our lives. Maybe not all preachers are equally affected by this disease of self-awareness, but there are enough of us who can't escape it, who live in bondage, and who have a permanent handicap. The awful, persistent question keeps being asked of my hidden self (or of my spouse): "How did I do? Was it OK? Reassure me." We ask these persistent questions because deep down inside, we're not sure we are OK. We persistently need reassurance that we are loved and acceptable as preachers. And that is what pulpit grace is all about: God forgiving our pulpit egotism and pulpit fears.

One factor that needs more attention is the preacher's attitude towards himself or herself as a preacher. I like what Paul Harms says about the importance of having a "baptismal attitude" towards ourselves, an attitude which sees ourselves graciously through the eyes of Christ. A "nonbaptismal attitude" is to magnify one's faults, shortcomings, and egotism. "Neither stars nor seas can deter him from seeing the darkness [egotism?] in his soul. We are too quick to magnify our impure motives, our egotism, and other marks of our humanity." Harms continues:

> God begins with a baptismal attitude towards people, including, especially including preachers. When God looks at preachers (or anyone), He does not see the preacher, He sees his Son. God begins with His Son. He sees the preacher through the crucified death of His Son. . . . Baptism works to reduce the preacher's self-consciousness and turns that self to ministry.[61]

Harms is right. Forgiveness is for preachers who struggle with egotism and self-consciousness, for preachers in whom the Old Adam is too strong for the young Melanchthon.

Brooks is the 19th-century sage who wisely advises us to focus on others and their needs as a way of reducing one's self-preoccupation:

> [Another] fundamental necessity of the preacher's power is the freedom from self-consciousness, . . . his forgetfulness of self. . . . [There are two questions:] "How shall I do it most effectively for others?" and second, "How shall I do it most creditably for myself?. . ." The second question disappears out of your work just in proportion as the first question grows intense. . . .
>
> Care not for your servant, but for your truth and for your people.[62]

Similarly, Erdahl suggests:

> The best pulpit communication results from forgetting ourselves and remembering just two things: our truth and our people. Self-preoccupation is the curse of preaching. As the purpose of preaching is to call people out of self-centeredness into self-surrender and self-giving, so also the call of the Lord invites us to let go of ourselves and to preach with the abandonment of self-forgetfulness.[63]

Bonhoeffer describes Jesus as "the man for others"; that quality of selfless love is desirable in any person, regardless of occupation. Stott compares the attitude of a preacher to that of a best man at a wedding, who doesn't want to be the star of the show, but does all he can to facilitate the marriage of the bride and groom. He also compares a preacher to a conductor of an orchestra whose primary task is to pull the music out of the orchestra. "A concert audience does not come to watch a conductor but to hear the music; a church congregation should not come to watch or hear the preacher, but to listen to the Word of God."[64] As has been said many times, preachers are to be like John the Baptist, pointing others to Jesus Christ who is the light of the world.

I once attended the ordination of a young man into the Anglican-Episcopal diaconate. With his distinctly British accent, a seemingly ancient archbishop growled out his *very* short elocution: "Three words you are to remember: Humility! Humility! Humility!" (quoting Augustine). Then he sat down. It is one of the few elocutions I will ever totally remember. Time passed, and the same Anglican archbishop was in town to ordain the same young man into the Anglican priesthood. At the highpoint of the ordination service, the candidate was kneeling before the altar. The old archbishop grabbed the back of the ordinand's collar and jerked his head down to the floor, his nose now pushing against the carpet. The old man then took a huge Bible and pushed it down onto his shoulders, neck and head, so that the young ordinand felt the weight of the Scriptures above him. With his distinct accent, the old archbishop again muttered words of wisdom to the young priest: "Humility! You are *under* God and the Scriptures!"

Jesus, when asked who was the greatest in the kingdom of God, said, "He who humbles himself. . . ."

SUMMARY

Needed in a pastor are: piety; passion; authentic humanness; sense of humor; selfless, caring love; and a gift or aptitude for preaching. Not needed in a pastor: egotism. And what is needed to combat the battle with egotism? Forgiveness. Focus on the truth; focus on the needs of others, as a way of moving beyond self-preoccupation. In other words, a seventh quality is needed within a pastor: humility.

4

The Preacher as Theologian

Theology is part of every sermon. It is impossible to have a nontheological sermon. No matter what its shape or form, every sermon is laced with theological presuppositions and prejudices.

Nothing is more certain than the fact that some theology will surface in every sermon. The danger is that it will do so without prior reflection.[1]

Spurgeon was his usually blunt self when he wrote:

If you are not theologians, you are in your pastorates just nothing at all. You may be fine rhetoricians, and be rich in polished sentences; but without knowledge of the gospel and aptness to teach it, you are but sounding brass and a tinkling cymbal.[2]

THE PREACHER IS A PERSON
WHO IS POSSESSED BY THE GOSPEL

It is crucially important that the preacher is grasped by the gospel, that a preacher knows what it means to be refreshed by the gracious love of God.

Whoever is grasped by the Pauline Gospel will preach credibly and authentically because it makes one a free person. . . . In other words, the need of the preacher is to be grasped by the message, . . . grasped by the word of the cross.[3]

The nerve center of the pastor's work is to emphasize grace in the pulpit and to minister from grace in pastoral relationships.[4]

In the Thursday morning text-study group that I attend, Al Stone is a pastor who persistently asks: "What is the shape of grace in this text?" That is the question we preachers always need to be asking.

Paul Harms is helpful when he talks about the importance of having a "baptismal attitude" towards oneself and the whole congregation.[5] The pastor preaches the truth of God in the spirit of genuine love for his parishioners; therefore, the sermon is not reduced to scolding or haranguing the flock. When the fundamental attitude of the preacher is gracious love, then the whole sermon reflects affection, gentleness and compassion, even when the law is preached. As Stuempfle noted, when a rock is warmed by the sunlight, it cannot fail to give off warmth; and likewise, when a preacher's inner life is warmed by God's gracious love, he or she cannot fail to radiate God's gracious love, especially in his preaching.

Luther was a man who had been grasped by the gospel. He knew what it meant to live within the promises of God, that God is gracious and good, that God loves sinners, that God freely forgives. Luther rings out the clarion call of the gospel:

A minister of Christ is a steward of the mysteries of God. He should regard himself and insist that others regard him as one who administers to the household of God nothing but Christ and the things of Christ. In other words, he should preach the pure Gospel, the true faith, that Christ alone is our life, our way, our wisdom, power, glory and salvation.[6]

Luther says we are to receive Christ in the same way that the earth receives rain. The earth does nothing to merit or deserve rain. The rain is freely given, and so it is with the love of God. God's love is freely and abundantly showered upon us.[7]

All of Luther's writings always return to that central theme: Christ, Word, grace, gospel, promise; and every text is viewed from a gospel perspective of God's good and gracious love, abundantly and freely given, like the rain.

Luther was also keenly aware of the alternative religion of law and reason. For him, the religion of law and reason was the religion of the papists, the fanatics, the schismatics, the enthusiasts, the sophists, the scholastics, and anybody else who subtly or conspicuously emphasized humankind's working, loving, choosing, willing, feeling, knowing, sacrificing, or dying in order to be saved, in order to be a worthwhile person in their own eyes or God's eyes. Such religion has the odor of rotten eggs. Luther's nose was like that of a K-9 police dog whose job it is to sniff out contraband; Luther's nose had the keen ability to sniff out a religion of Law and Reason, no matter where it was hidden or disguised. He wrote in a sermon in 1531:

> You [sectarians] preach the letter and the Old Testament, that is, the law. . . . It is impossible for the sectarian to preach the New Testament. . . . They do not know what the New Testament is. Even though they talk about it, they still run out into juridical legalism. . . . Paul calls all this the "letter" which "kills". . . . That's what it means to preach the letter which teaches nothing more than what I should do. . . . Where the only preaching is "do this," it remains only letter.[8]

The most natural thing in the world is to preach "do-this" sermons, and Luther had a nose for the foul odor of "do-this" religion wherever it might be found. Another has said: It is easier to preach "Good chidings" than "Good Tidings."[9]

By contrast, the religion of promise is a pure gift, given to humankind; and by the preaching of the Word, God creates faith and gives the Spirit of love. It is by Christ's working, loving, choosing, knowing, sacrificing, and dying that a person is saved, and as that Word passes through the ears and into the heart, God creates trust and a rebirth of love for the neighbor. That is the gospel. Luther proclaimed this gospel with clarity and power:

> Therefore we preach something better: the Spirit and the New Testament, which is that Jesus Christ has come for your sake and taken your sins upon himself. There you hear, not what you should do, but what God is doing through Christ, which means, of

course, that he works faith and bestows the Holy Spirit. This is what it means to preach the New Testament and the Holy Spirit.[10]

Whoever, therefore, does not know or preach the gospel, is not only no priest or bishop, but he is a kind of pest to the church, who under the false title of priest or bishop, or dressed in sheep's clothing, actually does violence to the gospel and plays the wolf in the church.[11]

Why was Luther a great preacher? Because he knew and preached the gospel? He was not a plague of the church nor was he a wolf in sheep's clothing. For Luther, the truth of every assertion and action was seen in light of the gospel. This gospel was not understood merely intellectually, academically, or theoretically, but this understanding of the gospel grew out of his life experience and was part of his own "life's native tongue." That's one reason why Luther was a great preacher. The gospel lived in, with, and under all he said and did. He was grasped by the gospel.

THE PREACHER IS A PERSON
WHO PROCLAIMS THE GOSPEL

The gift of many contemporary artists and poets is that they can describe the tragic condition of the world in which we live but may not have an equivalent ability to see grace, kingdom, and love. They often have a better eye for winter than spring. This struck me when reading Camus' *The Exile and the Kingdom.* Although Camus could vividly describe the exile, the desert, and the wasteland, he didn't have equivalent poetic power to recreate the kingdom, the power, and the glory. But that's what the preacher's task is all about—to be "fabulists," tellers of comedy and fairy tale, weavers of the Deep Magic![12] Our primary task is *not* to poetically describe the fallenness of the world. Our people live with that every day, inside and outside of their skins. We all know that world too well. Rather, a gospel preacher is called to put energy into imagining Easter, hope, freedom, kingdom. A gospel preacher loves the "re" words: renew, rebirth, restore, remake, reconcile. Henry Mitchell and Reuel Howe tell us that the laity are getting tired of "all that analysis that leads to paralysis," tired of the tirades about what's wrong with the world. It is as if many preachers are much more preoccupied with Romans 2 than with Romans 3.

Buechner encourages us preachers to rhapsodize with the gospel:

Stand up in his pulpit as a fabulist extraordinary to tell the truth of the Gospel in its highest and wildest and holiest sense. This is his job, but more often than not he shrinks from it . . . because the truth he is called to proclaim, like the fairy tale, seems . . . too good to be true, and so the preacher as an apologist instead of a fabulist tries as best he can to pare it down to a size he thinks the world will swallow. [13]

Homiletics becomes apologetics. The preacher exchanges the fairytale truth that is too good to be true. . . . He secularizes and makes rational. He adapts and makes relevant. He demythologizes and makes credible. And what remains of the fairytale of the Gospel in his hands, a fairytale not unlike the Wizard of Oz. [14]

The preacher is apt to preach the Gospel with the high magic taken out, the deep mystery reduced to manageable size. . . . The wild and joyful promise of the Gospel is reduced to promises more easily kept. The peace that passes all understanding is reduced to a peace that anybody can understand. The faith that can move mountains and raise the dead becomes faith that can help make life bearable until death ends it. [15]

The joke of it all is that often it is the preacher who as a steward of the wildest mystery of them all is the one who hangs back, prudent, cautious, hopelessly mature, and wise to the last. [16]

Yet the tears that come to our eyes at the joy of the fairytale are nevertheless essentially joyous tears because what we have caught a glimpse of, however fleeting, is joy itself. . . . [17]

Fleeting glimpses of joy. Just as we experience fleeting glimpses of a deer in the woods, so we experience fleeting glimpses of God's gospel: During the worship service when you see one person touch another person in love, maybe quietly and tenderly at the altar rail. During a visit to the nursing home, when you see an old man gently spooning melted ice cream into the mouth of his beloved wife of 60 years who is now incapacitated. During a conversation with an ex-Roman Catholic nun in Nicaragua who tells you story after story about her confirmation boys who had hope and yet were killed by the government death squads. Glimpses of joy in the midst of suffering and injustice! Wild and mysterious! Bitter and sweet! It takes high magic to experience the gospel in its highest, wildest, and holiest sense!

Extraordinary things happen when the gospel is experienced. Zacchaeus climbs up in a sycamore tree as a crook and climbs down a saint. Paul sets out as a hatchet man for the Pharisees and comes back a fool for Christ.[18] A man who looks in the "mirror all in a lather and sees at least eight parts chicken, phony, slob" is transformed by the deep magic of God's love.[19]

The deep magic of God's love is forgiveness. Forgiveness was at the very core of Luther's theology and preaching, and forgiveness needs to be at the very core of our theology and preaching. Whereas words like "atonement, propitiation, redemption, and justification" bounce off our hearts like hailstones dance off the pavement, the word of "forgiveness" seeps into our hearts like rain soaking into a garden. The language of forgiveness still gives life. We need to forgive and be forgiven. In our world today, people are crying out to understand and experience the reality of forgiveness. In the little corner of the world where I live, in the school district where the children of our church receive their education, 85% of the students come from fractured families. Only 15% of the children have their original mom and dad, brothers and sisters, grandmas and grandpas. In these homes, people have deeply hurt each other. I continue to be amazed how broken and bloody are relationships within the homes that surround our sanctuary. An American tragedy is that so many lives are being swept up into the values of our culture, into the disintegration of family and personal integrity. And in the real world of the people who are entrusted to my care and keeping, we need to hear, share, and experience the reality of God's forgiveness. The only way that imperfect people can live together with any happiness is when the forgiveness of God lives within them and between them. The gospel is the gift of forgiveness and that gospel needs to be given in preaching. Stuempfle tells us that the preacher will take time to interpret the dynamics of forgiveness and will tell stories of forgiveness. "A way must be found to break open for people the actual dynamics of the experience of forgiveness and to lead them into its reality." The meaning of forgiveness "can best be expressed through a 'story' in which people can be seen to interact in a way that is qualified by grace."[20]

The center of preaching is the proclamation of the gospel. Luther taught: "Nothing except Christ is to be preached."[21] Spurgeon had the same emphasis: "Preach Christ and him crucified. Where Jesus is exalted, souls are attracted. . . ."[22] "This is the sum: Preach Christ, always and evermore. He is the whole gospel. His person, offices and work must be our one great, all-comprehending theme."[23]

A preacher is a fabulist, a teller of the wildest mystery of them all, a proclaimer of the crucified and risen Christ, a weaver of the deep magic of forgiveness. A preacher is possessed by the gospel and proclaims the gospel. I love Spurgeon's metaphor, "However beautiful the sower's basket, it is a miserable mockery if it be without seed."[24] Preachers are to plant the gospel!

THE PREACHER HAS A THEOLOGY THAT STRESSES THE IMPORTANCE OF PREACHING

It is critical that a pastor understands biblically and theologically the role of preaching in the Christian faith. There would be no Christian faith without preaching. Christianity and preaching are connected to each other like a head is to the neck. You cannot have one without the other and still have life. Preaching and Christianity are inseparable; they are part of an organic whole. It has been said that Christianity lives by preaching, just as Confucianism lives by a code of manners, Buddhism by meditation, and Hinduism by rituals and social organization.[25] Preaching is indispensable to Christianity; this can be demonstrated from the Bible.

THE ROLE OF PREACHING IN THE BIBLE

A unique aspect of the biblical God is that God has a voice and speaks his mind. It is the very nature of our God to communicate, and for the people to hear and respond. If you open your Bible concordance to the word *voice,* you will find hundreds of biblical listings which remind us that our God is a God who talks:

> *Exod. 15:26* "If you diligently hearken to the voice of the Lord. . . ."

> *Exod. 19:5* "If you obey my voice and keep my covenant . . . ."

> *Deut.* 4:36 "Out of heaven he let you hear his voice. . . ."

> *Deut. 5:26* "Who has heard the voice of the living God speaking . . ., as we have, and has still lived?"

In contrast, the prophets ridicule the heathen gods precisely because they are "dumb"; they cannot speak; they have no voice. Habakkuk writes:

> For the workman trusts in his own creation when he makes *dumb* idols!
> Woe to him who says to a wooden thing, Awake; to a *dumb* stone, Arise!
> Can this thing give revelation?
> Behold, it is overlaid with gold and silver, and there is no breath at all in it (2:18-19).

In the New Testament, the apostle Paul writes: "You know that when you were heathen, you were led astray to *dumb* idols" (1 Cor. 12:2). The very nature of the word *idol* connotes dumbness, silence, inability to speak, whereas the very nature of God is that he has a voice. He speaks, he talks, he communicates his message orally and audibly—and his people are to listen.

Moreover, the biblical God speaks through his prophets. It is almost to be expected that a God with a voice has chosen to communicate through *human* voices, the prophets. The Hebrew word for prophet is *nabi* and means "spokesperson." These prophets become the mouthpieces of God. For example, in the story of the exodus, Moses complains that Pharaoh will not listen to his voice and will not believe that God appeared to him. Besides, Moses says, "I am not eloquent but I am slow of speech" (Exod. 4:1, 10). As the story evolves, God finally says: "Aaron your brother shall be your prophet" (Exod. 7:1); that is, Aaron will be your mouthpiece, your spokesman. The word *prophet* clearly means "mouthpiece." God continues:

I will be with your mouth and teach you what you shall speak.
. . . I will be with your mouth and with his [Aaron's] mouth and will teach you what you shall do (Exod. 4:12, 15).

A prophet is a voice, a mouth, a larynx, speaking a word from the Lord to the human situation. Moses and Aaron were mouths used by God to speak to Pharaoh and the Egyptians.

The office of prophet seems to have been instituted in Deut. 18:15-22. The Israelites had heard the voice of God on Mount Sinai, as he spoke out of the darkness and the fire, and they were very much afraid of his voice, and said: "Let us not hear again the voice of God . . . lest we die" (18:16). The Lord God agreed with them and said to Moses:

I will raise up a prophet like you from among their brethren; and I will put my words in his mouth, and he shall speak to them all that I command him (18:18).

Thus, the prophets became the living voices of God on earth, the mouths by which God addressed the ever-changing world. No longer would the people hear God's voice; the living voice they would hear would be the voice of the prophets.

The Old Testament prophets were rooted and grounded in the Mosaic covenant. Again and again, they spoke to their time in history. They didn't speak their own wisdom. They keenly understood the Spirit and substance of the Mosaic covenant and law; and based on that law, they were the voices of God to the particularity of their situation. The message of each prophet was unique because each prophet and each situation was different. The world was ever changing.

The prophets were people of God who were rooted and grounded in God's word and will and spoke God's word and will to the world in which they lived. That is what prophets did—and still do.

Today's prophetic preachers are rooted in the new covenant; and firmly grounded in that covenant, we address God's word to our time and place. Planted in the Spirit and in the substance of the Scriptures, prophetic preachers speak God's Word to the particular needs of our parish and world. Prophetic preachers are not clairvoyant predictors of the future nor do they simply deliver social-action sermons about political and economic exploitation. The issue is broader: prophetic preachers address the Word and will of God to the uniqueness of their contemporary situation. Thus the office of preaching finds its roots, not only in the nature of the voice of God and his speaking, but in his prophets and their speaking in God's behalf. Fant writes:

> Hebrew precedence for Christian preaching is evident . . . in the preaching of the prophets. In Isaiah, "proclamation" is used to describe the activity of the Servant of the Lord (Isaiah 61:1). Jesus later declared that his ministry was the fulfillment of these prophetic words and thereby traced his ministry of proclamation to Old Testament sources (Luke 4:21). Brilioth agrees that "A clear line extends from Old Testament prophecy to the sermon in the church."[26]

The prophet is the voice of God in human form (more on this theme later in this chapter).

Jesus came preaching the good news and sent his disciples out to do the same. Brooks wrote that "Jesus chose this method of extending the knowledge of himself throughout the world. . . . He taught his truth to a few men and then he said, 'Now go and tell that truth to other men.' "[27] Seventy times in the New Testament we find the verb *euangelizomai,* which means "preaching the good news."[28] Voicing the good news; proclaiming the good news: that is what Jesus and his disciples were doing.

Stott reminds us that "the evangelists present Jesus as having been first and foremost an itinerant preacher."[29] Mark introduces Jesus' public ministry with the words, "Jesus came into Galilee, preaching the gospel of God" (1:14); and Mark summarizes his Galilean ministry by saying, "He went throughout all of Galilee, preaching in their synagogues and casting out demons" (1:39). In Mark 3:12, Jesus sends out the Twelve in order to preach and heal. And in the "longer ending" of Mark's Gospel Jesus sends out his disciples and "they went forth and preached everywhere" (16:20). According to the Synoptic Gospels, preaching is a dominant priority for both Jesus and his apostles.

Farmer believes it is significant that the Gospels place preaching before healing. It is not that healing is of secondary importance but that preaching interprets the healing ministry. "A work of compassion even of the most devoted and sacrificial kind tells nothing per se about the gospel of the kingdom of God. It only begins to speak of that when it is associated with, and interpreted by, the preaching of the Gospel."[30]

Speech was essential to the incarnation and speech led Jesus to the cross:

> The words of Jesus, apart from his life, would be empty; but the life of Jesus, apart from his words, would be unintelligible. I cannot imagine a mute, silent, Jesus. The good news apart from words is inconceivable. Perpetual silence could have only led to ambiguity; speech led to the cross.[31]

Jesus is the Word of God in the flesh. He is the actual voice of God in human form.

The first apostles were preachers. In Acts 6 we read of the importance that the early church gave to preaching. There was a problem in the early church. The apostolic preachers were being distracted from proclaiming the Word by the need to care for widows and orphans, distribute food to the needy, and wait on tables at the agape meals. Finally, the congregation decided to select a group of deacons, loving and caring people, who would fulfill these pastoral ministries of human care, so that the apostles could "devote themselves to prayer and the ministry of the word." A definite priority was given to the apostles for prayer and preaching.

Stott especially focuses on Acts 6 as a model for pastoral ministry that emphasizes preaching. It is time to read slowly:

> That the apostles after Pentecost gave priority to the ministry of preaching is specifically stated in Acts 6. They resisted the temptation to get involved in other forms of service in order to devote

themselves to "prayer and the ministry of the word." For it was to this that Jesus had primarily called them.[32]

If we were to establish the "ministry of the Word and prayer" as our priority, as the apostles did (Acts 6:4), it would involve for most of us a radical restructuring of our programme and timetable, including a considerable delegation of other responsibilities to lay leaders, but it would express a truly New Testament conviction about the essential nature of the pastorate.[33]

That is why the program called Stephen Ministries, designed by Dr. Kenneth Haugk, is so important. Caring, loving, empathetic laity are trained to be healing individuals who can minister to widows, persons from broken homes, those undergoing divorces or who have drug problems, the hospitalized, and others.[34] Meanwhile, the pastor is able to find more time for prayer and preaching.

Life has always been busy for pastors of congregations, but the apostolic church found ways to create more time for its pastors, so their pastors could pray more often and preach more effectively.

During the worship services of the apostolic church, the preachers gave sermons based on the Scripture readings. The structure of the early Christian worship service was patterned on the synagogue service. The synagogue worship included psalms, prayers, readings in Hebrew from the Law and the Prophets, and readings from the targums (oral translations into Aramaic, the language of the people, and interpretations of the Scriptures by the rabbis). Each week, the rabbis would translate, interpret, and apply the Word of God to the needs of their hearers, teaching and exhorting them to live according to God's Word.

We find the same pattern of worship described in the New Testament. One example is Paul in Antioch:

On the sabbath day they went into the synagogue and sat down. After the reading of the law and the prophets, the rulers of the synagogue sent to them saying, "Brethren, if you have any word of exhortation for the people, say it." So Paul stood up, and motioning with his hand, said. . . (Acts 13:14-16).

Here we see this pattern of reading the Scriptures followed by exposition and exhortation. The same is found in the story of Jesus at the synagogue in Nazareth, when he read from Isaiah 61, after which "the eyes of all in the synagogue were fixed on him. And he began to say . . . " (Luke 4:20-21). The same pattern is found in Paul's instructions to Timothy: "Till I come, attend to the public reading of scripture, to preaching, to teaching" (1 Tim. 4:13). Stott comments: "The clear implication is that after the reading of the Bible, and arising out of it, there should be both *paraklesis* (exhortation) and *didaskalia* (instruction)."[35]

Fred Meuser shows that Luther linked teaching and exhortation in his sermons:

> Often Luther said that a sermon is comprised of teaching and exhortation. . . . Teaching lays out for the people what is true; exhortation encourages them to believe it and live it. [Luther said:] "Both parts are necessary for the preacher, which is why St. Paul also practiced both." It all sounds calm and intellectual: inform the mind and exhort the will.[36]

So we see that one of the roots of Christian preaching is the weekly rabbinic exposition and exhortation, immediately following the reading of Scripture. Fant writes:

> The origin of the Christian sermon, like nearly everything in the church services, is to be found in the Synagogue. We know from the Bible that it was customary to expound the lesson read in the services. In the Jewish church, this developed into the hortatory address, very near to a modern sermon.[37]

This brief survey of the biblical origins of preaching is indebted to John Stott, who is especially thorough and systematic in his use of Scripture and in his tracing of the biblical origins of preaching.[38]

Theologians, past and present, have clearly stated the importance of preaching within the pastoral office. Let us listen to a few voices out of the distant past. Again, it is time to read slowly.

> Unless you preach everywhere you go, there is no use to go anywhere [St. Francis of Assisi].[39]

Christ only once heard mass . . . but he laid great stress on prayer
and preaching, especially on preaching [Humbert of Rome].[40]

The highest service that men may attain on earth is to preach the
Word of God. This service falls peculiarly to priests. . . . And
for this cause, Jesus Christ left other works and occupied himself
mostly in preaching. . . . The Church is honored most by the
preaching of God's Word, and hence this is the best service that
priests may render unto God . . . [John Wycliffe].[41]

Whoever has received the call . . . to preach has the highest office
in Christendom imposed on him. After, he may also baptize,
celebrate mass, and exercise pastoral care. If he does not wish to
do so, he may confine himself to preaching and leave baptizing
and lower offices to others as Christ and the apostles also did
[Martin Luther].[42]

If I could today become king or emperor, I would not give up
my office as preacher [Martin Luther].[43]

There is only one obligation, that of preaching. . . . A pastor
who preaches is more than a bishop who dedicates bells and
churches, confirms children and sprinkles holy water. These ex-
ternals have no meaning to God [Martin Luther].[44]

Contemporary theologians and historians echo similar sentiments
about the value of preaching.

The Reformation gave centrality to the sermon. The pulpit was
higher than the altar, for Luther held that salvation is through
the Word, and without the Word the elements are devoid of
sacramental quality, but the Word is sterile unless it is spoken
[Roland Bainton].[45]

[I] see the value for every theology as determined by what it can
do for preaching [Paul Tillich].[46]

Preaching is the most distinctive institution in Christianity. . . .
With its preaching, Christianity rises or falls [P. T. Forsyth].[47]

The Christian cannot get away from verbal witness. . . . The
Christian is commanded to preach. Preaching is virtually a universal activity for the churches [Martin Marty].[48]

Proclamation is the Alpha and Omega of the church's praxis [Gerhard Ebeling].[49]

A student of the Bible knows that preaching was central to the mission of God's people. Moses and the prophets, Jesus, the disciples, the apostles, the missionaries, were part of God's grand design to accomplish his will through preaching. If preaching *was* part of God's means of salvation during biblical times, preaching still *is* part of God's grand design today. Farmer talks about the ecumenical conferences of the world (e.g., Madras), and how these conferences are a testimony to the truly international character of the church "which is in large measure the direct result of preaching of the Gospel."[50] There is no way to separate the spread of Christianity from the power of preaching.

THEOLOGICAL REASONS FOR PREACHING

We have referred to the emphasis on preaching in both the Old and New Testament. There are other reasons, theological ones, that underscore the crucial significance of preaching.

1. *In preaching, it is Christ himself speaking through the voice of the preacher.* One reason why preaching is so important is the awareness that it is God himself who is speaking through the lips of the preacher. The church has the audacity to believe that in preaching, we hear simultaneously God's voice and the preacher's voice. The mouth of the preacher is the mouth of Christ. Luther had the audacity to believe that his words were the word of Christ, the actual words of the Risen Lord, that Christ was actually present in, with, and under the voice, "the bodily voice" of the preacher. Numerous quotations of Luther illustrate this:

The sermon is the Word of God.[51]

When the preacher speaks, God speaks.[52]

So the pastor must be sure that God speaks through his mouth. Otherwise, it is time for him to be quiet.[53]

Now let me and everyone who speaks the word of Christ freely boast that *our mouths are the mouths of Christ.* I am certain indeed that my word is not mine, but the word of Christ. So must my mouth also be the mouth of him who utters it.[54]

Our Lord God himself wishes to be the preacher. . . .[55]

Again, I preach the Gospel of Christ, and with my bodily voice I bring Christ into your heart, . . . that the one Christ enters into so many hearts through the voice, and that each person who hears the sermon and accepts it takes the whole of Christ into his heart.[56]

The mouth of the man who teaches the Gospel is the hyssop and the sprinkler by which the teaching of the Gospel, colored and sealed with the blood of Christ, is sprinkled upon the church.[57]

From these specific quotations and from a general reading of Luther, it becomes clear that the word of the preacher is the Word of Christ. God himself is present in, with, and under the words of the sermon. Even if the preacher does not believe the Word himself, God can still take those words and make them Word for the hearer.

Other contemporary theologians have understood that the living voice of the preacher is the living voice of God. Karl Barth wrote: "Preaching is the Word of God which he himself has spoken." "Preaching is God's own Word. That is to say, through the activity of preaching, God himself speaks." "Preaching the Word of God is the Word of God."[58] Similarly, Bonhoeffer wrote: "The proclaimed Word is the Incarnate Christ himself. . . . It is Christ himself walking through his congregation in the Word."[59] Farmer stated that in the preaching event, "God is actively probing me, challenging my will, calling on me for decision, offering me his succour. . . ."[60] Bultmann wrote: "The crucified and resurrected Christ encounters us in the word of preaching, and never in any other way."[61] Gustaf Wingren wrote: "Preaching is not just talk about a Christ of the past, but is a mouth through which the Christ of the present offers us life today."[62] In other words, preaching is sacramental. God is really present in the living words of the preacher.

Fred Meuser speaks most pointedly about the "real presence" in preaching:

Much is made of the doctrine of the real presence in Luther's sacramental theology. He also had another "real presence"—the real presence of Christ in proclamation. . . . When the preacher speaks, God is really present and speaking. . . . If we are touched by the word, God has touched us.[63]

In spite of all this glorious-sounding theology of the Word, it is often difficult for us preachers to believe that our voices are the living voice of God on Sunday morning, knowing how capable we are of banality and boredom, insipidity and shallowness (these are the recurring words used by writers on homiletics to describe the average preacher in America). It is hard to believe that God's voice can be so banal and boring, so insipid and shallow, so . . . human. Yet it is true: God's design is to speak his word through his messengers, his prophets, his living voices. It is through the living voices of common and ordinary men and women, that we hear the voice of the living God.

Nor is preaching confined to the mouth of the minister. Proclamation of the gospel cannot be narrowly confined to preaching of the Sunday sermon. The mouth of the layperson is also the mouth of Christ, speaking the gospel in the world.

2. It is the design of God to save people through human relationships, and preaching is one form of an I-Thou relationship. Farmer says that when God saves a person through Christ, he insists on a living personal encounter with him or her here and now in the sphere of present personal relationships. "God never enters into a personal relation with a man apart from other human beings." "God insists on saving persons in a personal way." When he confronts us it is always closely bound up with an I-Thou relationship. This is not to limit God. It is merely to report the created order as it is. Why God chooses to save through human relationships "must lie in the inscrutable nature of the divine being itself."[64] God can save us through any means he chooses, but he has chosen the medium of human relationships, and preaching is one form of an I-Thou event.

Farmer especially seems to understand the importance of preaching as an I-Thou relationship. The more a preacher can adapt his sermon "to the personal approach, to the 'I-Thou' relationship, the greater will be his achievement." "I-Thou" preaching is more than speech techniques, such as "good matter, felicitous language, firm structure." "The closer your sermon . . . approximates the natural and spontaneous directness of serious private conversation, the better preaching it will be." Farmer gives the example of Whitefield of whom it was said that "his audience felt as though the message was intended for him and him alone."[65]

The Incarnation is *the* primary example of God's grand design to accomplish his will through I-Thou relationships. The Incarnation was God's ultimate act of communication.

> Even God himself had to become incarnate to communicate with man at the most profound level. The incarnation was the supreme revelation of God because it was the ultimate means of communication.

> The incarnation, therefore, is the truest theological model for preaching because it is God's ultimate act of communication. . . . The eternal word took on human flesh in a contemporary situation. Preaching cannot do otherwise.[66]

God, through the flesh and blood of Christ, communicated himself to the world. God, through the flesh and blood of preachers, communicates himself to the world today. It is the design of God to save through flesh and blood. Brooks understood this when he wrote: "The truth of the Gospel is 'preeminently personal.' However the Gospel may be capable of statement in dogmatic form, its truest statement we know is not in dogma but in personal life."[67] Preaching is person-to-person communication; it is an I-Thou relationship.

3. Christians are still nourished by the preaching of the Word. Craddock asks a question designed to make us preachers take notice: "Why do these people week after week return to their chairs before dull pulpits to hear a man thrash about in a limbo of words relating vaguely to some topic snatched desperately on Saturday night from the minister's own twilight zone?"[68] It's amazing, but people keep on coming back to hear preaching that is banal and boring, insipid and shallow. Even with these sermons of ours, the people of God are still fed. Fant entitles one chapter "The Stubborn Pulpit." In spite of all the attacks on preaching and the pulpit, it stubbornly persists; and one of the reasons it persists is that people are fed and nourished by the Word. Idolatries are challenged. Forgiveness is proclaimed. Lives are transformed. Sitting under the preaching of God's Word, the Holy Spirit consistently penetrates into the imaginations of our hearts and we begin to live anew. As the Lord God promises: "My word that goes forth from my mouth shall not return to me empty, but it shall accomplish that which I purpose" (Isa. 55:11).

In sum, why is preaching so important to the Christian faith?

● Preaching is important to the very nature of God and God's speaking to the prophets, Jesus, the apostolic church, and theologians of the past and present.
● In preaching, it is Christ himself who is speaking through the voice of the preacher.
● It is the design of God to save people through personal, I-Thou relationships such as preaching.
● Christians are still nourished by the preaching of the Word.

Pastors, then, take seriously the task of preaching and put time, energy, and soul into the preparation of the sermon. The event of preaching is at the very heart of the pastoral office, and preaching pastors manage time to reflect this fact.

THREE COMPONENTS OF THE PREACHING EVENT

What are the components of preaching? Phillips Brooks is the most lucid of authors on homiletics in his analysis of the necessary ingredients for preaching. He lists two: "message" and "witness."[69] His most famous statement is that preaching is "Truth through Personality."[70] Unfortunately, the word *personality* nowadays immediately triggers images of TV teeth, beauty queens, and the most popular teenager in the group. "*She* has personality!" Because of these connotations of the word *personality,* scholars occasionally caricature Brooks as the 19th-century "prince of the pulpit" who carried the gospel through the charisma of his personal charm. Of course, this is a result of a superficial reading of Brooks. He is convinced that "truth through personality" is the method God chose to spread his knowledge to the world, that every sermon falls short because of a defect in either the message or the messenger, and that the gospel is essentially personal and not dogmatic. The following are some of his major themes:

> Preaching is the communication of truth by man to men. It has in it two essential elements, truth and personality. . . . Preaching is the bringing of truth through personality. . . . It is in the defect of one or the other element that every sermon and preacher fall short. . . . Jesus chose this method of extending the knowledge of himself throughout the world. . . . He taught his truth to a few men and then he said, "Now go and tell that truth to other men," for that truth is pre-eminently personal. However the Gospel may be capable of statement in dogmatic form, its truest statement we know is not in dogma but in personal life.

> Truth through personality is our description of real preaching. The truth must come really through the person, not merely over his lips, not merely into his understanding and out through the pen. It must come through his character, his affections, his whole intellectual and moral being. It must come genuinely through him.

> With these two words ["message" and "witness"] I think we have the fundamental concept of the matter of Christian preaching.[71]

No other author says it like Brooks! Preaching is not just truth or biblical message; it is not just personality; but it is truth *through* personality—and that preposition *through* is utterly important. Arndt Halvorson echoes similar sentiments when he writes: "Every sermon is shaped as much by the interior world of the preacher's mind and imagination as it is by the text."[72]

I would like to add a third necessary ingredient for preaching: being involved in the struggle of life. Davis says it well:

Great preaching occurs when a man of compassionate discern-
ment, with the love of the Lord and mankind in his soul, himself
fully involved in the battle of existence, stands up on his feet and
lets his heart and head speak to his fellows.[73]

Through preaching, God addresses us in our situation—our worry about
nuclear holocaust, our abortions, our materialism, our deaths, our dis-
eases, our divorces, our drugs, our despair, our boredom, our kids, our
souls. Preaching is not only truth, and not only truth through personality; it is God's truth for us in our situation. I like Fant's definition:
"When the living Word touches the living situation, the preaching
event occurs."[74] God's truths are not simply timeless truths which the
preacher then parrots. Rather, the truth of God is always directed to
a specific situation or need. A faithful preacher attempts to understand
not only the text, but the Word and will of God for our context. This
third dimension, the contextual dimension, of preaching cannot be
lost. Recall Elizabeth Achtemeier's assertion: "Between the Word and
the world there is the figure of the preacher."[75]

Briefly then, there are three components of preaching: the message,
the messenger, and the mess in which we are living; or, the Word,
the witness, and the world.

SUMMARY

Theology is part of every sermon. It is impossible to have a nontheological sermon. Theologically, it is important that the preacher is
a person who is possessed by the gospel and that grace is the nerve
center of all he does. Theologically, it is important that the preacher
proclaims the gospel as a fabulist, a teller of the wildest mysteries of
them all, the death and resurrection of our Lord Jesus Christ. It is
important that the preacher understands, biblically and theologically,
the importance of preaching.

5

The Preacher as Textual Exegete and Interpreter

This is the way it has gone with preaching. . . . After the text of the Gospel is read, they take us to fairyland. One preaches from Aristotle and the heathen books, another from the papal decretals. One brings questions about his holy order, another about blue ducks, another about hen's milk. . . . In short, this is the art in which nobody sticks to the text, from which people might have had the Gospel [Luther].[1]

Unless spiritual knowledge and the Spirit himself speak through the preachers . . . the final result will be that everyone preaches his own whims, and instead of the Gospel and its exposition, we shall again have sermons on blue ducks [Luther].[2]

Preaching on blue ducks, Aristotle, hen's milk, pop psychology, ten ways to raise healthy children, four steps to successful living—the tendency of the preacher then and now is to avoid the text and the message of God within the text. Persistently and consistently in the history of the human race, clergy have departed from preaching God's message through the word.

Almost all authors on homiletics focus on the role of the pastor as textual exegete and interpreter; this chapter, like the others in this book, will be a compendium of their homiletical wisdom. Of all the authors, Keck, Halvorson, Davis, and Achtemeier wrote most thoroughly on this issue. Two particular chapters from this material are like a rich lode mine: Achtemeier's "Creative Exegesis" and Davis' "Tense and Mode."

There has been an erosion of biblical authority within the church. Laity and pastors are not reading the Bible as much as they used to. It is not that the Bible is totally ignored; rather, it simply does not have the authority it once had. Keck observes that "the Bible has seldom been rejected outright. Its place is more like that of an old grandmother who has a room in the house and who appears at meals but who has little real influence on the life of the family."[3] That's painful—but true. James Smart was right on target when he wrote *The Strange Silence of the Bible in the Church.* The Bible is rarely read daily or devotionally. It is no longer (or never was) the guiding book of our lives. Too often we live on Christian common sense—which often means middle-class values coated with a veneer of biblical piety.

Elizabeth Achtemeier writes about the indifference towards the Bible within the worship services:

> It is possible in this country to carry on the expected work of a Protestant congregation with no reference to the Bible whatsoever. The worship services of the church can be divorced from the Biblical models and become the celebration of the congregation's life together and of its more or less vaguely held common beliefs on some god. Folk songs, expressive of American culture, can replace the psalms of the church. Art forms and aesthetic experiences can be used as substitutes for communion with God. The preacher's opinions or ethical views can be made replacements for the Word from the Biblical text.[4]

Keck is concerned about the renewal of preaching in the church, and he is convinced that the renewal of biblical preaching will lead to a renewal of preaching as such. It is not the other way around. There are many books, he thinks, that are concerned about the renewal of preaching. These books often have to do with the renewal of the forms of preaching, e.g., storytelling, creative use of language, or imaging the gospel. Keck is convinced that the renewal of preaching will begin with the renewal of *biblical* preaching; that is, when the text becomes the source of God's message for the day. And biblical preaching begins

with the renewal of the preacher's relationship with the Bible, when
the preacher knows the Bible as a whole and then preaches from specific
texts. The church needs "the Bible in the preacher," "the Bible in the
pulpit," and "the Bible in the people."[5]

APPROACHING THE TEXT FOR THE SERMON

1. The preacher stands under the Scriptures, listens to them, wrestles with them, and finds authority in them.
A preacher stands beneath the text.

> The preacher himself must stand beneath the Word he preaches,
> not above it. To stand above it means to reject it, to ignore its
> message for ourselves, or to use it to manipulate people for our
> own ends. . . . We become Lord rather than the servant of the
> Word. . . . To stand beneath the Word means that we acknowl-
> edge our own humanity . . .,confess our sinfulness . . ., and
> make plain to the congregation that we stand beneath the very
> judgment of the Word we proclaim.[6]

A preacher listens to the text.

> The preacher sees himself first of all as a listener to the Word of
> God. . . . Paul outlined the plan of world evangelization, be-
> ginning not with the preaching but with the listening. Faith
> comes from what is heard. . . . Funk has succinctly expressed it:
> "He who aspires to the enunciation of the Word must first learn
> to hear it; and he who hears the Word will have found the means
> to articulate it." . . . Isaiah says the same thing, "Morning by
> morning, he awakens my ear to hear as those who are taught."[7]

A preacher wrestles with the text.

> Read the text as one involved with it *personally,* not as one involved
> only *professionally.* Read it as one who *seeks a message,* not as one
> who must *produce a sermon.* Become passionately involved with the
> text, as a wrestler with his opponent, as a debater with an ad-
> versary, as a friend listens to a friend. . . . Wrestle with the text:
> question it, fight it, quarrel with it—fully as much as you pray

about it, open yourself to it, receive it. Only in this way can the text engender communicative passion.[8]

The preacher should do combat with the text until it gives me a blessing. Not many texts yield easily. . . . Close scrutiny aids the process of working the sermon into the preacher's bones so that he will be able to deliver it with power.[9]

A preacher finds his authority in the text.

The one basis of our authority is the Holy Scriptures, and if we do not preach out of them, we should not be preaching at all.[10]

2. A preacher develops exegetical passion as he or she listens to the text in behalf of the congregation. Author after author expresses the importance of bringing to the text the congregation's questions and concerns, joys and sorrows, perceptions and insights. The people want a word from the Lord, and the priestly pastor brings their intercessions, not only his own, into dialog with the Scriptures.

Keck tells of the time he was invited to preach in another parish. He asked not to pray the prayer of the church because he didn't have a feel for the specific needs of that parish; for example, Al Jones had a heart attack and he didn't know Al Jones and his family very well. Not knowing the family, he could not shape the prayer as it needed to be. Analogously, Keck suggests the same is true for studying the text. The pastor knows his or her congregation and therefore studies the text on their behalf, asking their questions, bringing their needs under the light of the gospel. The pastor listens to the text vicariously for the people. It is *their text* as well as his. It is *their sermon* as well as his.[11]

Similarly, Craddock tells us the sermon grows out of a dialog between a specific text and the specific needs of a congregation.

The text is to be studied and shared, not in dialogue with the "human situation" in general but with the issues facing the particular congregation participating in the sermon experience. The familiar statement of Hermann Diem, "The congregation is born in preaching," is also true in reverse: "Preaching is born in the congregation." One only has to listen to sermons prepared for homiletics class with no congregation in view to realize how vital to preaching is the concrete situation. . . . The matter to be underscored here is the concrete situation of the particular congregation addressed.[12]

Pastors, whether we like it or not, soon discover that many of the laity's questions have to do with human relationships rather than divine relationships (although we cannot neatly separate the two):

The preacher today must turn away from easy answers, avoid addressing himself to questions people are not asking, and strive to recognize the questions people are asking, and the answers and clues for which they are searching. Today men are more interested in men than they are in God; and the questions they ask concern human relations more than divine relations.[13]

But the preacher also stirs the people to ask new questions, pertinent questions, God-questions:

I must deliver the *message* of this text to people living today. And therefore I must know these people; I must know at what point they raise questions, so I can "latch on" to these questions, and I know where they do *not* have questions, so that I must first stir them to ask the pertinent questions.[14]

Intimately knowing the people sets our hearts aflame with exegetical passion:

It is this passion, then; the passion of knowing that in the text which we will preach to our beloved people next Sunday, there is healing for the hurt of some broken heart, life for the dying of one guilty soul; hope for the despair of some woman as she looks at the future . . . *that knowing finally gives exegesis fire which sets our hearts aflame with the message.*[15]

The preacher, moreover, brings his or her own needs before the text:

Preaching gains power as the preacher scrutinizes the heart of his most immediate hearer—himself. Strange how often a pastor overlooks himself, the kind of person he is, his needs, his wants, his hopes, his dreams, his sins. . . .[16]

Obviously then, a preacher exegetes a text on behalf of the congregation. We bring our prayer lists with us into the study. The dialog is not narrowly confined to two parties, scholar and Scriptures. The congregation lives in the heart of the pastors, and we bring their needs before the Word, so that their needs (and the pastor's) can be addressed by the Word.

I would like to give an example of a person not consulting the congregation in preparation for a sermon. The illustration is drawn from *A New Look at Preaching,* a series of articles written primarily by Roman Catholic scholars. Dr. Walter Burghardt, at the end of his lecture on how to give a sermon, shared his own preparation for the First Sunday of Advent. He decided to preach on the texts for the Feast of the Immaculate Conception (three days from Advent I) and connect Mary, Advent, and waiting. He told us how he prepared for the sermon, consulting the scholarly works of Raymond Brown, pausing to

> read Shakespeare aloud, Gerard Manley Hopkins, T. S. Eliot, Tennessee Williams. I listen to Beethoven's *Ninth Symphony* or *Barber's Adagio.* . . . For the bare message can be deadenly dull; it must come alive, take wing. To play on the human heart, my words must leap and dance, quiver and shiver, burn and cool.[17]

As he continued to describe his preparations, I was swept off my feet by his words and insights. I sensed that this professor must be a good preacher, "a preacher's preacher," as the preface to the book indicated.

The lecture (and article) that followed Burghardt's was by Dr. Elizabeth Schussler Fiorenza, professor of New Testament studies and theology at Notre Dame. She said that she was impressed that Dr. Burghardt had consulted Brown, Shakespeare, Hopkins, Eliot, and Barber, but she continued:

> I was surprised that he does not think of taking into account the experiences of pregnant women and their sense of self. I wonder whether the male poets and artists he mentions can give his sermon the detail, sensitivity and insight that he would need for presenting pregnant Mary. . . . One might also listen to single mothers on welfare or to the woman at the checkout counter trying

to feed and clothe their children. . . . The Mary of Advent is the pregnant Mary, the unwed mother.[18]

Dr. Fiorenza then goes on to discuss the right of all the baptized to be part of the proclamation and not just the few, ordained clergy. She insists that "the silenced majority" must be heard and allowed into speech again if the richness and fullness of God's presence is to be articulated and proclaimed today.[19]

These scholars echo a similar theme: the right of all the baptized to be part of the sermon, "priestly listening," and the "silenced majority" being heard. Faithful preachers need to exegete the congregation as carefully as they exegete the text and bring their questions, perceptions, and stories into the study.

3. The preacher exegetes carefully and thoroughly. There is no excuse for us not doing our exegesis. The congregation is not trained to do exegetical study. That is one of our unique skills, and we must be rigorous in our exegetical preparation.

A preacher needs a good knowledge of the Bible as a whole:

Therefore, to understand a text, it is necessary to have a good knowledge of the whole Bible. . . . So know your Bible. Learn to feel at home in it. Let its message of God's love for you create in you a love for it. Then the Bible will fulfill what seems to be God's intent; it will become your main tool. . . . A sermon is *informed* by the Bible in its fullness; but a sermon is *created* by a text in its particularity.[20]

We know him through deep and sustained and continual study of the Bible. . . . We are to know God's Word through and through. It is the bread by which we live and with which we feed our people. It is the background commentary on every experience we have and every decision we make.[21]

Stott's familiarity with Scripture is impressive. He refers to the Bible again and again, pulling out verses from obscure places in the Old Testament to make a point. It was not until the closing chapters of his book that I discovered his secret. Early in his ministry, he had been convinced to read the Bible in its entirety every year. For him, that meant reading four chapters every day, three in the morning and one at night. He had found a lectionary which enabled him to do this systematically. He had been persuaded by the example of the apostles in Acts 6 prayerfully and consistently to read the Bible for nourishment and sermon preparation. He practices what he calls a "studied neglect of distracting duties" so that he has more time for prayer and preaching.[22] Likewise, the Anglican and Episcopalian traditions have "daily offices," morning and evening, whereby the priests are able (and expected) to read through the Scriptures every year. In the *Lutheran Book of Worship* a daily lectionary is provided so that one can read through the whole Bible every two years. It was obvious to me that Stott is a scholar who knows his Bible and is committed to the daily discipline of four chapters.

At the same time I was reading Stott, I happened to be reading *Faith and Ferment,* edited by Robert S. Bilheimer. One article, discussing family devotions and daily prayer, demonstrated that families either had prayer and devotions every day or not at all. Very few people maintained private worship weekly or monthly. It was a *daily* discipline or no discipline at all.[23] This same principle applies to a pastor's daily reading of Scripture.

The invitation of these scholars is for the parish pastor to spend more time reading the Scriptures. Listen to the wisdom of theological giants from the past, as they attempt to motivate us to spend more time reading the Bible:

> When your head droops at night, let a page of Scripture pillow it [St. Jerome].[24]

> To understand the Bible should be our ambition; we should be familiar with it, as familiar as the housewife with her needle, the merchant with his ledger, the mariner with his ship [Spurgeon].[25]

> Bishop Stephen Neill has written: "Origen, the greatest scholar of the early church, . . . seems to have held the whole of Scripture in solution in his mind.[26]

Many of us have learned our overview of the Scriptures by teaching the Bethel Bible Series, Crossways, or similar courses. It seems that these courses are a good introduction to a daily discipline of biblical meditation. I have found, however, that when I am preparing to teach biblical courses, because of the inevitable shortage of time, I read the Bible hurriedly; but if and when I read four chapters a day, I read much more slowly, thoroughly, and devotionally.

Preachers use their exegetical tools. Exegetical study is crucial to preaching. Spurgeon said, "He who no longer sows in the study will no longer reap in the pulpit," and Calvin wrote, "None will ever be a good minister of the Word of God unless he is first of all a scholar."[27] A man repeatedly asked Dr. Leslie Weatherhead, the famous English theologian and preacher, "What is the secret of the spell you can cast over a huge congregation?" Always he replied, "Preparation."[28]

Greek, Hebrew, theological word books, Bible dictionaries, and commentaries are all necessary tools for preparation. Each pastor has his own exegetical style. In the text-study group of which I am a part, a few of the 25 pastors use Greek and Hebrew well, and the rest of us benefit from them. Many pastors no longer have a scholarly use of the biblical languages and must rely heavily on good commentaries to handle the linguistic problems in the text.

Unless we do our exegesis thoroughly and "plum the details of the text," the sermons often sound like "generalized presentations of the gospel as a whole," "sounding the same themes over and over again, Sunday after Sunday."[29] We end up with homogenized, bland sermons on "sloppy agape." Doing careful and thorough exegesis accentuates the individuality of each text and sermon, creating diversity and particularity in our preaching. Keck tells us that redaction criticism "brings the distinctiveness of each writer's work into view . . . and increases the possibilities for preaching the Bible as a polychrome tapestry instead of a monochrome etching." "We must take the text as seriously as we take ourselves," and most of us take ourselves almost too seriously. A faithful exegete is like a person who listens to a tape recording over and over again until he or she understands what is on it. A faithful exegete resists the temptation to ask prematurely, "What does this mean for us today?" but instead first studies the text, trying to discover its *original* setting and meaning.[30]

Ronald J. Allen and Thomas J. Herin have written an exceptionally fine, step-by-step description of the exegetical process. Their work and Elizabeth Achtemeier's "Creative Exegesis" are most helpful on exegetical method. In their chapter, Allen and Herin compare the text to a visitor who comes to call:

> My text is rather like a visitor from outside my immediate but often quite limited world of experience. And whether he is an old friend or a virtual stranger, I have opened the door to him at this time, and I now want to hear his news, whether it calms me or upsets me. I also want to ask him some tough questions, to acknowledge my own hopes and fears in his presence, and to get to know him well enough to introduce him to my Christian companions. Rather than manipulating or using or talking about my guest in public, I want to enable my comrades to hear him on his own terms.[31]

Arndt Halvorson, with a slightly different perspective, compares the exegete to a detective searching for clues in an unsolved murder case. It is crucial to check all the evidence or you may mislead the jury:

> What does the text say? . . . Read it as if it were *the* clue to the whole story. Read it as a detective who has found a relevant but unclear scrap of paper in the wastebasket of the dead person's room. The success or failure of the whole enterprise—for the time being—rests on understanding this one clue, this text.[32]

> Graham Greene's novel, *The Human Factor,* . . . is the chilling story of the deliberate killing of an innocent man, because the detective made a premature decision without checking all the evidence. The detective was guilty of impatience, of taking the easy road. This can happen in our sermons when we avoid the crucial task of textual scrutiny and hurry to the sermon.[33]

Craddock reminds us that "the most important single, contributing factor to effective preaching is study and careful preparation."[34]

Preachers do their own research first before going to commentaries, a point emphasized by most writers on homiletics:

> Commentaries are better used as the last tool, not the first. They are helpful after you, the preacher, have come to some conclusions about the text on your own. The preacher is not simply a copy machine reproducing the thoughts of others about a text. Authenticity in the pulpit demands that the preacher reach his or her own conclusions.[35]

Farmer says of Jesus that he spoke with authority, rather than quoting the authorities, as the scribes were prone to do.[36]

A preacher discovers the central message of the text. When exegesis is thorough, rigorous, and complete, we usually can understand the central message of the text.

> Luther insisted on finding the *Sinnmitte,* the heart of the text. That heart, that *Kern,* or kernel is to save the preacher from getting lost in details. . . . The main point of a sermon is to be so clear in the preacher's mind that it controls everything that is said.[37]

> If we do careful exegesis, there is nothing vague about the meaning of the Biblical text. Rather, its principal thought, its setting, its intention, its function, and its theology are usually rather clear. It is the purpose of exegesis to make them clear, and those characteristics of the text uncovered by exegesis then become the controls for the content and the shape of the sermon.[38]

During exegesis, the preacher searches for the central message of the text, thereby enabling the controlling theme to grow out of the text. Thielicke calls this the "textual-thematic" sermon. Thielicke lists four reasons why we should preach "textual-thematic" sermons:

1. The sermon remains rooted in the text.
2. It helps the preacher achieve order and clarity.
3. The hearer retains the sermon better and can pass it on to others.
4. It is helpful to those hearers who are unchurched and interested in religious questions but have insufficient background to appreciate expository preaching.[39]

Several authors advocate that a preacher put the theme of the sermon into one clear sentence:

> I try to express the thrust of the present sermon in one clear sentence. . . . I live with that sermon idea and carry it with me wherever I go. . . . All other material to which I attend as the sermon comes together will be judged by whether or not it will directly help this sentence grow into a lively, sensitive, thoughtful whole.[40]

> Because the preacher can state his point in one simple sentence, he knows the destination of the trip which will be his sermon. . . . The contribution of the movement and power of a sermon made by the restraint of a single idea can hardly be overstated. . . . Like a magnet, it draws potentially helpful material from the current and remembered exposure to books and people.[41]

> The first step in preparing a sermon is to state in one sentence the content of the sermon, and in another sentence the purpose of the sermon.[42]

> I do not think that any sermon ought to be preached or even written until that sentence has emerged, clear and lucid as a cloudless moon.[43]

A preacher uses the Bible as a source and resource. In the past, there has been much debate about the role of the Bible in preaching and whether or not a sermon *must* grow specifically out of one particular text. It seems to me that Davis was correct when he wrote that we preachers can use the Scriptures as a source and resource. He suggests that there are two crucial questions in determining whether or not a sermon is biblical: (1) whether the sermon says what the Bible says; and (2) whether the Bible is the source of the sermon. He writes:

> . . . the dogmatic rule [is] that every sermon must have a text from Scripture. Normally, that rule is practical and sound, but we should not make a fetish of it. One of the problems with this rule is the possibility of the "comfortable delusion" that if a sermon has a text, it is sure to be Biblical. . . . The crucial question is not whether the sermon has a text attached to it, but whether the Scripture is the source of the sermon or not, whether

the sermon says what the Scripture says. . . . Every sermon that has a text falls into one or the other of these classes; it uses the text as a source or resource.[44]

The important questions are: Is the Scripture the source of the sermon? and Does the sermon say what the Bible says?

Similarly, in the past, there have been arguments about "thematic" and "topical" sermons. Achtemeier defines a "thematic" sermon as a sermon in which a theme is distilled from the text—repentance, prayer, faith, forgiveness—and a preacher then develops that theme rather than a specific text. She defines "topical sermons" as those in which the pastor preaches on the topic for the day, e.g., nuclear war, biblical pacifism, abortion, racism, apartheid, world starvation, self-respect and self-rejection. Often, in both the "thematic" and "topical" sermons, the *text* becomes a *pretext* for speaking on one's pet theme or topic.[45]

Fant helpfully reminds us that a textual sermon "may be full of texts but empty of the gospel." A textual sermon "can be all law, clobber the people with moralism, and abuse the gospel. On the other hand, a thematic sermon which is rooted in a myriad of texts [about sin, for example] can reflect the gospel and be fully Biblical."[46]
Fant also points to the confusion and difficulty in labeling sermons:

> He hears of "expository" preaching, "textual" preaching, "topical" preaching—but what does that mean? How much text does it take to turn a "textual" sermon into an "expository" sermon? How little text can turn a "textual" sermon into a "topical" sermon? Can "expository" sermons have topics? Can "topical" sermons have texts?[47]

> Karl Barth insists that the preacher must be faithful both to the text and to life, but it is always better to keep too close to the text if a choice must be made . . . . Harry Emerson Fosdick wrote: "Start with a life issue, a real problem, personal or social, perplexing the mind or disturbing the conscience; face that problem fairly, deal with it honestly and throw such light on it from the spirit of Christ that people will be able to think more clearly and live more nobly because of that sermon." . . . Barth's sermons consistently included references to the contemporary situation.

. . . Fosdick's sermons averaged about a dozen references to the Bible.[48]

Stott was most helpful in discussing the word *exposition*. People usually think of expository preaching as a "verse by verse explanation of a passage of Scripture. . . . Properly speaking, 'exposition' has a much broader meaning. . . . To expound Scripture is to bring out of the text what is there and expose it to view. . . . The opposite of exposition is 'imposition' which is to impose on the text what is not there. . . . The length of the text is immaterial, so long as it is Biblical . . . ."[49] The text could be one word, one phrase, one sentence, one passage, one theme. Luther says: "He who has only one word of the Word of God and is not able to preach a whole sermon on the basis of this one word is not worthy even to preach."[50] The important task of the exegete is to pull out from that Scripture what God is saying (exposition), rather than impose one's own wisdom and ideas (imposition) on that text.

Davis reminds us, however, that homilies in the early church were not expository in the strict sense of the term:

> In the early phase, it [the homily] was an informal, discursive talk, in which digression, passing from one subject to another was rather the rule than the exception. The early homily used no text and developed no particular theme. Later in the history of preaching the term came to mean almost the opposite: an ordered exposition of a passage of Scripture. The hundreds of sermons by Chrysostom, Augustine and the other fathers have come down to us as "homilies" in the later sense. . . . The homily is not a definite sermonic form.[51]

It seems that we will never solve the discussion about "topical" and "textual" but we do know that there are two poles in every sermon: Christ and culture, the Word and world, the Bible and Broadway, what the text meant and what the text means. There is an eternal oscillation between these two poles.[52]

A pastor avoids preaching his exegesis. The temptation of the preacher is to be fascinated with exegetical insights and begin to preach the message of the lexicons, commentaries, and dictionaries rather than the message of the Scripture.[53] Several authors warned of bringing exegetical gardening tools into the pulpit.

> Luther almost never used a Latin word from the pulpit, and he never used preaching to show off his amazing knowledge of Greek and Hebrew.[54]

> The expository sermon is a product of exegesis but not an exhibition of it. It is altogether wise to dig beforehand with your Greek spade and your Hebrew shovel but not to be digging while you are preaching.[55]

> Dogmatic words and terms are indispensable because they have stored within them the spiritual knowledge of a long history of faith. But as such receptacles, they can be used only in the theological laboratory. They are intended for internal office use only.[56]

> Like an iceberg, nine-tenths [of the sermon] is not visible.[57]

> Instead of a finished statue, we may offer our people the chips we made in carving it.[58]

Occasionally a preacher becomes a "biblical bloodhound" who sniffs out every detail of the text and then shares his sniffings with the congregation, as if exclaiming, "Aha! Look at this exegetical insight which I have discovered! How thrilling for me!"

John Doberstein, in his introduction to Thielicke's *The Trouble with the Church* (1965), is candid and forthright when he says that overemphasis upon hermeneutics and exegesis has led to a "complete sterility" in preaching and has "jammed the guns" of the younger generation of preachers.[59] Such local theologians were preaching what the commentaries said. The result was sterility and quoting of authorities rather than preaching with authority.

Lowell Erdahl has a helpful analogy. He talks about the difference between preparing *for* a dinner, and preparing *of* a dinner.

> Preparing a sermon is similar to preparing a dinner. The cook prepares *for* a dinner by shopping at the grocery store. The preparation *of* the dinner takes place in the kitchen, where the specific

grocery items are selected, cooked and combined. Without preparation *for* the meal, there is no food to serve. Without preparation
of the meal, there is only a pile of groceries on the table. Sermons,
like dinners, need both preparations.[60]

In preparation *for* a sermon, we do our exegesis and do it thoroughly,
so we understand the text. But when we begin preparation *of* the
sermon, we don't serve raw, exegetical horseradish as an entree or even
as an appetizer! Horseradish is normally something you mix in with
the other ingredients, and even then you know its taste is present.
Exegesis is mixed in with an entree; you don't serve it raw.

Preachers allow their exegesis to simmer. Spurgeon writes:

> . . . Get saturated with the Gospel. I always find that I can
> preach best when I can manage to lie asoak in my text. I like to
> get a text, and find out its meaning and bearings, and so on, and
> then, after I have bathed in it, I delight to lie down in it, and
> let it soak into me.[61]

Spurgeon also advises:

> It's a great thing to pray one's self into the spirit and marrow of
> a text; working into it by sacred feeding thereon. . . . even as a
> worm bores its way into a kernel of a nut.[62]

> The closet is the best study. The commentators are good instruc-
> tors but the author himself is far better. . . .[63]

Robert Louis Stevenson once said of himself: "I . . . sit a long while
silent on my eggs."[64] Simmering, brooding, praying, thinking, con-
templating: the Spirit of the text goes to work on the preacher.

*4. The preacher needs the courage and freedom to translate and
interpret the biblical message into the present.* There are usually two
poles to every sermon: past and present, what the text said and what
it says, what the message meant and what it means.[65] It is important
that during the exegetical process, we begin to understand what the
text means for today, and this also involves interpretation. It is safe to
proclaim biblical truths about the past, but God's concern is always

to address people in the present. Stott, quoting Ian Pitt-Watson, writes: "Every sermon is stretched like a bowstring between the text of the Bible on the one hand and the problems of contemporary human life on the other. If the string is insecurely tethered to either end, the bow is useless."[66]

With slightly different insights and emphases, several authors encourage us to exercise our freedom to interpret the Scriptures into today's situations; otherwise the sermon remains a repetition of biblical ideas and lives in a biblical past. These authors suggest that the church is always and continually interpreting the text anew. The New Testament itself is an interpretation and reinterpretation of traditions. Preachers are not to shy away from interpreting the Word of God for contemporary life.

> In fact, most of the New Testament can be viewed as interpretations and reinterpretations of the tradition in light of new situations faced on the mission field of a vigorous and growing church. . . . A real prophetic hope of today waits upon the release of the minister from the shackling hypercaution about interpreting the Scriptures as the Word of God to our situation. . . . The New Testament itself arose out of the continual interpretation of the Gospel for new situations. New interpretations are necessary because a new context of the hearer has to be addressed. . . . Without this continuing interpretation and reinterpretation, the text of the Word of God would be brief, old, dead, under glass protecting it from the soiling hands of tourists.[67]

Similarly, H. Grady Davis complains that two-thirds of most sermons he hears safely talk about the past—safely live in the land of Zion. Davis suggested that the primary difference between Jesus and the scribes was that the scribes were always talking in the past tense, teaching about the biblical past, whereas Jesus addressed the present. Davis suggested that perhaps we may have many scribes today who are still preaching in the past tense, who have developed the habit of looking backwards.[68]

For me, part of the attractiveness of Luther's preaching is his contemporaneity. He vividly applied the Word of God to the pope, papists, priests, and church of his day. He interpreted the text to his situation with great intensity and power. And that's one reason why his preaching was so enlivening and entertaining to those who heard him. We need to be equally free in interpreting and applying the Word of God to our life situations. Preachers who repeat the language, struggles, and ethos of the 16th century are like architects who build Gothic cathedrals in the 20th century. They are out of touch with their own milieu. Wilder writes:

> Every good sermon fortunately is an interpretation. To merely reproduce the words of the New Testament is to falsify their original meaning and to defraud the modern hearers of that meaning. To build a Gothic cathedral in the second part of the twentieth century is an analogous error.[69]

Our questions and concerns aren't simply the questions and concerns of Luther and his era. For example, Luther asked, "Is God gracious?"; we ask, "Is there a God at all?" Luther asked, "What must I do to inherit eternal life?"; we ask, "Is there life after death?" Luther asked, "What can I do to be saved?"; we ask, "What can we do to be saved from a nuclear holocaust?" (Or, if you are in Latin America, "What can we do to be saved from the death squads?" Or, if you are in central Africa, "What can we do to be saved from starvation?") We bring particularized feelings and questions to the biblical passages on which we preach. To repeat the concerns of Luther without interpretation for today is to build a Norwegian stave church in downtown Pittsburgh. However beautiful it may be, it is still merely a museum piece from the past. The freedom to interpret is the freedom to bring our particular questions and peculiar struggles to the text, so that God will speak to us afresh in our generation.

It·takes hard work to interpret God's Word for the present. It also involves a degree of risk, as Thielicke notes:

> The unfaithful witness is the one who simply transmits the conventional and familiar, unchanged and undigested. He is unfaithful in the first place, because he is lazy. For the labor of interpretation and contemporization, the work of "translation" is grueling work, and it is never done without abortive trials and

breathtaking risks. For he who dares to carry the Word into our time has given up all chance to retreat into the safety of tradition. He who simply repeats the old phrases takes no risks; it is easy to remain orthodox and hew the old line. But he who speaks to this hour's need and translates the message will always be skirting the edge of heresy. He, however, is the man who is given this promise: "Only he who risks heresies can gain the truth."[70]

Why was Thielicke such a great preacher? Why were people jamming into the cathedral in Hamburg to hear him preach? One reason was that he had the courage to interpret the Word of God to his situation. He was free from a shackling hypercautiousness. He knew that his task, as a spokesperson for God, was to speak God's message for today, for this people in this place. He wasn't preaching like a scribe, confining Jesus to biblical studies of the past.

Thielicke's pungent remarks about "boring blather" from the pulpit come right after his thoughts about the need for interpretation. If we don't interpret the Word of God for our day, our time, our place, the result is yawning indifference:

> Boresomeness paralyzes people, but it does not make them angry. And finally even the demons fall asleep. . . . Nobody is ever shocked by the lukewarm drip from the pulpit, but that temperature made him sick enough to wretch. . . . Not a single person was offended or upset; nobody protested. It was boredom that emptied the pews.[71]

There is a direct correlation between "boresome blather" and "scribal biblicism." We all need to hear God's message to us—with our questions and concerns brought to the text so that God can shine his light on our world through the preacher.

Keck has also written fully on the freedom to interpret. The following words deserve careful attention:

> The Biblical precedent for handling the tradition calls for a responsible exercise of freedom. . . . Matthew and Luke have little hesitation in changing Mark, nor is Paul afraid to reinterpret Jesus' sayings about divorce. . . . The New Testament treatment

of divorce is an instructive precedent. Not only do we seek the writer's struggle to be faithful to the word of Jesus while at the same time taking account of the actualities of their own situation, but we see them claim their freedom by avoiding a literal, legalistic application of Jesus' words. What Jesus said is not the end of the matter, but the beginning, so to speak. . . . In any case, Paul, like today's preacher, sought to articulate the import of the inherited tradition into a culturally different tradition where new issues arose. Being faithful to Paul therefore involves more than repeating what he said and then relating that legalistically to current situations. It also calls for claiming Paul's Gospel-given freedom to do as he did.[72]

Paul, Matthew, and Luke all had the freedom responsibly to apply the message of God to their situations, and we have that same freedom—and that same obligation. Ours is a different world, with threat of nuclear holocaust, massive world starvation, rampant family disintegration, a possible obliteration of the global village, growing secularism. It is the particularity of these issues that we need to address. John Burke, Roman Catholic theologian and teacher of homiletics, writes: "The problem of communicating the perennial message of the Gospel in the context of changing societies has had to have been addressed by each generation. Now it is our turn."[73]

Farmer is helpful in distinguishing between universal needs and contextual needs. He says that in the distant past, preaching focused more on the universal needs but today people are becoming more aware of contextual needs:

The life of any person is shaped by two great sets of factors: universal needs of individual human life and the immediate context, e.g., social, economic and industrial arrangements. The one set of factors has to do with the unchanging, universal needs of the individual human life . . . : death, bereavement, disease and pain, frustration and disappointment of ambition and desire. . . . The other set of factors has to do with the external setting of his life. I mean the social environment and context of his existence, including both the framework of his social, economic and industrial arrangements which so largely determine his existence, and those invisible influences which are soaking into him all the time. . . . This external setting varies from century to century, generation to generation, nation to nation. . . . Men have always died, always suffered bereavement, always had illness, always had bad consciences, always needed personal forgiveness, but they have not always lived under, say, industrial capitalism. . . . The Church, in the past, has on the whole concentrated on, specialized in, so to say, the application of its message to the first set of factors—the permanent and universal needs and troubles of the individual men and women whatever their situation. The Church has had little or nothing to say about the second set, which, as we have said, is more and more filling the horizons of the masses.[74]

These two sets of factors are not inseparable from each other. . . . They are relatively independent of each other, yet there is a close interrelationship. . . . We have to keep these two factors in balance and unity with each other. . . . Today . . . the second set of factors is so obsessive and so dominant in men's minds. . . .[75]

More than any other author I know, Farmer, writing during World War II, clearly saw the need for interpreting the Word of God to both universal and contextual factors. He also sensed the growing importance of contextual factors which "more and more are filling the horizons of the masses." It is these contextual and universal factors that need to be brought to the text, so that God's message speaks to the real world in which we live.

We preachers need to understand not only the text but the will of God for our context.[76] That is what exegesis and interpretation are all about.

SUMMARY

A biblical preacher can renew his or her sermons by:

1. standing beneath the Scriptures, listening to them, wrestling with them, finding authority in them;

2. developing exegetical passion as by listening to the text on behalf of the congregation;

3. exegeting carefully and thoroughly,

using knowledge of the whole Bible;
using exegetical tools;
scrutinizing the text like a detective;
doing one's own research before reading the commentaries;
avoiding preaching exegesis;
discovering the central theme and message of the text;
using the Bible as a source and resource;
discovering what the text meant and means; and
    4. translating and interpreting the biblical message into the present.

6

The Preacher as Prophet

As preachers we are ordained by God to speak God's message to the particular setting in which we live. We cannot do otherwise. That is our compulsion, our divine necessity, our spiritual calling. We speak a word from the Lord to the small portion of the earth on which we live.

AMERICAN SPIRITUALITY

What are some of the characteristics of our scene, in middle-class America in the 1980s? Most of us who read books on homiletics are part of Middle America and know our situation well. Steimle, Craddock, Rice, and Farmer are particularly helpful in identifying the hallmarks of our situation.

The trinity of family, career, and standard of living[1]

Most Americans live by this strict trinitarian creed. This is the primary creed of American life, and a preacher dare not challenge the sacredness of these three primary social values. Rice quotes the work of Dean Hoge, a sociologist from Catholic University of Washington, D.C.:

> Dean Hoge says that most of us live by values which express themselves in powerful social realities: family, career, standard of living. . . . Hoge believes that behind all ideological loyalties, religious confessions, public orations, and national creeds, this hierarchy, which can be understood as a creed and given creedal

form, is what actually determines our economic, political and religious behavior. . . . Among church members, there is a fairly easy identification of Christ with these values. . . ."[2]

Rice suggests that we moralize and allegorize Jesus' parables to "reinforce rather than to challenge" our cultural trinitarian religion. Preaching that does not reinforce this grid, will most likely "be tolerated as 'just preaching' or rejected outright as being irrelevant."[3]

My text-study group wanted me to add another tenet to the American creed of spirituality which should not be challenged: the nation. It seemed to be the unanimous consensus of these pastors that they could not criticize the nation from the pulpit without an immediate backlash from the congregation. There was no room in the pulpit to say anything negative about national policies.

Indifference, sloth, acedia

Steimle, Rice, and Craddock each believe that the "great sin" of an affluent society is not so much pride as indifference, sloth, and not caring. Steimle quotes Moltmann:

> Man's primary problem is fear, hopelessness, resignation, inertia, and melancholy. . . . Temptation consists not so much in the titanic desire to be as God, but in weakness, timidity, weariness, and not wanting to be what God requires of us.[4]

Steimle also quotes Dr. Karl Menninger: "This recognizes acedia as the Great Sin, the heart of all sin: . . . lack of caring, anxiety, indifference, sloth, . . . collective irresponsibility."[5] When faced with the overwhelming social sins and anxieties of our times (economic exploitation of Third World nations, massive global starvation, environmental pollution, nuclear holocaust), the reaction of the local congregation is often indifference. Many would rather focus on sins of private morality than public immorality.

Rice captures the essence of this indifference: life is acceptable as long as I can bite out of the shiny side of the apple and not from the bruised side. The rest of the world may bite from the rotten side, but as long as I can nibble from the shiny side, I am content with the apple the way it is.[6]

Passionless Christendom

Craddock's book, *Overhearing the Gospel,* is a study of Kierkegaard's Danish Christendom and American Christendom. The fundamental problem then and now is not the lack of religious knowledge. Christendom Christians have sufficient religious information ("Let's go one more time through the Bethel Bible series"). The problem is overfamiliarity, a complacent familiarity, a passionless familiarity. It is the problem of not being hungry for the gospel because people have been indulging on religious sweets. It is a problem of preaching to people who feel no need for food. Craddock writes:

> In another place, SK compares those Christians to a man growing thinner day by day. A physician looks at his wasted frame and explains to the family that it's not the fault of want. On the contrary, his sad condition has come from eating all the time, out of season, when not hungry, and thereby ruining his digestion to the point that it resembled a starving man.[7]

In American Christendom, there is "this lack of appetite," "this starvation amid plenty," "a deadly atmosphere of deadly predictability and low expectation." "In brief, it is easier to become a Christian when I am not a Christian than to become a Christian when I am one."[8]

Because of overaccessibility and overfamiliarity, there is little desire for true religion. There is no apparent need for it. Craddock tells a parable about an orphan in a school who unlike the other students is highly motivated to learn. The other children were much more passive and lethargic and said the orphan had the advantage: "She is an orphan. She *wants* to learn."[9] Most American Christians, because of the overaccessibility and overfamiliarity of Christendom, have little motivation to truly follow Christ. Our zeal is lacking. Our situation is *not* like that of Christians in Africa or Latin America where the stakes are costly, the passion intense, and the motivation high.

Americans prefer instant pudding, instant hamburgers, instant religion:

> Some would know God before the parking meter expires. . . . It is no wonder that those like SK who have understood this are rather reluctant to share the fruits of a lifetime of prayer and study

and discipline with someone who wants to talk religion while waiting for the light to change.[10]

Farmer echoes this same idea when he suggests that "today people, even in the churches themselves, think of religion, not as that which is relevant to and informs all activities, but as just one activity among others for those who happen to be inclined that way, like folkdancing. . . ."[11] Soccer, dancing, ballgames, church, choir, scouts; Christianity is just one more activity which is influential as long as it doesn't challenge the sacredness of my nuclear family, the importance of my career, and the pleasures of my standard of living.

Loss of meaning

Time is now measured in the billions of light years; the universe now contains billions of stars; the population of little planet earth has swollen into billions of bodies. Consequently, there seems to be a growing, gnawing sense of smallness, insignificance, and meaninglessness. Farmer describes this changing spirit of the human race:

> I believe that one of the most tragic consequences of the spiritual climate of our time . . . is a certain underlying, depressed, hollow sense of futility and meaninglessness of human existence. . . . What lies behind this loss of nerve and heart, this sense of futility? If we reply that it is due to the loss of the sense of God, that might appear to be just the sort of glib diagnosis of the world's ills that religious people are prone to give. Yet it is the truth, beyond question.[12]

Living in our 20th-century world, with billions of stars, billions of light years, and billions of people, there seems to be a growing futility and absurdity to human life. The disease of the spirit is that of nihilism, that nothing really matters under heaven, except living and loving for today—for my family, my career, my pleasures, my country.

Loss of personal significance and self-esteem

As the world is measured in terms of billions, as the American population has moved from the intimacy of the small villages and towns to the larger, impersonal urban centers, as families have become more fractured and have less quality time together, there seems to be a growing loss of self-worth and self-esteem within the individual. Farmer writes:

> I suspect that a very high proportion of individuals today are oppressed by a sense of their own personal insignificance, . . . that a very high proportion of ordinary folk have something in the nature of an inferiority complex. [13]

Forty years after Farmer's book, Robert Schuller published his best-seller, *Self-Esteem: The New Reformation*. [14] It is a thesis of this book that humankind has been diagnosed as having many fundamental drives. Adler claims the will of the human race is for power, Frankl for meaning, Freud for pleasure. Schuller asserts that the fundamental drive in 20th-century life is towards self-esteem, that a fundamental problem facing contemporary Americans is the loss of personal significance. [15] What is interesting to me is that both Farmer and Schuller describe the same phenomenon: people don't like themselves very well and are struggling to deal with their inadequacies, inferiorities, and incompetencies as persons, parents, workers, lovers, friends. This is a peculiar preoccupation of our present American milieu. In his preaching, Schuller intentionally and specifically deals with this fundamental human need, which partially accounts for his popularity.

Loss of healthy family life

It requires almost no intelligence to realize that devastating changes are going on in American family life. Divorces are epidemic. AIDS and herpes are new words to us. Illicit sexual expression is rampant. For example, on a confirmation retreat it is informative to hear junior high students talk about their close friends having sexual intercourse, the pressure on them to be involved sexually, and the sexual graffiti that is written by their friends on their school notebooks. Sexuality is part of their world, much more so than 30 years ago. Our American world has changed, in spite of the protests of some that "kids have always done it." Such people ignore the massive social changes in America, the transformation from a nation of farms, villages, and towns to a nation of suburbs, metropolises, and cul-de-sacs. Today's youth grow up in urban centers, often with both parents working, often themselves working by the time they are 16. Recent surveys tell us that teenagers value the influence of their peers more than their parents, with peer pressure increasing dramatically as parents have slowly abdicated their parenting roles. Küng could well be describing American family life when he writes: "We spend so much time dusting plastic flowers that we don't have time to cultivate the roses."[16]

It is extremely important for us to be aware of the studies of unchurched in America; 45–55% say they return or convert to the church because they need help with their family life. That is the number one reason given for converting to or returning to the church.[17]

An increasing sense of evil in the world

Whether it is due to television or media reporting, we Americans are becoming increasingly aware of the barbarism of the human species to our own kind. There is no doubt any longer that the human species is capable of being the most barbaric animal on earth. That has always been true about the human animal, but there seems to be an increasing awareness of it in recent years. Farmer observes:

> There is to be observed within men and women today a rather shocked, even frightened, awareness of the power of what can only be called the forces of evil and unreason which are at work in history.[18]

A person needs only to read Jacobo Timerman's *Prisoner without a Name, Cell without a Number,* or Penny Lernoux's *Cry of the People* to realize the depth of human atrocities.

Structural and governmental evil

In the book of Revelation, St. John describes what happens when the power of evil permeates a government. Evil can infect individuals, cultures, and governments; but when satanic powers spread like cancer throughout a government or among government leaders, the consequences are cruelly devastating. We need only recall Stalin's purges as described in Solzhenitsyn's *Gulag Archipelago* or the killings under Mao in China, Somoza in Nicaragua, Pol Pot in Cambodia, or dictatorships in Argentina, Guatemala, or El Salvador. We are becoming increasingly aware of how powerful evil becomes when it absorbs the hearts and heads of political figures and systems.

In the past we have often not cared about our government's political and economic arrangements with poorer nations, as long as those nations were allied with our interests. Somehow, deep down within our psyches, we have come to sense that we haven't cared about the suffering humanity beyond our borders. Now, however, American Christianity is becoming increasingly aware of structural sin and evil—even within our own political and economic system. In the past century, preaching was often involved in the struggle between science and religion, doubt and faith, atheism and Christianity. Increasingly today, the struggle is not with science so much as it is with injustice, starvation, and political exploitation. Increasingly, these issues will be part of American Christian life—in the pulpit.

Recall from the previous chapter Farmer's insistence that preaching involves both the universal concerns (death, disease, despair) and contextual concerns (nuclear holocaust, massive world starvation, rampant secularism). As American preachers struggle with the textual Word for Sunday, we always bring the questions, concerns, and struggles of our American scene, so that the wisdom of God may address us who live here in Middle America in the 1980s.

THE PROPHET CANNOT BE SILENT

We need to be aware of the sin of silence in the face of private and public moral injustice. Jacobo Timerman, while experiencing the hell of anti-Semitic and political persecutions from the Argentinian government between 1976 and 1979, vowed never to be silent again when confronted with social brutality. He remembered Auschwitz too well:

The Holocaust will be understood not so much for the number of victims as for the magnitude of the silence. And what obsesses me most is the repetition of the silence rather than the possibility of another Holocaust. . . . After the war, we began to fathom the magnitude of the Holocaust. And we promised ourselves that never again would this silent, methodical destruction of our people be repeated. We also promised ourselves, and swore repeatedly through the years, that never again would our own silence, passivity, confusion, and paralysis be repeated.[19]

Timerman's vow is the vow of every prophetic preacher: not to be silent when oppression exists. Thielicke also warns that the congregation cannot be silent about fundamental moral questions:

> When the state solved the Jewish question in the most horribly brutal way and delivered the mentally ill and retarded to euthanasia, apart from a few exceptions, there was silence. For after all, were not these "political questions" which were not the concern of the church?[20]

Phillips Brooks, a century ago, also admonished that "the pulpit cannot separate itself and confine its message to what are falsely discriminated as spiritual things." He urged that we ought to hear more sermons about the "right use of wealth, concerning the extravagance of our society, concerning impurity and licentiousness, . . . concerning political corruption and misrule."[21]

> I despise and call on you to despise all the weak assertions that a minister must not preach politics because he will injure his influence if he does, or because it is unworthy of his sacred office. . . . The ordinary talk about ministers not having any power in politics is not true. In a land like ours, where the tone of the people is of vast value in public affairs, the preachers who have so much to do in the creation of the popular tone, must always have their part in politics. . . . You will not turn the pulpit into a place where you can throw out your little scheme for settling a party quarrel or securing a party triumph. . . . But still, the ordinary talk about ministers not having any power in politics is not true.[22]

The preacher cannot be silent in the face of gripping private and public moral issues facing us in our global village. We cannot be silent in the face of "political questions" like the extermination of the Jews, the 12 million children who starve to death each year, the political and eco-

nomic oppression in the Third World, pornography, family violence—
the list goes on.

Spurgeon castigates the tendency to concentrate on trivia:

> I know a minister whose shoe latchet I am unworthy to unloose,
> whose preaching is often little better than sacred miniature paint-
> ing—I might almost say holy trifling. He is great upon the ten
> toes of the beast, the four faces of the cherubim, the mystical
> meaning of badgers' skins, and the typical bearings of the staves
> of the ark, and the windows of Solomon's temple; but the sins
> of the businessmen, the temptations of the times, and the needs
> of the age, he scarcely ever touches upon. Such preaching reminds
> me of a lion engaged in mouse-hunting. . . .[23]

Steimle is critical of the sermons of James Stewart because he was
preaching during World War II and he never mentioned the war in
any of his sermons.[24] It was as if he wasn't dealing with the real world
in which people were living and dying. Though helpful in many ways,
I have some problems with the *Augsburg Sermons* volumes. Too few of
the sermons refer to the immense misery which is part of our claustrophobic community here on planet earth. As Brooks so wisely cautions, "He who ministers to the same people always, knowing them
minutely, is apt to let his preaching grow minute and forget the
world."[25]

One reason for this prophetic silence is the fear of causing conflicts
for ourselves. Harry Wendt of Crossways teaches that the congregational
attitude towards the pastor is often: "If you say it right, we will pay
you right." Don't seriously challenge our family pleasures, our work
pleasure, and our life-style pleasure and we'll pay you right. Luther
echoes the same theme when he writes:

> Our bishops and clergy [are] the smartest people on earth . . .
> They preach in a manner calculated to keep them out of trouble
> and to gain for them money and property, honor and power.[26]

Luther also mentions a quality that the *world* wants from its preacher:
He tells them what they want to hear.[27] Brooks warns preachers: "If
you are afraid of men and a slave to their opinion, go and do something

else."[28] And Helmut Thielicke, who is attracted by the voluntarism of American Christianity, also notes the negative consequences of having our pastoral salaries paid by the congregation: "If a minister sets forth an opinion or conviction of conscience which is offensive to the congregation, he may lose his position."[29] One of the causes of our prophetic silence is that we want to be paid sufficiently well to enjoy a middle-class life like the rest of Americans.

Another reason given for this prophetic silence is the fear of causing division within the congregation—to which someone responded: "The morals of a congregation are more important than its morale." Anyone can foolishly polarize a congregation, but it seems that more congregational conflicts center on the personality of the preacher and lack of sufficient money for the budget, than on the preacher's speaking out on social injustice. And besides, as Brooks says, "The danger of the congregation to the minister comes more from their indulgence than from their opposition."[30]

Prophetic preaching needs to be preceded by pastoral love and care. Some preachers flail away at a congregation about their social convictions, and if those social convictions do not grow out of a pastoral love for the parish, such preaching will alienate persons. Under these circumstances, the source of alienation is not the prophetic word but the prophet's arrogance:

> Preachers able to take prophetic stands on controversial issues without alienating half the congregation seem to be those who understand prophetic ministry to be an extension of pastoral ministry.[31]

> Preaching in the prophetic mode involves love and compassion for those addressed. If prophetic preaching is not motivated and infused by love, it becomes harsh and scolding. . . . Just as preaching love without truth becomes chatter, so preaching truth without love becomes a shrill voice of alienation.[32]

> The militant and idiomatically fluent pastor of an adoring Black congregation is bound to suspect that his prophetic White counterpart gets cast out of his church because his flock are spiritually hungry, more than they are unalterably opposed to a justice never

presented in their language. As Dr. Miles Mark Fischer suggested to me in 1945, when I was already trying to change the South, "Brother Mitchell, don't *use* your influence 'till you *get* it."[33]

Don't use your influence until you have it! Prophetic ministry has its roots in pastoral ministry and spiritual feeding.

Dr. Ernest Campbell said in a lecture, "Tears become a prophet better than a scowl. . . . What passes for the prophetic is often a clogged colon."

The preacher as prophet also speaks with a heart of confession, with a self-honesty that realizes "I am part of the problem."

> The word of judgment is cast in the form of confession so that the preacher is clearly seen to be a participant in the guilt he describes. . . . We will address our common involvement in the social ills of our time. There is "solidarity of all" in the responsibility for poverty, hunger, environmental blight, malfunctions of government and the ultimate violence of war.[34]

> How much more then will preachers in all their frailty and vulnerability identify themselves with their people and make it crystal clear that the prophetic word is addressed to themselves as well as to others in the community of believers. The use of pronouns in the sermon will provide the clue. Prophetic judgment is never addressed to "you" but to "us." "We" are under the judgment of God. . . . Isaiah 6 proves a Biblical basis for prophetic preaching: "I am a man of unclean lips, and I dwell in the midst of a people of unclean lips, for my eyes have seen the King, the Lord of Hosts."[35]

The prophetic preacher is aware of the complexities of the issues to which he is addressing the word of God. It is not always so easy to understand the text nor is it always so easy to understand the word and will of God for our context. We are all keenly aware of giving biblical authority to our religious and social prejudices. Several authors speak about prophetic ministry in a complex world:

> I am less and less interested in preaching *to* them about the great social issues of the day than I am in struggling *with* them through

the complex dilemmas in which we find ourselves. . . . But the sheer complexity of life today requires that moral leadership be exercised less presumptuously than before. . . . I try to give my "prophecy" a probing, questioning inflection, rather than a dogmatic and authoritarian tone.[36]

Scherer suggests that many pastors stand in the pulpit, speaking "four feet above contradiction,"[37] uttering pious generalities. Laity often believe preachers are naive about politics and economics, that we are idealists who live in another world, that we speak in broad but not helpful generalities. We preachers are usually thought to be against war, sin, nuclear armaments, starvation, and pollution but we don't have the political savvy and wisdom to begin to solve these gigantic social cancers.

Specifically, Elizabeth Achtemeier cautions preachers who make economic pronouncements but have little understanding of the marketplace:

Nothing disturbs professionals or scholars or practitioners in some field quite so much as to have a preacher distort the facts from that field of knowledge. Their conclusion is that the preacher does not know what he or she is talking about, and that the Gospel as a whole is discredited. Especially has this been true in relation to American business practices. Many preachers don't have the foggiest notion about economics or how the American marketplace works. Yet the materialism and economic greed of society are favorite targets for criticism from the pulpit. The criticism would be much more responsively received if representatives from both management and labor in our congregations were convinced that the preachers understand money matters.[38]

Similarly, Brooks talks about the benefit of the "supercilious hearer." By "supercilious," Brooks doesn't mean proud or haughty, but is referring to men and women who listen to sermons carefully, intelligently, *and* critically. They keep us preachers on our toes, especially when it comes to political-justice issues. Religious political platitudes are often challenged by these hearers, and they keep the preacher honest. The supercilious hearer "keeps the atmosphere of the church fresh . . .

[and] makes the whole sermon more true and conscientious, more complete in the best qualities that belong to all good sermons."[39] Any preacher can benefit, as I have, from such articulate and forthright hearers in his or her congregation—persons who challenge caricatures and straw-man situations in sermons.

Knowing that we live in a complex world and knowing that we preachers are usually not familiar with sophisticated economic theory, we nonetheless can raise the difficult questions, especially questions of justice, greed, and complicity. Stuempfle writes:

> Our preaching will take the form of persistently raising the questions which many people would prefer to ignore. . . . The preacher is the one who keeps raising the awkward questions which will prevent us from being at ease amid the forces in modern life by which people are disadvantaged and dehumanized.[40]

Knowing that the human tendency is to be blind to our own complicity with evil, the prophet asks those naive and simple questions: Why is it right to destroy a whole nation of Russians when perhaps only 10 of them decided to bomb New York City? Why is it that our wealthy economy is becoming increasingly dependent on Third World nations? Why is it that 40% of our exports are to Third World Nations? Why is it that our business community seeks out cheap labor and then tries to inhibit labor movements in the poorest of nations? It's a complex world, but we keep on asking those questions of our own complicity with injustice, for the prophetic preacher is committed to the love and justice of God.

The prophetic preacher tells stories of persecution and oppression among fellow Christians. Life is usually changed more by stories than by any other form of communication, and so the prophetic preacher tells stories of fellow Christians who are being persecuted because of their commitment to the love and justice of Christ. Tell stories of Romero in El Salvador, and how he was shot while giving the sacrament, and why he was shot. Tell stories of parents escaping the death-squads in El Salvador and having to suffocate their children so their cries wouldn't draw the attention of the soldiers 15 yards away. Tell stories of the American physician who lives and works with the rebel forces in El Salvador and creates herbal medicines to drug the children so they won't cry out during an escape. Tell stories of Jean Marie Donovan ("A Rose in December," NBC), a young woman who had to go back to El Salvador and continue to work in her orphange "because of the children. I know it is safer for me to stay here in the U.S.A.," she said, "but I *can't* desert the children." She was raped and assassinated by the death squads and our Secretary of State claimed she was aiding and abetting the rebel forces (running an orphanage). Tell stories about fellow Christians in Namibia and their struggles with the South African government which is stealing their minerals, all the while shouting, "Anti-communism! We're protecting South Africa from communism!" which really means they are raping the uranium mines of our Christian brothers and sisters in Namibia. Tell story after story after story, specific with names and places, of Christians who are fighting for their rights. The present world is filled with millions of stories of Christians who are struggling for food and freedom. Indeed, theirs is the bruised side of the apple. The poetic, prophet preacher is a storyteller.

One night at the retreat center, Holden Village, I heard an effective example of prophetic preaching in story form. Charles Lutz, director of the Office of Church in Society for The American Lutheran Church, preached a sermon describing the origins of Christianity in Russia. It was July 15th, the appointed feast day to commemorate Queen Olga and Prince Vladimir, the founders of the Christian church in Russia. With a glint of humor in his eye, he reminded the heavily Scandinavian audience that the Christian church existed in Russia before it spread to Norway, and everyone laughed. He described the 60 million Russian Christians (including estimates of one million Lutheran Christians), and we all sang, "In Christ There Is No East or West." Chuck didn't say it directly—in fact, he never mentioned it—but the whole thrust of the sermon was: "Don't nuke the Russians who are fellow Christians, fellow human beings!" He was telling us indirectly about the peace of Christ. Not once did he mention "nuclear," but that is what the sermon was all about.

That same day, I had been reading about Kierkegaard's principle of "indirect communication" and what Craddock terms "overhearing the Gospel." You attract the listener into a story or narrative and let them draw their own conclusions. As we listened that night to Chuck Lutz, no one became defensive. No one became argumentative. It was not a harangue. You simply became aware of the long history of Christianity in Russia and the presence of millions of Christians living there. You, the listener, drew your own conclusions. Lutz's sermon was a good illustration of prophetic storytelling, "indirect communication," and overhearing the gospel.

GONZALEZ AND GONZALEZ

A most insightful book about prophetic preaching is *Liberation Preaching* by Gonzalez and Gonzalez. They discuss the dangers of leaving the interpretation of the Bible in the hands of the powerful or middle-class, knowing that we will read the Bible in such a way as to protect our vested interests. The Gonzalezes want to know why American middle-class Christianity is preoccupied with sexual sins rather than structural sins. They talk about their "ideological suspicion" which asks embarrassing questions: What is the hidden economic and political advantage of interpreting the Bible this way? In the lectionary, why do we use the prophets only for their predictions about the coming Messiah and never to hear their message of social injustice? Listening to the lectionary readings, the Sunday morning worshiper would think that Micah was solely concerned about the coming Messiah and not about social inequities. Again, being suspicious of how the lectionary was organized, why is it that the Ephesians 5 text is cut between submissive women and obedient slaves? Why do we *still* hear passages about women being submissive but not about slaves being obedient?[41] Is there some advantage for someone to keep women submissive? The book is a gold mine of insightful perceptions about our hidden power-prejudices.

Nothing is ideologically neutral: translations of the Bible, commentaries, lectionaries. None of these is ideologically neutral. The values and attitudes of the rich and powerful are unconsciously reinforced in our religious publications.

A key benefit of *Liberation Preaching* is that the reader can learn to read the Bible from the perspective of the poor of the Third World. For example, the authors quote from Cardenal's book, *Gospel of Solin-*

taname, which my wife reads for her morning meditations, trying to absorb a Christian "poverty perspective" while reading the Bible. Here you listen to the discussions of poor Nicaraguans as they interpret the Scriptures. The Psalms come alive for them, especially when the psalmist pleads and begs for protection from "my enemies." It is helpful to try to hear the Bible as interpreted "from below" since it is the conviction of the authors that the Bible was usually written by people from "below," in Babylonian captivity or during persecution (the Gospels, the Pauline corpus, Revelation, 1 Peter):

> God has a proclivity for speaking the Word through the powerless. The whole Bible bears witness to this. Is this an accident, or is it an essential ingredient of the Gospel itself? . . . The powerful have a difficult time hearing God accurately. . . . The powerless have readier access to an authentic understanding of the Gospel than do the powerful.[42]

Since the Bible was mostly written by poorer people, perhaps the poor of today have an eye for understanding Scriptures in a way that others do not. Our brothers and sisters in the poorer Christian communities then become our teachers. If we begin to read the Bible through the eyes of the poor, we will soon discover dimensions in the Bible we did not realize were there.

Earlier in this book, we discussed the importance of preaching to the needs of those in our parish. But Gonzalez and Gonzalez emphasize the necessity of preaching for the "powerless who are absent." We need to be aware of the needs of our poor, hungry, and oppressed brothers and sisters who are not physically present as we preach the gospel:

> If in a local congregation, our brothers and sisters in the faith who now stand in such a hostile relationship to us, were actually made present, we [would] begin to see the Gospel from their point of view. . . . The preacher of liberation has more opportunity to make this a reality than does almost anyone else of any church.[43]

We, the preachers of the gospel in affluent America, need to speak on behalf of the poorest Christians of the world who are not physically present with us on Sunday morning, but perhaps are quite angry with us. We need to see and hear the gospel through their eyes. We then preach in their behalf. We then pray on their behalf.

SUMMARY

More than any other place, the roots of the office of preaching are found in the prophets. Those men and women were rooted and grounded in God's word and will, and they spoke God's word and will to the world in which they lived. We preachers need to have the courage to do the same.

The sum of the matter is this: as preachers we are ordained to speak God's message to the particular setting in which we live.

7

The Preacher as Storyteller

THE IMPORTANCE OF FORM

The preacher needs to take seriously the form of the message. If there is no concern for form and style, the result is often boredom. A preacher may have many powerful ideas left unheard because of a boring form. Craddock writes:

> Undoubtedly there are many powerful and life-changing ideas lying impotent in pale paragraphs and slipping unheard past bored ears, written and spoken by great thinkers, who have no time or interest to give such marginal matters as how one communicates to another. On the other hand, who can deny that much of the lasting power of Nietzsche's philosophy is owed to his vivid and effective style?[1]

If a communicator of the gospel does not take form seriously, there is a great possibility that what is said will not be heard or absorbed, or enter into the imaginations of the heart.

Davis reminds us that all living things have form, be it a violet, a lily, a weeping willow, or a sermon. "All life, every living thing we know, comes in some organic form. . . . We cannot have life without form. . . . Likewise, every thought comes in some form. We cannot have thought without form. . . . The difference between chaotic thought and ordered thought is not the difference between form and no form; it is the difference between confused form and organized form."[2]

Davis suggests two reasons for a preacher to be concerned about form. First, to produce a response:

> The aim of preaching is to win from men a response to the Gospel, a response of attitude, and impulse, and feeling, no less than of thought. Since form does its work immediately and at deeper levels than logic, persuades directly and silently as it were, form has an importance second only to that of the thought itself.[3]

The *form* of the thought affects attitudes, impulses, and feelings which shape the mind and inner imaginations of the heart. If you convert a parable into a logical syllogism or dogmatic statement, you lessen the power of the truth to transform and change a person.[4] Davis' second reason why preachers need to be concerned about form is the "exceedingly complex nature of the people who hear the word."[5] So much is happening at one time in the mind of the hearer: thoughts, musings, wanderings. Hearing is a complex phenomenon, and the form of speech helps the listener actually to hear the words. The form enables a person to listen, comprehend, absorb, and respond; but for a person to comprehend, absorb, and respond, that person must first listen.

Both Davis and Craddock were critical of seminary training, seminary students, and young preachers for not taking form seriously. Davis suggests that seminary students often feel that the study of form is beneath their dignity and knowledge, that form is a secondary consideration, and that it is not worthy of the importance given to theological thought and truth. "They can give sixteen reasons why they should not be bothered with form." And yet, "only the apprentice preacher dares to think such things are beneath him, and expects to succeed in his work without knowing anything about how it is done." Just as an art student needs to study space and form, and just as a young poet needs to study the basic mechanics of the language, so also a preacher needs to understand the basic elements of the great art of oral communication. Davis reminds us that a large number of clergy were rhetoricians before they were preachers, among them, Ambrose, Augustine, and Chrysostom.[6]

Craddock writes about the "arrogant dismissal of methods in our churches, colleges and seminaries." When there are discussions about form and content, "invariably content is on the inside and form is on the outside; content is essential, form is accessory, optional." He suggests that the seminaries often hire the most brilliant minds, whether or not that person has the gift of teaching and communication; and these persons prefer to teach content (e.g., systematics) rather than form (homiletics).[7] He suggests there is a consistent and insidious bias against the strategic importance of form.

Dividing theological content from form results in a tragic separation: "The separation of method of preaching from theology of preaching is a violation, leaving not one but two orphans."[8]

In closely reading several writers on preaching, I sense they assume that a preacher knows and practices the elementary principles of oral communication. But in my experience with training interns and listening to other preachers, I have repeatedly discovered that they did not comprehend or practice the elementary laws of rhetoric, and their sermons were poorer for it. As we know, it is possible to graduate from seminary and never have had one speech class in college or seminary. It is possible to graduate and have taken only one or two courses in homiletics. It is possible to graduate and preach for 40 years and not take one course on the renewal of preaching. It is possible to be a pastor and avoid any systematic critique of our sermons. We often take numerous courses in the content of preaching, but rarely examine the form. Yet it is form which often gives power to the truth. The power of form is one reason why Jesus taught in parables and only rarely in syllogisms. Form must be taken seriously. Davis says that the preacher "is called to work in the great art of oral communication and is called to cultivate all the sense and skill he can."[9]

Most of the books which are required and recommended reading for seminary homiletics departments were written in the last 15 years. Most of these books are concerned about form. Fant writes:

First preaching learned that it must take the text seriously; then it learned that it must take the people [congregation] seriously; now it must learn to take the medium seriously.[10]

In these books there are more paragraphs and pages dedicated to the study of form than to any other topic. Consequently, the remaining chapters of this book will focus on form, including the importance of:

- stories, analogies, and images (Chapters 8, 9);
- language (Chapter 10);
- "living speech" (Chapter 11);
- variety of forms (Chapter 12).

JESUS LOVED PARABLES

Matthew tells us that Jesus "said nothing . . . without a parable" (Matt. 13:34). Jesus used stories, analogies, and images to communicate the message of the kingdom: The King is like a woman who looks diligently for a lost coin, a shepherd who searches for a lost sheep, a father who waits lovingly for his lost son to return home. Jesus couldn't resist. He had to tell a story or use a metaphor. It was his way of communicating the gospel.

It is for this reason that Wilder suggests the very nature of the gospel comes to us in the form of a story.[11] The structure of the gospel is not a series of well-argued ideas; the structure of the gospel is not a series of syllogisms. To convert the gospel into a syllogism or intellectual argument or collection of religious definitions is to alter the very nature of the gospel itself. Craddock writes:

> It is important that the very structure of the message be narrative.
> . . . Change the shape, for instance, into a logical syllogism and
> the question of whether the content of the message is altered is
> a moot one. The important point is the function of the narrative
> is now lost. . . . In its place are some ideas, well argued.[12]

That's what preaching often is: ideas well argued rather than stories, analogies, and images. We need to recall that H. Grady Davis said the Gospels themselves are 90% narrative, and our preaching needs to reflect that fact.[13] In the Bible, "we are not only told that God is love— that love is defined by a story. . . . Love is pictured through the events of a whipping, a trial, a mocking, a crown of thorns."[14] Mitchell, too, believes that a story is more powerful than an abstract idea. He advises that if you can't put your sermon into a story, don't bother to tell it. "No other form should be used in preference to a good story," and intellectual arguments and essays should be used as "adjuncts" to stories.[15] Similarly, Buechner writes:

> The way to preach is the way he did. Not in the incendiary rhetoric of the prophet nor in the systematic abstractions of the theologian, but in the language of images and metaphor, which is finally the only language you can use.[16]

Extolling the power of metaphor, Craddock writes:

> Among the aids for generating listening experience, none is more effective than a metaphor. . . . At the heart of the parables of Jesus is the metaphor.[17]

Wilder, Craddock, Davis, Achtemeier, Mitchell, Buechner, and others are correct: the very nature of the gospel is that it is communicated in the form of stories, analogies, and narratives; our preaching needs to use the same.

As was said previously, Jesus uses stories, analogies, and illustrations from everyday life. He referred to the most common and familiar of experiences: sheep, shepherds, fish, nets, boats, weeds, wheat, soil, flowers, children, parents, lost, found, treasures, enemies, friends, widows, blind, sick, temple, synagogue, Pharisees, money, lust, greed. His stories, analogies, and illustrations were drawn out of the common lives of the people. He didn't spend time giving an exegetical history of the text or doing a word study. He knew and used his Old Testament, but most often he illustrated his understanding of God and his ways by using the objects, images, and relationships nearest to the common lives of the people. Wilder writes:

> These stories are so human and realistic. One can even speak of their secularity. The impact of the parables lay in their immediate realistic authenticity.[18]

> Jesus brought theology down into the daily life and into the immediate everyday situation. Here is a clue for the modern preacher.[19]

". . . these sharply focused snapshots of life do reveal something very important about the storyteller himself and about the Gospel.[20]

Steimle also comments about the secularity of Jesus' parables:

When Jesus uses the parables as a teaching device, he uses essentially secular, worldly stories. They were not heard as "Bible stories" as we have come to think of them.[21]

Jesus drew his stories, analogies, and illustrations from the common lives of his hearers, and we are well advised to do the same.

Reuel Howe calls this the "principle of inclusion" or "inclusive preaching." By this, he meant that we include "their meanings," "their questions," "their hypotheses," "their affirmations," "their doubts."[22] Paul Harms wrote a chapter entitled, "Preaching Is for the People," in which he said that we preachers often overlook the obvious—the hearer. "If the hearer is the object of preaching, as he is most assuredly, then it is he who must be served."[23] Niedenthal is sharply critical but accurate when he writes:

I am tired of sermons that don't live where the people live. That don't connect with the real struggles by which their lives are shaped. That never touch earth or breathe the air that the congregation breathes.[24]

Mitchell echoes the same theme:

Most credentialed pastors arrive at their first parishes having been for three or four years acculturated away from the vocabulary and mental images, the frame of reference and basic concerns of that portion of the population which seminaries and others have pilloried as "the silent majority."[25]

Jesus *told* parables; he didn't read them out of a book. The very nature of Jesus' stories, analogies, and illustrations is that they are "living speech." Wilder remarks that "even when written, a story, like a dialogue, is not far removed from oral communication, from living speech."[26] In preaching, you don't read stories; you tell stories. The very telling of the stories, analogies, and illustrations is at the heart of the preaching event. The nature of the gospel encourages "living communication," and the very nature of stories, analogies, and illustrations encourage "living speech."

Wilder points out that the word *parable* is not a rigidly defined category when used by Jesus. Jesus' parables include metaphors, similes, short stories, and long stories. There was no single pattern to his parables, in contrast to the rabbis who had a very rigid set of rules on how to tell a parable.

> Jesus uses figures of speech in an immense number of ways. The variety of the parables is only one aspect of this variety. As Hermaniuk observes, "by contrast with the rabbinic *mashalim,* the parables of Jesus are largely free of rigid and stereotyped formulas. They move with a great freedom and are not constrained by any rule of schools."

> Indeed, we may say that the term "parable" is misleading, since it suggests a single pattern and often distorts our understanding of that special case. [27]

Jesus was free when it came to the use of stories, analogies, and images. This is part of the pleasure of listening to Jesus; you sense his freedom of form. Jesus was not constrained by a static design of parable, nor should we be.

WE LOVE STORIES

How the ear loves a story! When the ear hears such phrases as "Let me tell you about the time when . . ." or "I remember when I was a boy growing up . . ." the ear perks up and begins to listen. Steimle mentions that as soon as the ear hears these liturgical phrases, "the ear bends to the speaker, wanting to listen."

> The storyteller and the circle of listeners *bend* to each other. There is in the very nature of storytelling a posture, a leaning forward. And this is true of both the listener and the storyteller, as if the story cannot be told without this attentive *bending* to each other. . . . A good storyteller is bending to the circle, modifying the

details of the narrative, perhaps adding to it and modulating the voice for these particular listeners. . . . [The story] is not frozen in print; it is alive in the imagination of the storyteller. . . . Speech is flexible enough to bend spontaneously to the attentive circle so that the story can become a shared story. Is it too much to say that the story, in the telling, is a *new* story which happens between storyteller and listeners who, all ears, bend to each other?[28]

I have come to love the word *raconteur:* one who excels at telling stories or anecdotes. The preacher is a raconteur of the gospel.

I remember hearing Helmut Thielicke speak a number of years ago. His English was not very proficient, and my mind would wander. But as soon as he would say, "I have a story to illustrate," immediately my ears would pick up and begin to listen.

When a story is being told, graphic detail helps the ear in listening; colorful details make the storytelling and the listening more enjoyable. Frederick Buechner and Clarence Jordan are two masterful storytellers (raconteurs). Listen to Buechner's description of Pilate:

On that day that he asks his famous question, there are other things that he has seen and done. He makes his first major decision before he has even had his breakfast. While still in his pajamas, he walks downstairs to the bar closet where he keeps extra cigarettes, takes the two-and-a-half cartons that he finds there and puts them out with the trash. . . . After dinner the evening before, the talk turned to politics and he was up for hours, talking and smoking, so that when he awoke, his tongue felt hot and dry, his whole chest raw inside like a wound. He knows about the surgeon general's warning. He has seen the usual photographs of a smoker's lungs. He has been a three-pack-a-day man for better or worse for thirty years so his prebreakfast decision is a decision for life against death. . . .[29]

Notice all the graphic detail used to describe Pilate. The ear knows better than to take this detail literally; the ear senses that the detail is merely telling us that Pilate is a real human being like us. This graphic detail makes a link between past and present; so when speaking about the past, it becomes a present event because we can easily visualize this three-pack-a-day government bureaucrat. He's probably sitting in our pew. The ear loves it and wants to listen, thereby helping the mind and heart to begin to hear and understand.

Clarence Jordan knows how to tell a story so that his congregation delights in listening. His sermon on the rich man and Lazarus immediately links his southern congregation to the biblical scene. Although Dr. Jordan has a Ph.D. in Greek, this does not inhibit him from retelling the story with graphic colorful detail in such a way that tantilizes those Southern ears:

> Jesus told the story one time, of a very rich man who liked to give a big party and invite a lot of his cronies and serve them mint juleps out under his big magnolia trees, and just be the real aristocrat old gentleman with his little goatee and pince-nez glasses.
>
> . . . And many a time Abraham would invite old Lazarus over to his house for an evening of fried chicken, black-eyed peas, gravy, rice, and collard greens. . . .
>
> Now it so happened that the rich man found that he no longer had his table set with all the dainties and delicacies of the South. He found that he didn't even have a drink of water, and the temperature was unseasonably hot, and getting even worse, along with extremely high humidity. And in this rather parched state, the rich man said, "Ooh, I wonder where my water boy is. Boy! Bring me some water!" And no boy comes. . . .[30]

How the ear loves every graphic detail, smiling as the preacher links the past with the present, so that the past becomes alive. Not all stories need this graphic detail, yet the ear appreciates colorful short stories such as told by Luke in his gospel.

Mitchell describes this as "eyewitness preaching," where the storyteller has so absorbed himself in the story that he tells it like a firsthand, eyewitness account. He himself is reliving the story as it is told for what seems like the first time.[31]

I remember an intern a few years ago who was preaching on a text about "plowing and not looking back." He used an illustration of a farmer plowing the field in North Dakota and the need to keep his eyes on the furrow in front of him. It was a good illustration. Two days later, as we were evaluating that sermon, I discovered that *he* was the person on the tractor. When he told me that same illustration again, he told it in the first person, with all the feelings and exhilaration of a young boy on a huge tractor. The graphic detail made the story come alive. It became an eyewitness story, rather than an impersonal analogy. The analogy was fine, but his eyewitness story would have been more powerful and vivid as a means of communication.

STORIES HELP US REMEMBER

Stories help the mind and heart to remember. The ear, mind, and heart love these vivid, firsthand stories and analogies because they are often easier to remember than Bible verses or serious-sounding theological truths. The story "is a form which lends itself to wide popular diffusion. It is easier to remember than a homily, or moral talk or a poem."[32]

This reminds me of a story about caring that Mary Schramm told at Holden Village and is published in her book, *Gifts of Grace*. It is a story which I have labeled, "The Nun and the Nightie," and I would like to retell it as I remember it being told.[33]

How this young nun loved pretty things! Especially lace! Especially pretty, delicate, soft, *silk* lace! The vows of chastity and obedience were possible for her to fulfill, but the vow of poverty was most difficult for her. She loved things, especially pretty feminine patterns and designs. One year her mother sent her a lovely new nightgown. When she opened the box, she immediately fell in love with it. Silk. Lacey fine silk. She took it to her Mother Superior to ask for permission to keep it. "Hrrumpt," was the reply, "You have one nightgown already and that is sufficient." The young nun left, quietly obedient but secretly despondent. Another older nun, overhearing the conversation, approached the young woman and suggested, "My nightie is all worn out, and I need another. Could I have your old one? I would be most grateful if I could." Permission was granted and the young nun felt new silk on her skin each night, touching it pleasurefully like a three-year-old touches a silk pillow at night in her sleep.

Months have flown by since I heard that story. My ear, mind, and heart have enjoyed that parable, that story, that illustration. And who is to say what it precisely means? Like most parables, it works on the inner imagination of one's heart over time. What that story means to me today won't be quite the same as it means to me a month from now, when I am facing a different day. Stories, analogies, and images are easier to remember than Bible verses, witty sayings, clever speech patterns, and beautiful language. How I love to read Buechner and Achtemeier! Their words are majestic and heavenly; they lift me up as I hear their beauty; and yet I can remember few of their lovely phrasings. But my mind can remember "The Nun and the Nightie" and other vivid stories, analogies, and images.

SUMMARY

Preachers need to take form seriously. If they do not, the sermon usually cannot even penetrate past the eardrums. The form of an idea helps it slip through the ears and into the mind and heart. The very heart of the gospel usually comes in story form because human beings intuitively love the truth as expressed through stories and analogies. Jesus often used the form of the parable, and the source of Jesus' metaphors and stories were the common and ordinary experiences of daily life.

8

The Importance of Stories, Analogies, and Images (SAIs)

I have coined an acronym, SAI (pronounced "sigh" as in Saigon), and it stands for parabolic stories, analogies, and images. Often the word *parable* has too narrow connotations and is primarily associated with the biblical past. The word *stories,* on the other hand, has broad connotations and often leaves out the concept of analogies and images. In this and the following chapters, I will refer to SAIs as Jesus would have referred to parables. A SAI is a contemporary story, analogy, or image which is used to communicate God's message about the kingdom.

Even though people often disdain the creation of another acronym, I hope that SAI will become part of our vocabulary about preaching. While "talking shop" with pastors, I found SAI to be a good shorthand word. It is cumbersome to say "parables, similes, and metaphors," to use Spurgeon's words. SAI is easier and simpler. Also, creating a new acronym suggests the importance of using contemporary stories, analogies, and images in sermons.

One of my colleagues responded to all of this by asking, "Does this mean that the Holy Spirit intercedes for us with SAIs too deep for words?" As I recall, he produced a chorus of groans.

What is a story? We all know what stories are, but the term is difficult to define. It's like asking what a leaf or a flower is. We all know what they are; we also know that there are a great variety of them. There are short stories, long stories, tall stories, light stories, heavy stories. Stories usually have beginnings, middles, and ends. Stories usually have a plot. We all remember and love good stories, even if we can't define the word.

What is an analogy? An analogy is a comparison. God is like a good car mechanic who loves his work, understands engines, and knows how to repair them. God is like an X-ray machine; he sees right through you. God is like the radio waves in the air; he is always present but you hear him only when you tune him in. Our mind thinks in terms of what is familiar to help us understand that which is intangible or not so familiar.

What is an image? The preacher uses both stories and analogies to imprint an image or picture in the heart and mind. For example, Jesus told three consecutive stories—about a lost coin, a lost sheep, and a lost son (Luke 15). These stories created and can still create an image or picture of what it means and feels like to be lost and found. The image of lost and found was being imprinted on our minds and emotions as he told one story after another on one theme. The image is the picture remembered by the head and heart, and is created by a vivid story or analogy.

SAIs are contemporary stories, analogies, and images that convey the message of God.

Spurgeon says that "similitudes" (SAIs) are like windows in a house; they let the light in. Windows bring in freshness, happiness, and the pleasure of sunlight. A house without windows is like a prison, closet, or basement; it is dark, depressing, and claustrophobic. Likewise, a sermon without SAIs is usually dull, boring, and even depressing. A sermon with good SAIs can be fresh, interesting, and even uplifting. Spurgeon writes:

> Reasons are the pillars of the fabric of a sermon, but similitudes are the windows which give the best lights.

> The chief reason for the construction of windows in a house is . . . to let in light. Parables, similes, and metaphors have that effect; and hence we use them to illustrate our subject or, in other

words, to "brighten it with light," for that is . . . the literal rendering of the word illustrate.

A building without windows would be a prison rather than a house.[1]

Personally, I would much rather be in a house with windows than a house without them, and I would much rather listen to a sermon with SAIs than to a sermon without them.

Reason and points of theological truth are *absolutely necessary* in every sermon; just as structure and walls are necessary in every home. A house needs to be solidly built, with good supports and load-bearing walls. A house cannot be all windows; there must be proportion. Likewise, a sermon must have proportion; it cannot be all SAIs. If a sermon is to be solidly built it must use fundamental theological truths as its structure. But, as pointed out in Chapter 2, the laity's persistent complaint about modern preaching is that there are too many theological truths, too many intellectual supports, and too many solid walls of thought— but not enough illustrations (SAIs) and not enough windows that bring light, freshness, and clarity into the sermon. We need more windows in our preaching.

THE POWER OF SAIs TO TRANSFORM

Latent within SAIs there is power to transform. In fact, the primary purpose of a vivid SAI is to change us. Jesus told parables (SAIs), not to entertain people with good illustrations, not to keep their mind listening to his religious speech, but to transform them—and that is still the purpose of stories, analogies, and images today.

Several authors refer to the power of SAIs to move, shape, and change people, more so than religious-sounding lectures. Read the following quotations slowly, as these insights are perhaps the primary key to this book. This is not the time to skim. As usual, each author has a slightly different and uniquely helpful way of describing the power of SAIs to transform:

The aim of preaching is to win from people a response to the Gospel, a response of attitude and impulse and feeling no less than thought. Since form does its work immediately and at deeper levels than logic, persuades directly and silently, as it were, form has an importance second only to that of thought itself [Davis].[2]

Teaching and preaching that stay in the conceptual world of ideas and doctrines, however true or right or current, leave hearers essentially unmoved. The consciousness in its imaginative depths is unaltered [Craddock].[3]

The Bible does not push dogma upon us. It lets us enter into the events by imagination until the story becomes our story and we are transformed. . . . If we are to proclaim that story, we should do so in words and forms that will produce the same telling effect. Why turn God's love into a proposition? . . . Propositional and moralistic preaching both have one fault in common: they fail to mediate the actions of a saving Lord, because they fail to allow us to experience those actions for ourselves. They tell us about them; they never let us enter into the imaginations of our heart [Achtemeier].[4]

It is good to be a Herschel who describes the sun; but it is better to be a Prometheus who brings the sun's fire to earth [Brooks].[5]

Almost invariably, the [white] preacher/student will say that "The goal of a sermon is to show . . . to enlighten . . . a 'head trip. . . .' Black preachers have historically set out to *move* persons, even if they did nothing else. . . . It is time for all of us honestly to embrace the goal of a *complete gospel,* which includes the deep *moving* of persons. . . . When Jesus spoke of the forgiveness of God, he always had a human goal of more than simply "showing." . . . Nothing important should ever be said by syllogism which is not also stated more comprehensively in symbolic story, poetry or picture. The latter is better remembered as well as moving of persons [Mitchell].[6]

My message is one that concerns not only all men but the whole man: the man of feeling, the man of intellect, the man of will, and the far larger contingent of those who are a mixture of all three [Thielicke].[7]

We have learned anew that the presence of a full set of emotions is not evidence of the absence of intelligence nor is the ability to feel strongly about a matter to be interpreted as a lack of maturity. . . . From the time a baby reaches from a crib to catch the sunbeam streaming through a keyhole until the day when he sits old and among the pigeons in the park, the significant turns in the long road are marked by images with emotional force that linger in the memory long after the factual details are faded and dim. The preacher must be a whole person to admit such material without distortion or apology into his sermons [Craddock].[8]

[The television miniseries] *Roots* moved me. It moved all kinds of people. . . . Why can't preaching be like that? Why can't preaching be more like *Roots* in its power and impact and less like a cold, unemotional book? . . . Couldn't we learn to tell stories in such a way that people's lives would be changed? Changed lives, transformed people—that's what the gospel is all about. Couldn't the storyteller's art aid us in our preaching task? [Jensen].[9]

The one who moves people must first himself be moved [Cicero].[10]

Mood is as important as logic. . . . Christian mysticism uses feelings and moods to engender the dimensions of awe and wonder and longing. Christian mysticism unashamedly addresses the heart, for as Pascal reminds us, "The heart has reasons that reason does not know." . . . Sermons must not only address the emotions, they should be preached in the awareness that divine love creates emotions. . . [Halvorson].[11]

My favorite quotation on this theme is a paraphrase of a remark by Paul Holmer:

Bad literature [or sermons] describes emotions; good literature [or sermons] creates scenes and situations which evoke emotion.[12]

Each of these authors is emphasizing that the goal of a sermon is to move, shape, change, and that the vehicle for such transformation is a vivid SAI which speaks the message of God. Power to change usually comes in SAI form because that is the shape of the gospel.

It is interesting to me that a 19th-century Bostonian (Brooks) and a 20th-century black Baptist from Los Angeles (Mitchell) sound almost alike when they talk about the goal of preaching: *to move people* towards the fullness of Jesus Christ. I think Brooks and Mitchell would have enjoyed each other's preaching.

Stories trigger the listener's participation in the message and thereby stimulate our creative imaginations which underlie our motivation to change. Stories "move" our creative imaginations, and it is from within our creative imaginations that change quietly begins in us. For example, during engagement counseling I often tell the story about Irving and Jennie. Irving was a retired machinist, age 65, bald, round, and shy. Irving was married to Jennie who had been blind for several years because of diabetes. Every afternoon, they could be seen walking the streets of Des Moines together, Irving gently guiding Jennie along. What care he had for his wife! What compassion! Time passed and Jennie died. Time passed again, and six months later, I began seeing Clara over at Irving's house—more and more often. Clara was Jennie's sister, a widow. Months passed and soon the wedding bells were chiming, and Irving and Clara were married. It was a grand day! But it was only two months later that I discovered that Irving was dying of cancer. Clara had known it for months, and that was a primary reason she had married Irving—so she could care for him in his home during his illness and death. She loved Irving for many reasons, but especially for the way Irving had cared for her blind sister. Clara's quality of love for Irving was a similar kind of love Irving had for Jennie. The love of Christ lived in their love. These are examples of "sacramental marriages"; their marriages were visible signs of the invisible God. Such marriages build us up and strengthen us. Irving, Jennie, and Clara have been an inspiration for my life and marriage for years. Their lives are stories which help my mind imagine what my marriage can be. Such stories energize our imaginations about our own marriages. Stories "move" our creative imaginations which are often the source of the motivation to mature, grow, and change. SAIs are intended to touch both the mind and the heart.

While at Holden, I had several experiences with the power of SAIs to mold people; I recall one in particular. At breakfast one morning, a young adult, about 21, gave devotions. He told the story of how he and his cousin were struck by a car six years earlier. His cousin was killed, and he was in a coma for three months. He had been emotionally vulnerable since the accident. A source of strength for him during the past six years was the parable "Footprints" (attributed to Dathan Moore). You see it on posters nowadays, and it can be purchased in almost any gift shop. It has become as common as some of Jesus' parables. Briefly, the parable is this: A young man has a dream in which he sees two sets of footprints on the ocean sand as they were walking side by side. One set of footprints belongs to God and the other to the young man; but suddenly, there was only one set of footprints in the sand instead of two. In the dream the young man accused God of deserting him and God replied: "No, I did not desert you. The time that you noticed one set of footprints in the sand was the time I had picked you up and was carrying you." This story was the source of strength that helped this young accident victim get through his troubles. It was both the truth of the story and the story itself that sustained him during those six years. The young man didn't tell us about any Bible verses; he didn't quote "God is our refuge and strength, a very present help in time of trouble." What he said helped him was that SAI. This is not to minimize the power of actual Bible words and stories. Biblical words and stories always nourish us. But as Jesus did not rigidly repeat parables out of the Old Testament, but created new parables which were alive, fresh, and contemporary, you and I need to do the same. We need to create contemporary parables (SAIs) which become the vehicles of God's truth and transformation for us in our moment of human history. Jesus used secular SAIs more than stories from the Old Testament, and we need to use secular SAIs more than stories from the New Testament.

"Footprints" happens to be one of those SAIs that do help God's people. Like so many parables of Jesus, "Footprints" is not inherently Christological; but like the parables of Jesus, it too can be used in service of the kingdom. In my pastoral work, I find that especially the unchurched know and love this parable.

It is good to remember the advice of Mitchell: If you can't put the truth into a story, don't bother to tell it. There is always a central message from God in every sermon, but that central message is enfleshed in stories, analogies, and images . . . so that we will be fed and not given a recipe; so that we will be served a meal and not merely a menu; so that we will be given medicine and not a lecture about medicine. For the very nature of the gospel itself is story, narrative, or SAI. It is then that the ear begins to listen, the mind begins to hear, and the heart begins to imagine the truth about God's kingdom.

That's why good or vivid movies and plays are so powerful. They touch not only our head, but our mind, feelings, and will. Poor plays, movies, or sermons have the opposite effect; they do little to us and are easily forgotten.

Craddock talks about "overhearing" vivid SAIs. He gives several examples of situations where he overheard SAIs. Once he overheard a group of deacons in his house praying for his father who was sick and dying. Another time Craddock heard a Jewish person tell of his experience with Polish Jews during World War II. There were times when he "listened in" on wedding sermons, funeral sermons, and children's sermons, and times when he visited the theater and experienced a powerful movie or play. In each of these situations, Craddock was engaged by the gospel. He was moved by the power of a story that was approaching his heart indirectly.[13] Reason assaults the fortress walls of the mind, but stories slip gently through the back door into the heart—and begin to change us. "Truth, like love and sleep, resents approaches that are too intense. Truth must be approached gently [W. H. Auden]."[14]

All of us preachers should be keenly aware that it is God who creates faith; we don't. It is not the vividness of our SAIs. It is not our eloquence or lack of it. If and when a person comes to believe in Christ and live in his kingdom, it is because God has done his creative work. I like a paraphrase of Rice: "The foolish rooster thinks he causes the sun to rise, and the foolish preacher thinks he causes faith to grow." Luther, more than most, emphasized the divine initiative:

> For it should be left to God and his Word should be allowed to work alone, without our work or interference. Why? Because it is not in my power or hands to fashion the hearts of men as the potter molds the clay and fashion them at my pleasure (Eccl. 33:13). I can get no farther than their ears; their hearts I cannot touch. And since I cannot pour faith into their hearts, I cannot,

nor should I, force anyone to have faith. That is God's work alone, who causes faith to live in the heart. . . . We should preach the Word, but the results must be left solely to God's good pleasure.[15]

It is easy enough for someone to preach the Word to me, but only God can put it into my heart. He must speak it into my heart or nothing at all will come of it. If God remains silent, the final effect is as though nothing had been said.[16]

If God remains silent (to use Luther's phrase), no matter how good the sermon, a life will not be transformed. I think a preacher is always amazed when someone comes to faith or renews faith through a sermon. You know it was God's miracle and not your own. So much was happening in that person's life before she arrived at church that day. God was working on her long before she sat in a pew in front of the pulpit.

There is another aspect of the power of SAIs to transform. We preachers work hard at designing a sermon, so there is coherent unity to the whole sermon; but to be honest, we rarely listen to a whole sermon and the people don't usually take the whole sermon home with them. Often within a sermon, there is a moment, maybe 15 seconds, 50 seconds, maybe two minutes during which time our hearts are opened up to God's penetrating presence. For example, I think of the movie *Hiroshima-Nagasaki*. It's a story of those cities immediately after the bombs were dropped, a series of old film clips about that awful devastation. In that movie, there was one scene in which a young, 10-year-old boy was standing in a line in an emergency ward of a hospital. His arms were totally burned. For one moment, for a fraction of a second, this young boy turned his head and looked into the eyes of the camera and deeply into my eyes. I was crucified. That was my son. My 10-year-old son. And in a fraction of a moment, God reached deeply down into my heart and I made a vow that I will always oppose the use of nuclear weapons. In my life, that movie and moment helped change my heart. And I think that is often true of SAIs, whether they be in a movie, a play, or a sermon. Often, from a sermon, it may be a line, a twist of a phrase, a story, some fraction of a second in which the imagination of a heart is moved. In his studies of the laity, Howe informs us that two-thirds were not able to state even the central theme of the sermon immediately after the worship in the post-service discussion group.[17] If that is true, it reinforces the conviction that only a few SAIs in any given sermon may actually deeply touch a person's heart.

SAIs can have the power to transform; and often only a few SAIs from a whole sermon will touch deeply.

SUMMARY

SAI is a new acronym for the preacher's vocabulary, and it refers to contemporary stories, analogies, and images. The way in which the Bible uses the word *parable,* with its several layers of meaning, is the way I have attempted to use the word *SAI.*

SAIs are like windows of a house; they bring light, freshness, and pleasure to a sermon. A persistent theme echoed by all authors we are surveying is the power of SAIs to move, change and transform a person. Reason appeals primarily to the mind; SAIs appeal both to the mind and the emotions. As someone said, "Reason assaults the fortress walls of the mind, but stories slip gently through the back door into the heart . . . and begin to change us."

9

Characteristics of Good SAIs

A reminder: I am now using the term *SAI* the way Jesus used the word *parable*. A SAI is a contemporary story, analogy, or image used to communicate God's message about his kingdom.

FIVE CHARACTERISTICS OF GOOD SAIs

Good SAIs serve God's message.

What good is a SAI if it doesn't serve God's message? What good is a skyscraper sermon, one story on top of another, if those SAIs don't communicate God's word to his congregation? Just to tell a SAI for interest, entertainment, or diversion does not help. The central message of a sermon is like a magnet that draws certain SAIs and repels others. An effective SAI serves God's message for the day.

Often in preaching you build one SAI on top of another that echo the same theme. Luke does this in Chapter 15 where he tells the story of the lost coin, the lost sheep, and the lost son. Often, parables are clustered together on a theme. For example, in a sermon, "Afraid of the Unknown," I told three stories about the fear of the unknown— stories about E.T., swimming in deep water, and being in dark basements. Most people could identify with these images and stories. In their guts, they started to recall those feelings of being afraid of the unknown. These stories were not told to entertain but to engage the person in a central thesis of the sermon: we are afraid of death because we are afraid of the unknown. If a SAI does not serve the central message of the sermon, it should not be used.

Good SAIs are vivid and memorable.

A good SAI not only serves God's truth, but is vivid, sharp, and pointed. As we all know from experience, SAIs can be boring, banal, and insipid. SAIs can be "dull, duller, and dullest." SAIs can lack punch, impact, and confrontation. Dull preaching is often the result of dull SAIs.

Part of the magic of Jesus was the vividness of his images. Wilder said of Jesus' speech that it "had the character not of instruction and ideas but of compelling imagination, of spell, of mythical shock and transformation."[1] Images need to be vivid, and Buechner is the master of the vivid metaphor:

> It is harder for a rich person to enter paradise than for a Mercedes to get through a revolving door. It is harder for a rich person to enter paradise than for Nelson Rockefeller to get through the night deposit slot at First National Bank.
>
> What is the kingdom of God? . . . To find a ring you thought you lost forever . . . to win the Irish Sweepstakes. Jesus suggests rather than spells out, he evokes rather than explains, he catches by surprise. . . . He speaks in parables [which] were antic, comic and often more than a little shocking.[2]

Shocking, antic, comic, evocative, vivid! That's one of the reasons why Jesus told such good SAIs. They had all of those qualities, and therefore they penetrated deeply into the imagination of our minds and hearts. The more vivid the SAI, the greater the impact.

One example of a vivid SAI is the story about Lady Astor and Winston Churchill. Churchill had insulted Lady Astor, and she fired back, "Mr. Churchill, if you were my husband, I would poison you." To which Churchill retorted, "Lady Astor, if I were your husband, I would drink it." It's a vivid SAI, and when placed in the right setting can be used to serve God's message.

One night at Holden Village, we experienced an unusually vivid homily, entitled "A Sermon in Stones." The preacher used slides of rocks, accompanied by appropriate biblical narration. We saw a slide of a foundation wall of an ancient civilization while we heard a reading from the Bible about God as our foundation. Another slide was of a high rock cliff that gave relief from the burning Palestinian sun, and we heard that God was our refreshing shade. Another slide was of a cave, and God became our hiding place. It has been months since I experienced that preaching event, but those words and slides still haunt the imagination of my mind and heart. The Word continues to live on in the hearer, with God slowly working his miracle of transformation on us.

Good SAIs need to be vivid, and if they are vivid, the mind remembers.

Good SAIs inform and teach.

Jesus was the master of analogy, and he used his creative analogies to inform and teach about the kingdom of God. Many would agree with Wilder that "the distinctive feature in the teaching aspect of Jesus' proclamation is his analogical power."[3] In teaching by analogy, you use what is known to communicate what is not known; you use what is close at hand to help understand what is far away. The Psalmist says, "The Lord is my shepherd." Shepherding was part of David's youth and was "close at hand"; it helped him to understand God.

Elizabeth Achtemeier is extraordinarily helpful in explaining the function of analogies:

> It is in such pictorial language that we preachers must finally learn to speak, in order that our people can see new images in the imagination of their hearts. The question is, How do we learn to do that?

> We do so by constantly using similes and metaphors. You will notice that several of the lines in the psalms begin with "as," while the next lines start with "so"; that is a *simile*. God's forgiveness is compared to something else—to the immensities of space. Then there is a comparison of man to grass and the flower of the fields: that is *metaphor*—a longer comparison of two things.

> Similes and metaphors enlarge our vision and understanding and allow us to experience a new world by speaking of the unknown in terms of the known.[4]

Analogies can help us to understand who God is. The Bible often piles images on top of images. God is like . . .

> A shepherd, a father, a husband, a king, a lover, a bridegroom, a warrior, a master, a vineyard owner, a lord, a consuming fire, a redeemer of slaves, a savior, a never-failing stream, a rock, a fortress, a lion, a bear robbed of her cubs, a moth, a fountain of living water. . . . These are the similes and metaphors by which the Bible lets us experience the reality of God. They describe him with images with which we are already familiar, and through them, we begin to know who God is.[5]

I once had the privilege of hearing a lecture by Kristine Carlson, a pastor and, at that time, a new mother. She spoke on Psalm 131, focusing on the metaphors of that psalm: God is like a nursing mother and Israel is like a weaned child who is 10 years old but needs to return to her mother's breast. The analogies were especially powerful that day because of Pastor Carlson's experiences of being a new mother. If an old man would have taught that psalm that day, I would have forgotten it by now. But the speaker's life at that moment was a living out of the analogy. Months later, the image of God as a nursing mother stays with me.

Kristine Carlson was marvelous in her ability to freshen biblical metaphors. Unfortunately, we have lost the freshness of many of Jesus' metaphors because they have become too familiar—like watching the same movie over and over again or like watching reruns on TV. As soon as the rerun starts, you turn it off. That's the way it is with many biblical metaphors, and it is the mark of a good teacher to be able to freshen and recover biblical analogies—and create new ones.

Jesus was creative in his use of analogies. Just to repeat Jesus' analogies can become ineffective, especially knowing that Jesus gave us the freedom to spin off new analogies and comparisons that help us and our people understand the gracious love of God. Preachers need to put energy into creative new analogies, using the stuff of our daily lives as a resource.

It is also beneficial to be reminded that Luther felt that Link was the best preacher among his colleagues—precisely because he knew how to use analogies that were helpful to the laity.

Good SAIs help move a sermon along.

SAIs contribute to movement in a good sermon. Like any good play, movie, or novel, sermons can become boring if they don't move.

Steimle uses the analogy of a fire in a brick fireplace. Why is it that your eye watches the fire and not the bricks? The fire is alive and moving and the bricks aren't. Or why is it that people love to watch a lake, the ocean, or the waters of Puget Sound? Or why do elderly people often enjoy living on a busy street so they can watch the traffic? The eye and the ear both love movement.

Two factors help move a sermon along: vivid SAIs and unity of theme:

> Good illustrations may grab a congregation at the beginning of a sermon by showing them that the text is about their lives, and then more illustrations may sustain interest through the entire length of the delivery by making every point crystal clear and by forming pictures of its concrete meanings in the people's minds. Good illustrations, by personalizing the biblical message, may drive it home to some reluctant heart.
>
> Illustrations also may serve a function in the structuring of the sermon. If they are well placed, they can add to the variety of pace in the sermon. . . .
>
> Never let illustrations alone carry the thought of a sermon.[6]

Achtemeier's whole book is superb, but the chapter, "The Use and Abuse of Illustrations," is indispensable. Also, in Craddock's *One without Authority,* the chapter entitled "Inductive Movement" is must reading for a sharpened understanding of what moves a sermon.

It is important to understand Craddock's concept of "the *inductive process* of preaching."[7] His basic ideas may be sketched as follows: In past generations, the way people learned was primarily through deduction. That is, an authority figure would stand before the audience and tell them his conclusions or deductions. People would trust his authority and memorize those truths. Today, the world has changed and more people are learning inductively or experientially. At least two generations of Americans have been brought up with hands-on learning. We now have "touch and feel" tanks at the aquarium and "touch and feel" pens at the zoo. Our whole mode of learning today is more through experience than memorizing deductive truths about sea anemone or piglets. We now touch sea anemone and pick up the piglets and closely examine them ourselves.

This change in learning style has affected preaching as well. Preaching today is more inductive and experiential than it used to be. Rather than intoning deductive biblical truths from the pulpit, the preacher often builds his sermons inductively, describing God-given experiences in people's lives. Preaching inductively involves the creative use of analogies and draws on the immediate and concrete experiences of the lives of others.

This inductive, experiential preaching helps the listeners to be more attentive as they identify with the experiences being described, and it also helps move the sermon along. What Craddock labels "inductive preaching" I call vivid SAIs.

John Stott discusses at length the negative impact of television on our ability to listen. Studies have concluded that television tends to make people physically, emotionally, and intellectually lazy. The more we watch TV, the more it inhibits our ability to focus our attention and listen to speeches; and adult Americans watch 23.3 hours per week.

Television makes it harder for people to listen attentively and responsively, and therefore for preachers to hold a congregation's attention. . . .

Whatever is dull, drab, dowdy, slow or monotonous cannot compete in the television age. Television challenges preachers to make our presentation of the truth attractive through variety, colour, illustration, humor and fast-flowing movement.[8]

Whether or not the movement needs to be "fast flowing" may be open to debate. But in this age of television, when people's ability to listen to speeches has lessened, our sermons need vivid SAIs to help the mind focus its attention on what is being said.

H. W. Beecher once said, "The true way to shorten a sermon is to make it more interesting."[9]

Good SAIs are often personal.

You can borrow SAIs from other preachers—we all do—but the best SAIs usually grow in the garden of one's own personal life. If I read a good SAI in another preacher's sermon and want to borrow it, there is usually a parallel experience (or SAI) in my own life, so that SAI can be adapted and personalized. Good SAIs are usually but not always part of one's own personal experience.

When using SAIs out of one's personal life and experience, these SAIs are to point to the message and not the messenger. If SAIs become self-serving and self-inflating it is due to the preacher's egotism, not to the use of a personal SAI. A self-serving preacher will use his material to inflate himself, no matter what his resources for preaching are. We all understand that preachers can use exegetical chips, theological books, and quotations from famous philosophers in such a way as to inflate themselves. Personal SAIs are not inherently egotistical and self-inflating. Some preachers will never directly mention their own lives in their sermons, and their preaching still seems self-centered; other preachers can tell SAIs out of personal life and experience and remain selfless. The key issue is the degree and shape of the preacher's egotism, regardless of the form of materials he or she uses.

In recent generations the tendency was for the preacher not to use SAIs out of his own personal life. The preacher was never to use the pronoun "I" in his preaching. In those days, preachers were often the authority figures of the village or city, and they intoned their imper-sonal, deductive truths from the Bible, and people listened apprecia-tively. But the world has changed and, increasingly in America, there is a new sense of personalism. People are willing and wanting to share stories out of their own personal lives. This is not only true for preachers but for persons in other occupations as well. Preaching is part of this new American personal transparency and, consequently, there is a greater use of personal SAIs in preaching today.

There is also a curious correlation between what is personal and what is universal:

> Carl Rogers writes, *"what is most personal is most general."* This same thought can be expressed in different words: "Repeatedly I have found to my astonishment that the feelings which have seemed to be most private, most personal, and therefore the feelings I least expect to be understood by others, when clearly expressed, resonate deeply and consistently with their own experience. This has led me to believe that what I experience in the most unique and personal way, if brought to clear expression, is precisely what others are most deeply experiencing in analogous ways."[10]

What are characteristics of good SAIs? They serve God's message, vividly illustrate, inform, move a sermon along, and are often personal.

SAIs ARE NOT . . .

- replacements for sound reasoning and biblical truth;
- substitutes for generalizations, concepts, ideas;
- a combing of secular literature for Christian meanings;[11]
- skyscraping (telling one story on top of another);
- substitutes for exegetical insights and biblical teaching.

I am not suggesting that the whole sermon become a story or parable. Storytelling is a good form for the preacher and needs to be done. But a story sermon can be as boring as any other form of sermon if it lacks vividness and freshness.

The same is true with the Aristotelian sermon (introduction, three points, conclusion), about which Craddock, Jensen, and others complain. But the Aristotelian outline, too, can come alive *if* there are vivid SAIs that serve God's message. These authors are simply encouraging us to be more imaginative and creative as we attempt to put more SAIs into the sermon, so that the message has a narrative-like quality to it.

Communication may be narrative-like, yet contain a rich variety of materials: poetry, polemic, anecdote, humor, exegetical analysis, commentary. To be narrative-like means to have the scope that ties it to the life of the larger community. [12]

WHERE DO WE FIND GOOD SAIs?

It seems that we preachers are always looking for more effective SAIs. These authors consistently criticized the use of sermon-illustration books, and I certainly would agree with them. It seems to me that there are at least six good resources for vivid SAIs.

We discover good SAIs in our own creative imaginations.

Good SAIs primarily grow in our own garden, in what we see, feel, and hear.

H. W. Beecher, the father of the Beecher lectures on preaching at Yale, entitled a section of one lecture "The Power of Imagination." He insisted that "the first element on which your preaching will largely depend for power and success, you will perhaps be surprised to learn, is *imagination,* which I regard as the most important of all the elements that go to make the preacher." [13] Arndt Halvorson contends that "if you compare two preachers of comparable ability and training, the better preacher will always be the one who has and uses the gift of imagination." [14] He also says that "creativity is simply the eye for seeing the familiar from a new perspective or in a different context. It is a spontaneous thing, not an imitative skill." [15]

Imagination begins with the capacity to receive images—to see and feel sights and sounds and smells and stories. Craddock is most helpful:

The place to begin discussing the function of imagination in preaching is not the point of using imaginative words or phrases but at the necessary prior point of receiving images. . . . So preaching begins not with expression but impression.

This requires first of all an empathetic imagination in the preacher, a capacity to receive the sights, sounds, tastes, odors, and movements of the world about him.

[Imagination] involves thought, emotion, aesthetic appropriation, humor, laughter.

As far as preaching is concerned, it is better to have a child's eye than an orator's tongue.[16]

Craddock is right. *Imagination has two faces: impression and expression.* Imagination does not begin with the use of imaginative words and phrases. Imagination begins first with receiving impressions and then with expressing those images with evocative SAIs.

Dr. Ernest Campbell says that imagination has to do with your "angle of vision." An imaginative author wrote about the sinking of the Titanic from the point of view of the iceberg, and that was an imaginative angle of vision. Imagination in preaching involves seeing the text from a slightly different angle, for example, the story of Noah's ark from the point of view of the carpenter's union; the story of Zacchaeus from the perspective of his wife and her unexpected guest for dinner; or the story of the good Samaritan, five months earlier when Jericho had a town meeting to discuss the robbings on the Jericho road and nobody cared enough to come to the meeting, raise taxes, and hire more policemen to control the violence on that road. Find a new angle to look at the text, and let your imagination go to work.[17]

Dr. Campbell suggests that imagination is helpful in overcoming the use of boring abstractions (the curse of much preaching). "Poverty" is a boring abstraction which needs to be personalized. "Poverty is being at the welfare office. Poverty is putting off visits to the doctor. Poverty is wondering if the heat will be on during cold days." Campbell says: *Feel your way into what you know.* Let your imagination go past the abstraction of poverty to various concrete examples of poverty which are part of the experience of your parishioners.[18]

Is "empathetic imagination" purely a gift (like having perfect pitch, the ability to read music, the talent to draw portraits), or can preachers like you and me develop it? Arndt Halvorson is most blunt about creativity as a gift:

You may not be a creative person. Not many people are. And those who are not are the ones most prone to think that creativity is a skill to be learned. They are usually corny.[19]

"Empathetic imagination" is a gift. For example, one day I was with a group of people in a sanctuary, listening to an organ. We were in need of a new organ at our church and so we were listening to the sounds of this particular instrument. The organist pushed a button on this "digital computer organ," and it made a slight change in sound. The musicians around me asked, "Did you hear that? Did you hear that?" I didn't. And so the button was pushed again, and for a second time, I couldn't hear what the others heard. My ear wasn't as keen as theirs. Similarly, I believe that some people have a gifted eye that sees human condition for what it is, an eye which sees the subtleties of life, the shades, the nuances, the small glimpses of truth in human experience. And this gift contributes to the power of preaching.

All would agree that imagination is a gift, but these authors also insist that the creativity found in every one of us can be developed. Elizabeth Achtemeier is helpful here:

> The Christian Gospel has spread through the world because it is possible to communicate it, because it is possible to make creative preachers out of people like fisherman Peter and tentmaker Paul and tens of thousands of other ordinary folk with the talents of you and me.[20]

God does choose what is foolish to shame the wise. Craddock, Halvorson, Achtemeier, Brooks, others—they all suggest that *broad reading and pastoral involvement* are the two primary resources for developing creative, empathetic imagination. (A good friend of mine also suggests that a person must do something daily that touches the soul.)

We obtain good SAIs from other preachers who have the gift of vivid imagery

We all have the gift of seeing and expressing good SAIs but there are some preachers who have a greater measure of that gift and we need to read them, talk with them, borrow from them. For example, Jim Bjorge's books (Augsburg) have a wealth of good SAIs which can be adapted to your time, place, and understanding of the gospel. I may not always agree with Bjorge's positivism and his apparent avoidance of talking about gut political issues that are facing us here on Mother

Earth; yet his sermons are loaded with vivid SAIs. I have borrowed several from him and adapted them to our needs in our parish, just as the New Testament authors took Jesus' parables and adapted them to meet the needs of their community in their time and place.

Even though pastors are forever borrowing ideas, stories, and phrases from each other, I still appreciate the warning from Spurgeon: "Gather flowers from your own garden with your own hands; they will be far more acceptable than withered specimens borrowed from other men's bouquets, however beautiful those may once have been. . . ."[21]

We experience good SAIs in our lives as pastors among the flock.

Our preaching gains power and effectiveness as it comes out of the heart of true and deep pastoral relationships. Several authors advise us to draw on the lives of those whom we know and love. Farmer, with his own heart immersed in I-Thou relationships, was most eloquent on the preacher being a pastor:

> Preaching is essentially pastoral activity. . . . An old book asks, who can lawfully preach? . . . Answer: priests, deacons, and sub-deacons who have the care of souls.
>
> Don't succumb to the temptation to rely on your pulpit powers to make up for the deficiency on the pastor side. This is fatal. In the end, it leads to what I only call "French lacquer preaching," bright and interesting, but lacking in depth and tenderness and searching power.
>
> You cannot love people from the pulpit. You can love them in concrete personal situations wherein there is cost.
>
> On the other hand, for those of us who have no marked pulpit gifts, there is surely here great encouragement. Our preaching, poor as it may be, can gain power and effectiveness if it comes to people out of the heart of a true and deep pastoral relationship.[22]

Other authors echo the same theme:

> If Phillips Brooks and Harry Emerson Fosdick could not preach without in-depth contact with persons, we probably cannot either. Preaching is enriched through visiting and counseling, and

we do well to get involved with groups such as Alcoholics Anonymous and Emotions Anonymous, which help people face the problems and possibilities of life. To have something to give, we need to be perpetual sponges, soaking up insights from everything and everyone. . . . [23]

Preaching both can and must emerge out of pastoral caring. [24]

The work of a preacher and a pastor really belong together and ought not to be separated. I believe that very strongly. . . . The two parts of a preacher's work are always in rivalry. . . . I assure you, the two things are not two but one. . . . The preacher who is not a pastor grows remote. The pastor who is not a preacher grows petty. [25]

To draw from the analogies of the lives of others, those about us and those who belong to history. . . . It cannot be overemphasized that the immediate and concrete experiences of the people are significant in the formation and movement of the sermon. [26]

Craddock tells of preachers who draw their SAIs from faraway places and times. Their heroes become Dietrich Bonhoeffer and Martin Luther King Jr. and their villains become Stalin and Hitler. It makes for safe preaching. He writes:

But if the preacher makes normative the sacrifice of Polycarp, the conversion of Saul, the stewardship of St. Francis and the service of David Livingstone, then he will leave his most serious listeners wishing they were someone else, somewhere else. In the meantime, the Kingdom does not come to dull little towns where God's lightning never seems to strike. [27]

I like that last line. We need to quote the lives of present-day saints, to draw on the concrete and immediate experiences of our own people—with their permission of course. For example: A good friend of mine died recently. His name was Ray Osterloh, age 47, stockbroker, good husband, father of two tall, lean young men. Ray was a good man. As his wife, Jan, was going through his clothing after his death, she was cleaning out the top drawer of their armoire. She opened Ray's jewelry box where men often keep their old tie tacks, cuff links, class rings and other minor valuables from the past. There in that jewelry box, she discovered the following poem, a clipping from the newspaper which was now yellowed with age.

Dad's Greatest Job

I may never be as clever
    As my neighbor down the street,
I may never be as wealthy
    As some other men I meet;
I may never have the glory
    That some other men have had,
But I've got to be successful
    As my little fellow's Dad.
I may never get earth's glory,
    I may never gather gold;
Men may count me as a failure
    When my business life is told;
But if he who follows after
    Is a Christian, I'll be glad,
For I'll know I've been successful
    As my little fellow's Dad.

(Author unknown)

It just so happened that Ray was an inspiration to my life and others by the quality of man, husband, and father that he was. Ray, by his example, lifted up our lives and made us better. Recently we preached a dialog sermon on the Fourth Commandment. In that sermon we were discussing the transmission of faith to our children. With his wife's permission, I retold that story and read Ray's poem. This is an example of what could be called "quoting from the lives of saints." Our pastoral lives are filled with similar day-to-day encounters that make for vivid and powerful preaching if we handle them with care and discretion. Howe says that congregations are usually more attentive during these sermons, and they "carry extra authority because they come out of the life of the community, and it is a word to the community."[28]

One other example. It was the men's breakfast and Bible study. Mother's Day was the next day and so we were discussing the theme of mothers, parents, children. The leader would look up an appropriate passage; it was read and then discussed. The leader asked the question, "Do we love our parents if they make mistakes, if they are imperfect?" Before the question came off his lips, Cal spoke: "I wanted to find my mother to spit in her eye." He then told this story.

> I was five years old when my mother abandoned us. There were seven of us. It was depression years and she dropped us off in an orphanage. Every day of my life I thought, "When I grow up I will find my mother and spit in her eye." After I finished the military, I went looking for my mother. I wanted to spit in her face and tell her what she had done to me. I finally found her house. Seventeen years of hate were ready to unleash on her. She opened the door, looked at me—and called me by name. She called me by my name . . . after all those years! How can you spit in the face of someone who calls you by name?

He went on to talk about his mother and other mothers who do the best they can under the given circumstances. His mother wasn't perfect, but she tried her best. Cal didn't mention the word "forgiveness" or even "reconciliation," but that's what the story was all about.

All the men left the room that morning, talking about Cal's story and the line "I wanted to spit in my mother's eye." It was a powerful and vivid SAI for the group. Somewhere along the line, that particular SAI will service the theme of a biblical text, and I will telephone Cal and ask for permission to use his story. This is another example of "quoting from the lives of the saints."

Lightning does strike here, in our little town, out near the corner of nowhere. And here at our men's breakfast, one dreary Saturday morning, I unexpectedly heard a powerful SAI that needs to be used someday.

Howe's research shows that the primary resources preachers use for sermons are commentaries, notes from the seminary classroom, and sermon books. He observes, "the pastor's relationships and experiences with people and their reflections are not consciously explored and used as resources."[29] It seems almost impossible to me that preachers don't see sermons in the lives of their saints.

Earlier we discussed Craddock's concept of "overhearing the gospel"—those times when you happen to listen in on SAIs that were meant for others, such as at a wedding, funeral, or children's sermon. He told the well-known story about Søren Kierkegaard who overheard a grandfather, while standing over the fresh grave of his own son, tell his grieving grandson about the meaning of his father's death. The sensitivity of that event moved SK, and it moves us as he retells it. It was a powerful moment for SK, and it became a powerful SAI for him. That famous story is simply SK quoting from the lives of the saints. It was overhearing the gospel as it was daily enacted in the lives of the people. SK's story is similar to Reuel Howe's story, telling of a father who secretly felt his son was killed in a car accident because the father loved the son too much. This kind of preaching moves people because the preacher himself is moved. He has been touched by the gospel.

There is truth in what Arndt Halvorson writes: "A sermon is a product of our pastoral concern as well as an expression of our pastoral concern."[30] Craddock says: "It cannot be overemphasized that the immediate and concrete experiences of the people are significant in the formation and movement of the sermon."[31]

Good SAIs are found in reading.

There is no replacement for reading, and author after author encourages us pastors to read. Reinhold Niebuhr, in *Leaves from the Notebook of a Tamed Cynic,* tells what happened in his early ministry when the well ran dry: he sat alone, discouraged, and heard God say, "I'm the only one who can create *ex nihilo*. Get busy and read!"[32] And Arndt Halvorson comments, "There is no substitute for reading, if we would generate an imaginative approach to life and our preaching. There is no justifiable excuse for a nonreading preacher!"[33] It is important to read, not only in preparation for a specific sermon, but to grow as a person and be part of the world in which we live. Otherwise, our reading is reduced to scanning books and looking for sermon illustrations. You rarely find them that way. Phillips Brooks stresses the importance of reading to develop as a whole person.

If you are like me, you often lack quality reading time. You just don't have enough time for general reading. Recently, I did a survey of pastors in the Pacific Northwest, asking them to rank the comparative importance of their resources for preaching. I listed 15 possible resources. It was interesting to me that many pastors aren't reading, or don't feel that reading is an important resource (I mean reading beyond commentaries, dictionaries, and other homiletical aids).[34]

This was true of my own life until I formed a reading group at our church. Belonging to a group forced me to read books. There is no choice not to, as I am responsible for leading the discussion. I want it clearly understood: I did this for me—to force me to read. It happens that ours is a "political action" reading group in which we read literature which connects faith to the pursuit of justice. These books and discussions have become a rich source of SAIs for me. I have pulled numerous SAIs out of the following books which I heartily recommend:

Pilgrim, *Good News for the Poor*
Sider, *Rich Christians in an Age of Hunger*
Nelson, *Hunger for Justice*
South Africa: Time Running Out (Rockefeller Study)
Tutu, *Crying in the Wilderness*
Namibia (numerous papers from Wartburg Theological Seminary)
Timerman, *Prisoner without a Name, Cell without a Number*
Lernoux, *Cry of the People*
Erdozain, *Romero*
Gettleman, ed., *El Salvador*
Nuclear War: What's in It for You? (Ground Zero)
Schell, *Fate of the Earth*
Dayton, *Discovering Our Evangelical Heritage*
Rasmussen, *Economic Anxiety and the Christian Faith*
Brandt, *North-South*
Gilder, *Wealth and Poverty*

There is an advantage in reading these books with laypersons rather than just with clergy. Clergy tend to be more liberal in political orientation, and an intelligent conservatism is most beneficial when reading these books together. Sometimes, I have been in clergy discussion groups when we have discussed these same books. The tone of discussion in the lay group is not at all like that of the clergy group. There seems to be a greater diversity of opinion in the lay groups, as political liberals seem to be more outspoken among the clergy and dominate those discussions.

We also have a group of divorced men and women in our church, and occasionally we read books together for a monthly meeting. One of the classics for these people is *How to Survive the Loss of a Love*. I didn't especially like the book, but the group loved it. Seeing the power of this book on the lives of our divorced people, I then read that book much more closely and now use it as a resource for vivid SAIs. The group had other suggestions of good books to read and their suggestions are helpful to my reading.

In his book *Between Two Worlds* I was pleased to discover that John Stott also relied heavily on a reading group to enrich his ministry. He and his group read such books as Ellul's *The Meaning of the City*, Schumacher's *Small Is Beautiful*, and Bonino's *Christians and Marxists*. The group itself chose many titles, and their choices weren't quite as religious as Pastor Stott's: Reich's *The Greening of America*, Pirsid's *Zen and the Art of Motorcycle Maintenance*, and Toffler's *Future Shock*. His group also attended films together such as *Kramer versus Kramer*, *Autumn Sonata*, and *Star Wars*. I was pleased that he, too, found immense value in his lay study-group.[35]

Paul Scherer advised pastors tactfully to inform their congregations of their study habits and then hold fast to those habits:

> Let your congregation know, tactfully, at the outset of your ministry, that your habitual and unfailing practice is to devote yourself to study for some stated period of each day; and you will find, I think, that they will not only understand but will give you their hand [of blessing] on it. . . . Keep for your own sober use the first precious hours of the morning.[36]

I have found Scherer's advice a description of my own ministry. Each fall in our parish paper I publish my work schedule, e.g.: "Emergencies, telephone any time. Mornings, 8:30–12:00, Tuesday-Friday, study time. I will return calls later." These mornings are mine, and they are precious for study and meditation. Also, every year after Vacation Bible School is out in mid-June, I take four weeks for concentrated reading.

I still do parish ministry, but I change my pastoral focus and read at least six hours per day. I long for these weeks to arrive and enjoy the pleasure of them. All pastors have their own style for managing time, but these blocks of time have been important for *uninterrupted* study. I also recall Phillips Brooks' advice: Form good work habits early in your ministry because those habits will rule you slavishly until the end.[37]

Neaves describes the trends of his reading habits:

I have always enjoyed reading, but never in my life have I done as much reading as I have *had* to do since becoming a parish minister. It is a major priority in the budgeting of my time each week, because it supplies me with the images and stories which I need if I am to deal with deeply personal issues. . . . Increasingly, however, I find that the bulk of my reading centers more and more in novels, plays, short stories, articles and biographies, and I have become much more discriminating in watching television and movies. It's not that I'm no longer interested in systematic theology and biblical exegesis. I am quite interested in both and spend significant portions of time in each. But neither has much meaning for me anymore apart from the life issues which real human beings are encountering.[38]

We find good SAIs through watching films, television, and plays.

As I look back over sermons from the past years, films have been a source of many SAIs. Again, a person doesn't go looking for SAIs but you can't help but experience them when you are seeing a fine film. We had a hunger-justice film series at our church. A few of us watched perhaps about 20 films through the years; the following 6 are classics which were deeply appreciated by the laity of our parish. These films evoked vivid SAIs:

Remember Me
The People Next Door
Everyone, Everywhere
Excuse Me, America

Last Grave at Dimbaze
Hiroshima-Nagasaki

Television can be helpful. Some pastors disparage using television. They say, "It's not weighty enough." To which a friend of mine replies, "Even a lightweight can pack a strong wallop." Again, a person doesn't go looking for SAIs, but when watching television, you can't help but experience them.

We find good SAIs in other life-shaping experiences.

In the questionnaire that I mentioned, most pastors referred to the annual pastor's conference as a source of preaching material. For other preachers, it's course work they take through a university, college, or seminary. For others, it's vacationing or other stimulating environments. And for still others, it's traveling to Third World countries, not on a pleasure trip but as a learning experience. From my perspective, traveling to the Third World is crucially important today, much more so than a trip to Germany or the Holy Land. We can take our congregational members on trips to religious shrines in Israel and Germany, but visiting Christians in the Third World is much more transforming. My conversations with Christians in Mexico and Nicaragua have been much more memorable and sharing than my visits to "holy places" with the tourist crowd. This is not to minimize contacts with Germans and Israelites and the sacred places of Jesus' life, but Jesus is still being crucified today on the cross of violence, oppression, and injustices, and most often we experience that in Third World nations. The Lutheran World Federation is an enormous international organization, second only to Catholic Charities in its scope and influence. We have numerous opportunities to visit and work with Third World Christians and experience their vitality of faith and commitment to Christ and his work in this world. I suggest we need more trips to Tanzania, Zimbabwe, Namibia, India, Colombia, and other places where we have contacts, but especially we need encounters in Latin America. Latin America will dominate the political scene of our nation for the next 20 years, and we need our people and pastors visiting. Perhaps more study leaves should be in Cuernavaca, Mexico, and Madras, India, than in St. Paul or Berkeley.

SAIs don't just happen. They grow in the many gardens of our lives. As Thielicke says:

> Every conversation I engage in becomes at bottom a meditation, a preparation, a gathering of material for my preaching. I can no longer listen disinterestedly even to a play in a theater without relating it to my pulpit.[39]

And Burghardt:

> There is hardly an experience in your day that is not grist for your proclamation. . . . I do mean that everything you see, hear, touch, taste and smell is part of your human and Christian experience, can therefore shape the word you preach and the way you preach it. *Chariots of Fire, On Golden Pond,* and *E.T.*; the photo of Mother Teresa cradling a naked retarded child in West Beirut. . . . These experiences and a thousand more combine to fashion the person you are. Let them fashion your homily as well.[40]

Through all of this—

praying;

struggling with the Word;

worshiping with the congregation;

being a pastor totally immersed in the lives of the people;

reading widely and wisely;

traveling;

participating in struggles for justice;

being a husband, father, son, wife, mother, or daughter;

being a friend;

imaging glimpses of the gospel all around you

—through all of this, inevitably, there will be *growth in the person* of the preacher. If the preacher's life is shallow, no matter how electrifying the text, the sermon probably will be shallow. It is from the fullness and emptiness of our God-shaped humanity that we speak.

One final comment about SAI preaching: Preachers who put God's message into story form, who use SAIs, may be accused by the "theological heavyweights" of being "lightweights." Craddock warns of this:

> The imaginative preacher may have to endure such comments as "his sermons don't seem theologically weighty" or "it was much too interesting to have contained much truth," or perhaps such inverted compliments as, "I was much involved with your talk or whatever it was. It didn't seem like a sermon."[41]

Of course, the theological heavyweights of Jesus' time probably felt the same way about his preaching!

Two final questions: Do you remember who Luther said was a good preacher? And why? Link. Because, in preaching the gospel he used analogies the laity could appreciate and understand.

PREACHERS NEED TO HAVE A METHOD OF STORING AND RECALLING SAIs

Several of the authors suggested it is wise to have some method of storing SAIs. Some people put them on 3 x 5 cards, others in notebooks. Dr. Ernest Campbell always carries a small notebook (without a spiral wire on the top, because the wire ruins his shirts and suitcoats) to record SAIs. Sometimes a momentary inspiration comes whizzing through the mind like a sudden squall and then it is gone. It is important to capture those momentary inspirations on paper. Each pastor develops his or her own system of filing. The point is that we need a method for both recording and storing SAIs.

SUMMARY

In his preaching Jesus never said anything without a parable (Matt. 13:34). And so it is with today's preachers of the gospel. While in the pulpit or teaching podium, we never say anything without using SAIs. Contemporary stories, analogies, and images are the means by which we proclaim the gospel in our preaching and teaching. Reason assaults the fortress walls of the mind, but SAIs slip gently through the back door into the heart—and begin to change us.

10

The Importance of Language

PREACHERS NEED TO TAKE LANGUAGE SERIOUSLY!

We preachers need to take language seriously. There are three primary reasons for doing so:

1. The gospel comes through languages.

2. Language is the foundation of all communication and is at the heart of all I-Thou relationships.

3. Language is one of the crucial tools of our trade.

Authors on preaching have captured the importance of language in the art of preaching. Again, it is time to read slowly:

> Although the Gospel came and comes everyday through the Holy Spirit alone, nevertheless, it came by means of languages, spread through them, and must also be maintained through them. . . . And let us realize that we shall scarcely be able to maintain the Gospel without languages. Languages are the sheath in which the knife of the spirit is contained. They are the case in which the jewel is borne. They are the vessel in which the drink is held. They are the room in which the food is stored. And as the Gospel itself tells us (Matt. 13:20), they are the baskets in which the bread and fish and fragments are gathered up [Luther].[1]

> Speech is absolutely central and indispensable in the world of personal relationships. . . . The spoken word is right within the

core of the I-Thou relationship and the written or printed word is always a poor substitute for it.[2]

A preacher's tools are words, shaped into the rhythms and cadences, the fortissimos and whispers, the conversation and confrontation of oral speech. To neglect the mastery of words is to be like a carpenter who throws away his saw and sets out to fashion a piece of fine furniture, using nothing but an ax. We may hack away at a congregation with tools totally inappropriate to their purpose—dull words, misleading sentences, repetitious paragraphs, ineffective illustrations. Or we may take up the fine tool of language, honed and polished to the cutting edge, and then trust that God will use it to fashion his people—his "work of art in Christ" (Eph. 2:10). The committed preachers—the faithful servants of God—do not neglect their tools.[3]

About the prophet-preachers: they put words to things until their teeth rattled. . . . Deep within their words, something rings out which is new because it is timeless. . . . They put words to both the wonder and the horror of the world. . . . They say what they feel in language that even across the centuries and through all the translations causes us to feel them too. . . . So let him use words, but in addition to using them to explain, expound, exhort, let him use them to evoke, to set us dreaming as well as thinking . . . to stir in us memories and longings and intuitions."[4]

They sit there waiting for him to work a miracle, and the miracle they are waiting for is that he will not just say that God is present . . . but that somehow he will make it real to them. They wait for him to make God real to them through the sacrament of words.[5]

Store ideas in a rich vocabulary. . . . You must be masters of words, they must be your genii, your angels, your thunderbolts, or your drops of honey. Mere word-gatherers are hoarders of oyster shells, bean husks, and apple parings; but to a man who has wide information and deep thoughts, words are baskets of silver in which to serve up his apples of gold. See to it that you have a good team of words to draw the wagon of your thoughts.[6]

What a wealth of insights is found in these quotations. Language is the sheath in which the spirit is contained, the cup in which the drink is held. Language is the way that God talks to us. God makes himself known to us through the sacrament of words. Words are the essential tools of all I-Thou relationships. Of course, knowing all of this, we preachers then *must* take language seriously. The Word himself loves words.

JESUS WAS FREE TO BE SECULAR IN HIS USE OF LANGUAGE

Wilder is *the* seminal theologian who discusses the secularity of Jesus' language patterns. He is the fountainhead of the recent appreciation of Jesus' linguistic secularity and freedom. He writes:

> The first Christians were conscious of a new endowment of language, both freedom of speech and powers of communication.

> We have seen that the coming of the Christian Gospel was in one aspect a renewal and liberation of language. It was a "speech event," the occasion for a new utterance and new forms of utterance, and eventually new forms of writing. . . . These signs will accompany those who believe. . . . They will speak in new tongues.

> There was no flight from the vernacular. . . . The common language of men was itself the medium of revelation. . . . But passion in him used the common speech and did not dissolve it. His human self-identification with his fellows evidences itself here, too, in the matters of speech.

> Jesus taught in the living dialect of his time, Aramaic, not in the language of the Scripture, Hebrew. The early church had no hesitation in translating his words into Greek or the language of whatever population was evangelized: Latin, Syria, Coptic, etc. The idea of a holy language was unknown.

> It offers no precedent for what is sometimes spoken of as the "language of Zion," that is, a particular vocabulary and imagery thought of as sacred or pious.

All such heavenly discourse remains rooted in the secular media of ordinary speech.[7]

Thus Wilder underscores what we already know about the speech of Jesus: his use of everyday Aramaic, the secular, vernacular language of his family and friends. He did not use some sanctified, "Bible-speak" of the Old Testament. If you could have tuned Jesus in on the radio, you would not have known he was a preacher by the sounds of his religious tones or by his phrasing of biblical cliches. His language was fresh, secular, and part of the world in which he lived.

LUTHER AND LIVING LANGUAGE

Luther is a strikingly good example of the creative use of language. Luther was the first notable theologian in 12 centuries who had a commanding use of Hebrew.[8] It is important to note that Augustine and Aquinas did not have use of Hebrew. The vivid imagery of the Hebrew language helped free Luther to translate the Bible into common pictorial German.

Luther loved his native German. He was critical of the papists whose minds thought in Greek and then translated woodenly into Latin. It was the vividness of both his Hebrew and German language that made his translation of the Bible normative for Germany:

> Luther's great genius lay in his uncanny and inspired ability to forge a language which was idiomatic and natural. His was not the first translation of the German Bible; there had been fourteen translations into High German and four into Low German. The first of these—that of John Mentel—in 1461—had gone through seventeen editions. But it was Luther's translation which was destined to become the German Bible.[9]

Why was it that Luther's translation of the Bible became the official German version and not John Mentel's? It was because of Luther's creative genius in his use of language, his deep love for common German, his sense of freedom to translate the sacred text into a secular idiom, and his knowledge of Hebrew. Gerhard Ebeling has assessed Luther's great genius as linguistic innovator of the faith:

No one who knows what a language is can come face to face with
Luther without venerating him. There is no nation in which one
man has done so much to form its language. . . . It is he who
awoke the sleeping giant of the German language. . . . It is of
no account that Erasmus, perhaps the most precise scholar the
world has ever known, accused him of having brought Latin
literature to an end. . . . Friedrich Schlegel made this judgment:
"Equally, we owe an unmistakable debt to him personally for his
forceful language and the spirit of his writing, his lofty and powerful mode of expression in German. For even in his own writings,
there is an eloquence such as has rarely appeared in any country
throughout the centuries."[10]

Luther wrote two fascinating treatises on the art of translating:
"Against Latamus" and "On Translating: An Open Letter." In both
there is provocative analysis of the use of figurative and metaphorical
language in Scripture. Luther claimed that it was not wise for a linguistic scholar to translate "too properly and literally" when so much
of the biblical language is metaphorical and figurative.[11] In translating
Deut. 4:19, he compared the use of the words "caressed" and "allotted."
Luther expressed a preference for the Germanic, homey, down-to-earth
word "caressed" over the proper and literal, Latin word "allotted." He
was critical of the "assheads" who did not have a sense of either the
Greek or German language but thought, felt, and dreamt in the scho-
lastic language of Latin. Because the papists didn't "know" Greek and
Hebrew and because German wasn't the lifeblood of their soul, it was
impossible for them to be good translators.[12] In contrast, Luther's language was simple and earthy, rich in expression, "a reflection of everyday life—of the market, the guild hall, the hearth, and the home."[13]
Luther had a sense of freedom in his use of language and was not
constrained to use Latin "Bible-speak."

PREACHERS ARE TO USE THE LANGUAGE
OF THEIR PEOPLE

If Jesus preached in Aramaic and Luther preached in common German, you and I are called to preach in our own native idioms.

In the book of Acts, we hear the story about Paul speaking in the language of his people, and consequently, "they listened more willingly." Having been rescued by the Roman guards from the Jewish mob who believed he had desecrated the temple, Paul asked the soldiers if he might speak to the crowd. They agreed:

> He spoke to them in the Hebrew language saying, "Brethren and fathers, hear the defense which I now make before you." And when they heard that he addressed them in the Hebrew language, they were more the quiet (Acts 21:40—22:2).

Fant translates Acts 22:2 more clearly: "And when the people realized that he spoke their language, they stopped their shouting and listened more willingly."[14]

When interviewing several unchurched people who had recently joined congregations, I asked them why they joined a particular parish. One idea was consistently expressed over and over again: "I heard preaching in words and thoughts I could understand." As the book of Acts says, "When the people realized he spoke their language, they listened more willingly."

Henry Mitchell's chapter, "Preaching as Folk Language," is worth the price of his book. His basic thesis is the "obligation to translate all theological ideas into folk-type language."[15] But he also has another fascinating insight: speech patterns reveal you as an understanding friend or betray you as a distant stranger. For example, he talks about Simon Peter seeking to join the servants by the fire:

> Peter (Luke 22:55-62) . . . was excluded because his speech betrayed him to be a stranger (Matthew 26:73). From his first few phrases, his identity had been established, and the first impression was never overcome.[16]

In Jerusalem, Peter's speech patterns betrayed him as a stranger. Life is the same today: our speech patterns reveal who we are. As preachers, our speech patterns quickly tell the congregation whether we are a friend or a stranger in their midst, whether we are with them or above them. Clarence Jordan's use of "black-eyed peas, gravy and collards, mint julip" was a way of communicating to his people that he knew them. Jordan's people understood he knew them because he knew how to use the subtlety of their language system. His congregation knew his soul lived in their land, and they appreciated that. Because he spoke their language accurately, they knew that he knew their inner feelings and soul.

Edmund Steimle, in *Preaching the Story,* has a fine section about the "language of Canaan." If the tendency of many preachers is to preach in the language of Zion, Steimle suggests that Jesus preached in the language of Canaan, in the vernacular and vocabulary of the world in which he lived. It's not only the words themselves that need to be secular; the whole fabric of the sermon needs to be secular. That is, if Jesus talked about moths and rust, contemporary preachers will talk about inflation and tax-bracket creep.

> This means in explicit terms that the sermon will be studied with allusions to the facts and fancies and news events which make the newspapers: international tensions and conglomerates, Northern Ireland, the Middle East, the energy crisis, abortion, legislative tangles in the Congress, Dear Abby . . . Peanuts, NFL . . . sleazy nursing homes . . . the flush of joy at falling in love . . . the ethical dilemma of a businesswoman trying to be a Christian. . . . The fabric of a sermon will, like the fabric of the Bible, reflect the actual world in which we live—all of it.[17]

The language of Canaan *and* the living conditions of Canaan are the warp and woof of the sermon. Thielicke writes:

> I would say that the more a man speaks in modern terms the more he will be heard. And the more he is heard, the greater will be the acceptance and the rejection of his message, the more provocative it will be, and the more emphatic will be the decisions and separations that result . . . when the word becomes flesh again, that is to say, when it enters into our own time, wearing the dress of the present.

> A consequence of the Reformation doctrine of justification seems to me to constitute the core of the thesis that there must be no fundamental dividing wall between the sacred and the profane, and that therefore the message of the Word become flesh must

be spoken in worldly terms, that it must meet people where they are.[18]

I have noticed that quoting Bible verses or extended portions of Scripture encourages people to turn off their mental hearing aids. As Paul Harms says:

> By the time the preacher has said, "For God so loved . . . " the listener has already added, "the world that he gave his only begotten son, that whosoever believeth in him. . . . " While the preacher is enchanted with quoting one of his favorite Bible passages, the hearer, the object of all that quoting, has long ago become disenchanted.

> The point is, religious language does not engage the listener's mind because it is religious. In fact, religious language, recognized as such, often discourages the listener's mind, effecting the opposite of its intention.[19]

As soon as the preacher begins a long biblical quotation, or even a short one, I sense that the hearer drifts off, waiting for the moment when the preacher himself starts talking again. Biblical preachers will always quote Scripture, but let us be aware that too much quoting causes people to turn off their hearing aids.

The point is: we are to preach in the language of the people. If there is no listening, there is no persuasion.

PREACHERS ARE TO USE THE LANGUAGE OF THEIR OWN HEART

Obviously, we preachers need to express our thoughts and feelings and we are to use our own speech patterns and vocabulary. As Buechner says so well:

> Drawing on nothing fancier than the poetry of his own life, let him use words and images that help him make the surface of our lives transparent to the truth that lies deep within them.[20]

Using nothing fancier than the poetry of our own lives is the way to preach and teach. It was said of Luther that he "wrapped the Gospel in the language of his home, his hearth, his heart."[21]

Phillips Brooks describes the importance of a preacher being true to himself and his own language:

> It is most desirable that every preacher should utter the truth in his own way, and according to his own nature. . . . The solemnity of the minister's work has often a tendency to repress the free individuality of the preacher and his tolerance of other preachers' individuality. His own way of doing his work is with him a matter of conscience, not of taste.[22]

Brooks warns against the temptation to try to convert one's sermon into a work of art, to try to write beautiful sermons or great sermons:

> The sermons of St. Peter, St. Stephen, St. Paul . . . were all valuable solely for the work they could accomplish. They were tools and not works of art. To turn a tool into a work of art . . . is bad taste. . . . Without knowing it, many ministers are trying to make them not only sermons but works of art.[23]

After reading the poetic language of Buechner and Achtemeier, I sometimes wish I had their poetic gifts. Their sermons are works of art, and I want my sermons to be more artistic. They put words together as Rembrandt puts paint on a canvas. They are gifted artists. Let's be honest: most of us don't have such poetic gifts. As Achtemeier says, "Illustrations are, for the ordinary preacher, our substitutes for not being poets."[24] Because most of us are not poetic by nature, we put more energy into the use of illustrations and stories rather than the beauty of language. We need to resist the temptation to convert our sermons into works of art.

We also need to resist the temptation to be someone we are not. Luther warns of the danger of comparing oneself to other reputable preachers:

> When you are to preach, speak with God and say, "Dear Lord God, I wish to preach in thy honor. I wish to speak about thee, glorify thee, praise thy name. Although I can't do this well of

myself, I pray that thou mayest make it good." When you preach, don't look at Philip, Pomeranus or me or any other learned man, but think of yourself as the most learned man when you are speaking from the pulpit. I have never been troubled by my inability to preach well, but I have often been alarmed and frightened to think that I was obliged to speak thus in God's presence about his mighty majesty and divine nature. So be of good courage and pray.[25]

I love Luther's line: "Although I cannot do it well myself, I pray that you would make it good."

Good preaching has always used "the native language of the heart" (Hawthorne), language that is nothing fancier than the poetry of one's own life, language that grows up in the soil (or from the cracks in the concrete) of one's childhood and home. Good preaching helps people see, feel, smell, and touch the truth, so that the Word does not remain some doctrine to be memorized and recited on confirmation day. Beauty of language is not a goal in and of itself. Language serves the message and does not draw attention to itself, but rather to the message.

PREACHERS NEED TO LEARN TO USE VIVID LANGUAGE

Preachers need to develop greater skill in using vivid language and concrete images; we do this by reading well and writing well. Almost all the authors encourage us as preachers to develop greater skill in using pictorial language, words which you can see, smell, touch, taste, hear, and feel.

The minister would do well to check his sentences to see if his words convey that which can be heard or seen or smelled or touched or tasted. If a sermon revives the memory of the odor of burped milk on a blouse, it evokes more meaning than the most thorough analysis of "motherhood."[26]

The minister says, "All men are mortal," and meets drowsy agreement; he announces that "Mr. Brown's son is dying" and the church becomes the church.[27]

Human beings learn through specific, concrete experiences. Not beauty, but a golden American Rose or Candace Bergen. Not strength, but the Russian weight-lifting champion leaning and jerking hundreds of pounds at the 1976 Olympiad in Montreal. Not devotion, but Mother Teresa ministering tirelessly to the dying in the streets of Calcutta, India, year after year. Not discrimination, but the South African government providing no eating places for blacks, so they must eat their noontime lunch on street corners and sidewalks pictured in *The Last Grave at Dimbaze*. Concrete, specific references go a long way towards impact as well as clarity.[28]

. . . A smile . . . like the breath of a May morning.[29]

. . . Preaching the king who looks like a tramp, the prince of peace who looks like a prince of fools, the lamb of God who looks like something hung up at the butchers.[30]

Almost every author encourages us to improve the vividness and pictorial concreteness of our words.

We preachers need to labor over our words, so that they may mirror at least a hint of such a God of glory, though we know that heaven and the highest heaven cannot contain him, much less our awkward phrases.[31]

But how do we do that? How do we learn to use language more effectively and evocatively? How do we learn to preach more pictorially? Elizabeth Achtemeier, who is both a gifted homiletician and a creative author, has several suggestions. She encourages us to master the basic grammatical structure of English. Most of us don't like preachers making grammatical errors while speaking, and we want to correct them when they do.

The very first step in the discipline of learning to be a preacher is that of mastering basic English usage. American schools are now turning out, year after year, hundreds of thousands of students who cannot write a proper English sentence, much less a well informed paragraph. Congregations are hearing such phrases as "between he and I," "there are less Christians today". . . .

The list of grammatical errors could be extended almost indefinitely.[32]

She warns of four dangerous pitfalls for all speakers:
- dull words;
- misleading sentences;
- repetitious paragraphs; and
- ineffective illustrations.[33]

Poor communication can often be attributed to one of these four errors in rhetoric.

Further, to improve our linguistic abilities, we are encouraged to read the literary masters of the English language and even to borrow some of their colorful phrases, such as T. S. Eliot's "I have measured out my life with coffee spoons." Write down these phrases, study them, store them, learn to use them. A preacher learns to write well by reading well.

> The preacher should listen to others' words in order to improve his own, and the major source of such improvement is literature. Constant reading helps us to find the words to engage the hearts and minds and wills of the congregation. . . . Write them down, store them up, study them. Preachers, unfortunately, often read simply to find illustrations; far too few read with the purpose of expanding and improving their use of the English language. We can learn to write well by reading well.[34]

As I have been working on this book, I have typed certain lines and paragraphs four or five times, such as Brooks' phrase, "a smile as fresh as a morning in May." By typing these lines over and over again, I thought they would begin to etch themselves into my mind, but they didn't. Rather, these poetic phrases began to imprint themselves into my mind when I put them *orally* into a sermon, conversation, or class. It was when I spoke the lines orally that the words began to sink deeply into my psyche. I learned Küng's line, "Some of us are so busy dusting plastic flowers [or writing sermons, running to meetings] that we don't take time to cultivate the roses" by repeating it in many conversations. These words, then, gradually became part of my inner person; they became part of my imagination. But if I merely write down these phrases—two, three, four, or five times—I forget them within a month.

GOD USES LANGUAGE TO CHANGE PEOPLE

One way that a person is changed is by changing that person's images. Give people new images, and they may begin to see the world differently. For example, after years of watching television's Mr. Rogers with my children, I became used to the phrase, "God loves you just the way you are." I was aware that Fred Rogers had been through seminary training (Presbyterian), and that he is a devout Christian who expresses God's grace during his television program. His grasp of grace has permeated the life of my children: "God loves you just the way you are." And yet for me, there was something missing. It wasn't quite sufficient. It was true, "*but!*" One day while reading *Preaching the Story* I ran across a statement by Morris Niedenthal: "God loves you just the way you are, but never leaves you the way you are, because he loves you."[35] "Aha," I thought. "That is helpful." And that simple phrase, "he does not leave you the way you are because he loves you," became an image-change for me. I began to see the world slightly differently because a metaphor by which I was living was changed. Language changes images, and when our images are changed, we are changed.

Achtemeier is most lucid about the power of language to change the images of the heart:

> What does language do? It not only bears ideas but it brings reality into being for a person and orders and shapes a person's universe. . . . Human words, like God's word, brings our universe into order and being. . . . Human beings live by the images of reality created by their words.

> If we want to change someone's life from non-Christian to Christian, we must change the images—the imaginations of the heart—in short, the words by which that person lives.

> The inner imaginations of the heart are changed when a person's language is changed, and the images by which that person lives are altered into a new experience of reality. And everywhere the

Bible insists that new life involves this change of heart—this inner transformation of personality by the working of the Word.[36]

Craddock also talks about the power of changing images within a person:

> The galleries of the mind are filled with images that have been hung there casually or deliberately by parents, writers, artists, teachers, speakers, and a combination of many forces. . . . Images are replaced not by old concepts but by other images, and that quite slowly. Long after a man's head has consented to the preacher's idea, the old images may still hang in the heart. But not until that image is replaced is he really a changed man.[37]

C. S. Lewis refers to the same objective: "to render imaginable that which before was only intelligible."[38]

Of course, we have already discussed the purpose of vivid SAIs to inform and transform. Vivid SAIs are another way of talking about changing images.

SUMMARY

Preachers need to take language seriously because language is the vehicle of God's message, the heart of all I-Thou communication and a tool of our trade. Jesus was free to use secular language, and we need to exercise the same freedom. Preachers are to use the language of their people, so that "they will listen more willingly." Preachers are called to be ourselves and use nothing fancier than the poetry of our own lives. We need to develop greater skill in using pictorial, vivid images. People are changed when the images in their hearts are changed.

11

The Importance of "Living Speech"

WILDER'S FIRE

Amos Wilder quietly ignited a small fire in 1964 when he published *Early Christian Rhetoric,* and the insights of that book continue to smoulder; but it wasn't until the 1970s that the small fire began to spread into a major blaze. By then, Steimle, Jensen, Craddock, Fant, Achtemeier, Erdahl, Halvorson, Mitchell, and others seemed to find inspiration from Wilder's seminal insights into "oral communication" or "living speech."

Wilder lists several features of this early Christian communication which was primarily "oral." The words of Jesus and his followers were not written down for decades, as it was a time of "living speech," reminiscent of the Hebrew God who *speaks* through the prophets. Jesus, himself, as far as we know, never wrote a word "except on that occasion when, in the presence of the woman taken in adultery, he 'bent down and wrote with his finger on the ground.' "[1] Jesus was oblivious to any concern for transcription and recording his world for posterity. He was a "voice not a penman, a herald not a scribe." A living voice is more malleable, more personal, more searching. A living voice is extemporaneous, dynamic, immediate, direct, engaging, demanding, urgent, face-to-face.[2] Wilder quotes Fuchs who "makes the observation that Jesus wrote nothing and adds that even Paul wrote reluctantly," expressing regret that he had to write and indicated he would come soon to speak in person. Wilder reminds us that oral speech—living speech—was the early medium of Christian communication, and even when it came time to write, the written words were very close to the patterns of living speech.[3]

> Oral speech is where it all began. Jesus and his followers used the different modes of language which we know as dialogue, story or poem, well before it occurred to anyone to set anything down on papyrus or leather tablet. Even when they did come to write, we can overhear the living voices, speaking and praising. This kind of writing is very close to speech. . . . The Gospel represented a new and living speech. For this dynamic and prophetic word, the conventionality of writing was inappropriate. The Word must not be bound.[4]

Continuing in the same tradition of "living voices," Papias (ca. 135) wrote: "I did not suppose that information from books would help me so much as the words of a living and surviving voice." And even in the third century, "we find Origen reluctant to write. He prefers oral instruction, face to face with his students and congregation. In his view, the Gospel as the Word of God is properly addressed to the ear and not written for the eye. . . ."[5]

Why is there so much emphasis upon "living speech"? Because oral speech is personal, firsthand communication; and the very nature of the gospel is personal, firsthand encounter.

LUTHER'S "LIVING VOICE"

Luther had a deep appreciation for the "living voice" or the oral word:

> Where the oral proclamation of the Gospel ceases, the people will revert to heathenism in a year's time. . . . The devil cares nothing about the written Word, but where one speaks and preaches it, there he takes to flight.[6]

Christ himself did not write his teaching, as Moses did his, but delivered it orally, also commanded to deliver it orally and gave no command to write it. . . . For before ever they wrote, they had preached to and converted the people by word of mouth.

And the gospel should not really be something written but a spoken word which brought forth the Scriptures, as Christ himself did not write anything but only spoke. He called his teaching not Scripture but gospel, meaning good news or a proclamation that is spread not by pen but by word of mouth.

[The gospel] is an oral preaching, a living Word, a voice which sounds into all the world, and is openly heralded forth, so that it may be heard everywhere. That Gospels had to be written was itself a weakness, "a great quenching of the Spirit."[7]

Luther said that the church is a "mouthhouse, rather than a 'penhouse' even as the New Testament Gospel was preached before it was written down."[8]

Perhaps it is for these reasons that Luther in his preaching used very sparse notes and rambled freely and perceptively on the text. He spoke in a slow, methodical manner, allowing his students to transcribe him almost word for word.[9] Luther's preaching had the marks of "living speech" and not written communication.

A SHIFT TO THE WRITTEN MODE

Unfortunately there have been numerous times throughout history in which the "living speech" dimension of the gospel has been diminished. Several homiletics authors refer to the 19th century as a time in which there was a gradual shift from the oral to written mode. What was written became more authoritative than what was spoken. Fant describes this gradual shift from an oral to a literary medium:

Following the nineteenth century and the advent of popular literacy, the sermon was steadily transformed from its original oral medium into a literary, written medium. This change was partly due to the impact of printing as a medium of communication. . . .

The influence of these men upon the form of the modern sermon is incalculable. The sermons of Robertson, Spurgeon, and others were printed and distributed to millions. Homileticians subsequently used those written sermons as models of excellence for their preaching classes. And although this approach unquestionably produced many good results, it also had one unfortunate effect upon the sermon. Students were encouraged, directly or indirectly, to *write* sermons like the ones they were reading.

As a result, the sermon was increasingly prepared for the eye rather than the ear. Devices suited for reading—paragraphing, formal syntax, tightly fitted logical arguments, complex outlines, literary language—were superimposed upon the sermon. Of course, the sermon continued to be delivered orally, but increasingly from a manuscript really prepared for reading.[10]

We in the 20th century forget how popular these written sermons were. In 1877 Brooks tells us that there was a high demand for these printed books of sermons, that these sermon books led to competition with Sunday morning worship attendance, that people were staying home from church because "they can read better things of the same sort at home. . . . The competition of printing has interfered very much and is destined to interfere even more."[11] (This almost sounds like the complaint of the 1980s, that people stay home to worship in front of the TV.) Books of sermons were the rage in the 1880s, and sermons gradually became prepared as written medium which were then read rather than the "living speech" of oral communication.

But there is a vast difference between the principles of "living speech" and written communication. People intuitively sense that. Phillips Brooks says that "in general, it is true that the sermon which is good to preach is poor to read, and the sermon which is good to read is poor to preach. There are exceptions but this is generally true."[12] For example, Erdahl mentions the fact that printed sermons of Luther and Wesley were only the "written corpses of the sermons and only those who heard them preached experienced the living sermons."[13] Fant tells the story of "John Brodus who preached an excellent series of sermons at Calvary Church in New York which he was urged to publish, but when he saw the stenographer's transcription of them, he was so horrified that he called off the project."[14] What is alive orally may be totally flat in print; and what is alive in print may be totally flat orally. This may explain why some readings of great short stories from the pulpit often sound flat because they have not been adapted to the oral medium. For example, I recall several boring readings of "Barrington Bunny" but the story came alive when it was *told* orally, when it was *adapted* to "living speech."

Wilder, Mitchell, Davis, and others such as Luther are trying to encourage "living speech." They are suggesting that we preachers develop more fully the art of oral communication, that we do not write out our ideas on a piece of paper, read them, and then call it preaching. "Living speech," which was part of the earliest Christian community, is concerned for direct, personal, engaging conversation about Christ and the kingdom. To paraphrase Luther, sermons that are written and then read reveal "a weakness, a great quenching of the Spirit."[15]

THE NEEDS OF THE EAR
AND THE NEEDS OF THE EYE

H. Grady Davis suggests that there is a radical difference between the hearing situation and the reading situation—that we can't understand the problems of oral communication until we understand the substantial difference between the needs of the ear and eye. He also states that one standard of excellence for written communication is that it can be read over and over again and still make an impact on us. This is not true for oral communication. A sermon is *not* intended to be read over and over again. He says that one test for excellence of oral communication is that in the first and only presentation, the sermon is heard, comprehended, and then lives on in the mind of the hearer.[16]

So what are the features of "living speech"? What are the needs of the ear which help it to listen more effectively to a set of words that are heard only once? What are some of the essential principles of oral communication?

To help us understand the principles of "living speech," let us carefully examine three paragraphs from a sermon by Mitchell. These paragraphs were transcribed and not edited for publication; they are therefore a good example of "living speech." As you read the words, you sense that they were not written for the eye but were spoken to meet the needs of the ear.

Title: "To Sit Where They Sit"
Then I came to them of the captivity at Tel-Abib, that dwelt by the river of Chebar, and I sat where they sat and remained there astonished among them seven days (Ezek. 3:15).

If somebody were to ask you what is the hardest job in the King-dom of God, what would you answer? What *is* the hardest job in the Kingdom of God? I know a lot of people who would say parent to a teenager; there is no harder job in the world. I know some others who would say, teacher in the inner city schools, for there is no more difficult task anywhere than that of trying to teach children with the difficulties which some of them have had to suffer. I know some people who would say that the hardest job in the world is to be a pastor of a church, any church. And quite a few others would say, the hardest job of all is not the pastor's but the pastor's wife, because she has all that responsi-bility and no authority. And there are some among us who would say the toughest job in the world is to be a teenager in the midst of all these crazy adults . . . .

. . . Well, I was socking it to the old folks, and there were about thirty-five youngsters in the choir behind me. They were rooting for me because I was saying how old folks claimed to believe many principles they didn't actually practice. All those kids were having a great time, until I turned around and said, "Well they aren't the only hypocrites. I have a suspicion that if I asked most of you where you were last night, Saturday night at twelve o'clock, I might get a 20% accurate response. The rest of you would lie just as fast as you could put it together."[17]

THE NEEDS OF THE HEARER

It is interesting to me that none of the twenty-three authors I read gathered together in one subchapter the primary, essential principles of oral communication. I have attempted to do this in the following pages. It is important that oral communicators compose for the ear and not the eye.

Speakers Immersed in the Message

The hearer needs a preacher who is totally immersed in his message, who has absorbed what he or she is going to say and therefore doesn't have to read it sentence for sentence. As you listen to Mitchell, you can feel that he isn't reading. You know that he is free-flowing, that his is "living speech," that he is in direct communication with his congregation in an I-Thou relationship, that he is talking with them and not reading his ideas from a page. Certain words may be jotted down on that paper, e.g., "hardest job in the world," "parent," "inner city teacher," "pastor," "pastor's wife," "teenager"; but he has absorbed his material and he knows what he is going to say after each of those "help words." Farmer, Brooks, Harms, and so many of the other authors talk about this need for the inner form of the sermon and the inner form of the preacher to be one. The preacher is immersed in his message, and even if he lost his notes, he still would be able to proclaim that sermon because that sermon has become a living part of his inner soul. The ear appreciates this "living speech" of direct oral communication. This is not to suggest that a person avoid a manuscript. A manuscript preacher is also capable of absorbing the material so that the sermon fully lives within himself. Farmer writes:

> It is, I think, a capital error which many make, to suppose that when a sermon has been written, it is ready. It is not. The writing is merely the preliminary. As a sermon indeed, it does not at that stage exist at all. It is merely a manuscript [or outline]. The important thing is to absorb it, through your own person. . . . On the desk, it is an "it." [As it] becomes part of you as a person, [it becomes] a "thou," God's "thou," to another "I." This reabsorption will be for most of us no easy matter.[18]

Farmer goes on to talk about spending one or two hours prior to the worship service, rearranging, pruning, correcting, *"until it is in your mind and heart, and your mind and heart are in it."* Then the sermon becomes part of God's I-Thou communication.

Potent image/story/metaphor

The hearer needs a potent image/story/metaphor that will linger in the heart and mind long after the sermon is delivered. The ear wants a vivid image that works on the inner imagination of the heart, long after the sermon has been completed, for the heart and mind want to be nourished, fed, challenged, changed, enlarged. After the sermon is delivered, Mitchell's primary image, "to sit where they sit," will linger in the mind. In that sermon, Mitchell suggested that we should not be combative with people who have a different point of view from our own, but rather try to understand life from their unique perspective, to sit where they sit; then perhaps we will have a greater appreciation for them and we, in turn, will learn and grow.

The ear needs an image to help it remember. Hopefully, from any sermon there will be one or two potent images that live on in the hearer. A person usually cannot remember the whole complexity of a sermon, all the stories, all the illustrations, all the points. Only a few images will remain and live in the mind and begin to shape the heart.

The mind wants to remember and feels cheated if it can't remember. Laypersons sometimes complain, "By Sunday afternoon, I can't remember a thing the preacher said." When teaching interns to improve their preaching, I tried to convince them that people need a handle to carry a suitcase. People need some kind of handle—a dominant theme, image, or story; they need some aid to help them carry the sermon home with them. Harley Swiggim in the Bethel Series and Harry Wendt in Crossways use the same principle; they give you pictures or diagrams which help you remember. Luther was pleased with Master Morlin's preaching because the "common people . . . could take it home with them." [19] The point is that the mind does want to remember a sermon and feels cheated if the sermon doesn't linger in the heart. So in preaching, a dominant image, theme, metaphor can serve as a handle to help carry the sermon home.

Order and Clarity

The hearer needs order and clarity. Intuitively and naturally, the ear and mind will try to impose some logic and clarity on what is being said:

> The desire for unity is the law of the listener's mind. It is his own sense of form at work, trying to bring order out of the chaos of impressions. [20]

By its nature, the mind works logically and feels uneasy when logical connections aren't being made. Davis uses the analogy of a jigsaw puzzle in which you hand a person first the blues from the sky, then the greens from the meadow, and then the blacks from the plowed earth at the bottom of the painting. But if you hand a person a green piece, than a black piece, then a blue piece, the mind begins to be confused. Intuitively, the mind wants order. "If I hand him the pieces one at a time in the right order, if he does not have to pick the right one out of the handful of various shapes and sizes, the connection of each will be obvious, and he can put them together as we go along."[21] That is the purpose of an outline: to give order and clarity to thought. The ear and mind will naturally resist if order and clarity are not present.

Repetition

The hearer needs repetition. The ear needs to hear the same sentence twice. Referring back to Mitchell's sermon, you will notice that he repeats his opening line but in slightly different ways: "If somebody were to ask you what is the hardest job in the kingdom of God, what would you answer? What is the hardest job in the kingdom of God?" When reading the sermon for the first time, you may not have even noticed the repetition because it seemed so natural. But if that same sermon were to be refined for publication, the repeated line would have been omitted. "Redundant! Repetitive!" would have been the criticism. If you are working orally, however, you intuitively sense the need to repeat sentences in slightly different ways.

The ear needs repetition of words and thoughts. In the first six sentences, Mitchell has repeated the phrase, "hard job," six times. Who has the hardest job? A parent? An inner city teacher? A pastor? A pastor's wife? A teenager? Quickly, six times, he repeated the two words, "hardest job" with each category of persons.

The title of Mitchell's sermon was "To Sit Where They Sit." Intuitively and immediately, as soon as the bulletin was read, the congregation began to imagine what the sermon was going to be about. "To sit where they sit" reminded his audience of the old familiar adage, "don't criticize until you have walked in another person's moccasins."

Throughout the sermon, that phrase was repeated, and was gradually imprinted on the mind.

One particular form of repetition is parallelism. Martin Luther King was a great Christian orator who understood the power of repetitious parallelism. In a film about King's life, a person was able to hear him preach in his powerful, parallel rhythms:

> We are tired of living in dilapidated, run-down, rat-infested flats and slums.
> We are tired of sending our children to overcrowded and inferior schools.
> We are tired of having our men not be able to be men because they cannot find jobs.
> We are tired.
> Somewhere I read about the right to freedom of assembly.
> Somewhere I read about the right to freedom of speech.
> Somewhere I read about the right to freedom of voting.
> Somewhere I read that we have the right to protest for those rights.[22]

It is not merely parallelism or repetition that gave King authority and power. King wasn't reading these parallel lines; they were flowing from his heart and head. He was a man filled with the passion and truth of God.

But passion and truth always express themselves in some kind of form. *If the form is not powerful, then the truth and passion are often not heard or remembered.* Form is important to truth and passion. King's powerful parallelisms helped make him a great preacher.

Familiar Language

The hearer needs familiar language. In the paragraph addressed to teenagers, Mitchell used words such as "socking it," "old folks," "rooting," and "kids." Not just in this section of the sermon but throughout the whole he used the language of his hearers. He was speaking as if he lived in their homes, schools, streets, backyards, factories, businesses, offices, bedrooms. Elizabeth Achtemeier advises us to "labor over our words, so that they may mirror at least a hint of such a God of glory,"[23] and her language is glorious. As you read Achtemeier and

Buechner, you wonder how people can create such beautiful thoughts fashioned by words. Mitchell isn't like that. His words do not give a "hint of God's transcendent glory" but seem to reveal the immanence of God, God with us in the messy business of living in our streets, homes, schools, and factories. His language is down-to-earth, not fancy. Obviously, there is a place for both "high English" and "common English." If a preacher has the poetic gifts of an Achtemeier and Buechner, use them. Most of us don't. People essentially enjoy hearing the language they use in everyday life.

Because the ear has only one chance to listen to a sermon, the ear needs language it can quickly understand.

Facial Honesty

The hearer needs facial honesty. The ear needs facial expressions which convey honesty, integrity, concern, passion, and involvement. When reading a book, obviously you cannot see the facial muscles of the writer, but these facial muscles are extremely important in oral communication. In fact, Paul Harms reports that "careful research shows that more often than not [by a wide margin] the hearers trust the preacher's face more than the preacher's larynx."[24] When watching any television commercial, especially by a used-car salesman, you watch the face to see if you can trust the speaker. A trustworthy face is not something that a speaker can normally manufacture (unless that person is a consummate actor) but is derived from facial tones and miniscule muscle movements. Harms reports that the body is capable of 700,000 different movements and it is the subtle variations of these body movements that help create trust.[25] The speaker needs credibility:

> Credibility is highly important in communication. The listener's acceptance of the message of a high credibility communicator can be as much as four times greater than that of a low credibility communicator, the one who was perceived as seriously lacking in trustworthiness and expertness.[26]

There are many factors that contribute to trustworthiness, but one of the most strategic is facial honesty.

Good Eye Contact

The hearer needs good eye contact. Eye contact is usually not possible in written communication but is absolutely essential in "living speech." In an I-Thou dialog with another person, communication between the eyes of the two people is essential. A wife doesn't normally tell her husband that she loves him as she casually looks away from him. The impact of that statement is much more powerful when two people are looking at each other eye to eye. When a parent is talking with the children about a serious matter, a parent will say, "Please look at me." By doing so, the power of the communication event is enhanced. Another reason why a preacher needs to absorb his sermon is to enable him to look into the eyes of his parishioners so they can read his eyes. This helps the sermon become an I-Thou dialog instead of an I-it address. That's hard to do when you are reading ideas off a page or when your head is bobbing up and down like a kiwi bird.

Wilder and Luther emphasize the need for living communication, and eye-to-eye exchanges are at the heart of living communication. It is often through the eyes that you receive glimpses into the heart.

Variations of the Human Voice

The hearer needs variations of the human voice. The ear needs tones, pauses, inflections, silences—and these qualities often can't be heard while reading a story. Harms tells us that the human voice is comparable to an orchestra with a range of 10,000 different tones and qualities and that we preachers need to use a greater range of the orchestra that is available to us.[27] We need only to listen to Martin Luther King's famous sermon "I Have a Dream" to recall the wonderful orchestral power that helps us to remember those inspiring lines. It is said of George Whitefield that he addressed 30,000 people at one time in Philadelphia with similar orchestral power. Benjamin Franklin, who was present, reported that

> his delivery was so improved by frequent repetition that every accent, every emphasis, every modulation of the voice was so perfectly well tuned that without being interested in the subject, one could not help being pleased with the discourse, a pleasure of much the same kind with that received from an excellent piece of music.[28]

This "musicality of delivery," this "sonorous tonality," is a quality often appreciated by people in oral traditions who fully enjoy the immense range of the human voice. In contemporary, middle-class, white America, it seems as if the voice is often more flat, with only an octave range at most. Middle-America often tends to be self-conscious of tonal diversity. This is not to advocate being a grand orator in a small sanctuary; but following Phillips Brooks' advice to do your best for every occasion, whether it be in a grand cathedral or small sanctuary, we need to speak of Jesus Christ with all the tonal possibilities of living, conversational speech. Common and ordinary conversational speech is often filled with a greater variety of tones than we hear from the pulpit. Reading ideas from a page encourages vocal monotony. You, the listener, sense that the preacher is not talking to you but reading creatively. The listener senses the loss of living speech that is found in everyday conversation.

I once heard a sermon by a colleague of mine, and it was a good illustration of the versatile power of the human voice. The preacher, Charlie Mays, had God asking, "Elijah, what are you doing in that cave? Come out into the world and be my spokesperson." The sermon repeatedly asked that one question, "Elijah, what are you doing in that cave?" which became the potent image that lingered for weeks. Why did that sermon linger in the mind? One reason is that the preacher asked the same question in many tones of voice. He imitated God's voice, how God may have sounded when he asked the question in demanding tones, pleading tones, inviting tones. The lasting impact of this particular sermon grew out of the preacher modulating different tones on one question. The end result for me was: "Edward, get out of that cave and into the world and be God's spokesperson." That one theme haunted me for weeks, and my mind and heart enjoyed being haunted by God's continuing presence.

Importantly, the tone of the voice is the carrier of emotion: passion, intensity, joy, sorrow, seriousness. Authority is often revealed by the tones of the voice. The intonation of our voices reveals who we are, our degree of commitment to the truth we are proclaiming.

Pacing, rhythm, and timing

The hearer needs pacing, rhythm, timing. Black preachers often ask

of other preachers, "Can he tell a story?"[29] In other words, does he
have the gifts of pacing, pausing, timing, rhythm—all of which serve
to enhance the quality of the story. Pacing, pausing, and timing are
not only important in telling a specific story but are also important in
the movement of the whole sermon. Wilder writes:

> Rhythmic speech, of course, plays a large part in all religions
> from their earliest beginnings. . . . From the beginning, Chris-
> tianity selected forms of utterance and communication which were
> dynamic. . . . The new speech-freedom of Jesus and his followers,
> this new fruit of the lips and new range of meaning, inevitably
> adopted the rhythmic mode.[30]

It may be that these abilities of pacing, timing, and rhythm are
natural gifts, much like singing or painting. But like singing and
painting, these storytelling gifts can be developed. Listening to other
good storytellers and oral communicators is a good way to develop the
art of pacing, pausing, timing, all of which help the ear to listen.

SUMMARY

H. Grady Davis is correct when he suggests that there is a radical
difference between the hearing and reading situation, that we can't
understand the problems of oral communication until we understand
the substantial differences between the needs of the ear and those of
the eye. To summarize, the ear needs:

1. a preacher who is immersed in the message;
2. vivid images and analogies which can be remembered;
3. order and clarity;
4. repetition of words, phrases, and sentences;
5. familiar language;
6. facial honesty;
7. good eye contact;
8. conversational variations of the voice;
9. pacing, rhythm, timing; and
10. good SAIs.

What the ear really needs is a living voice or direct, person-to-person
conversation, as is found in an animated conversation between two
friends.

12

The Importance of Variety of Forms

In the Bible there is a variety of forms which communicate the message of God. A person doesn't have to teach the Bethel Bible Series to realize that there is a variety of literary and oral expressions in the Scriptures: sagas, poems, parables, visions, songs, legends, parabolic histories, history, letters. The list goes on and on. Wilder observes:

> The New Testament writings are in a large part works of the imagination, loaded, charged, and encrusted with every kind of figurative resource and invention. The Apocalypse, again, is a master of surrealism. . . . The Gospel of John offers a series of incomparable unveilings. . . . For its part, a Gospel like that of Mark is a book of epiphanies, a tragedy yet not a tragedy, a sacred drama . . . carrying with it a reversal of the story of the race as hitherto understood.[1]

Among the authors I studied, Keck and Stott mention Paul's use of the diatribe method of communication. The diatribe features the counterquestion. That is, the speaker anticipates the question of the hearer, asks the question for the hearer, and then answers it. The Stoics used this method all the time. The Roman world was accustomed to the diatribe method, and so Paul used that method when speaking to his Roman world. Based on his experiences with his listeners, he could anticipate their questions, acknowledge their questions, and then "use them to lead their thinking deeper into his own understanding of the matter." Keck goes on to say that "the sermon which takes into account the people's reactions to the text and incorporates them into the discourse itself will be conducive to the occurring of the Word among the people."[2]

Jesus used the parable, but the Jewish parable was not the best form for Paul. That wasn't his style, his way of communication. So he used the diatribe method which was natural to him and his Greco-Roman world. Paul didn't have to continue Jesus' use of the Jewish parable. He was free to use his own forms which were uniquely rabbinic and Roman.

Just as Jesus and Paul used the forms of communication which were indigenous to their personalities and culture, we are free to do the same. Each pastor has his or her own unique preaching style. In the text-study group of which I am a part, as we worked through this book together, it was clearly apparent that each member had a unique way of exegeting, creating, forming, and delivering sermons; yet we could learn from each other and expand our natural inclinations.

THERE IS NO IDEAL, STANDARD, FIXED FORM FOR SERMONS

We need only to read sermons from the last four centuries to realize that there is no fixed sermon form. The form varies with every individual, generation, and culture.

> There is no ideal or standard form which every sermon should take. The sermon is not a species with fixed and invariable characteristics, as the form of the violet, the lily, the leaf of the red oak, the twig of the weeping willow is fixed. There is no pre-existent mold into which the substance of thought must be poured in order to make a sermon.[3]

It seems that the typical form of the sermon in recent decades has been the standard, three-point outline. Craddock writes:

> It will not take a lengthy exposure to such studies of the lively modes of discourse used by Jesus and the early Christian evan-

gelists to cause the average preacher to look upon his own stand-
ardized sermon outline with a new lack of appreciation. When
he begins to ask himself why the Gospel should always be impaled
upon the frame of Aristotelian logic, when his muscles twitch
and his nerves jingle to mount the pulpit not with three points
but with the Gospel as narrative or parable or poem or myth or
song, in spite of the heavy recollection of his training in homiletics, then perhaps the preacher stands at the threshold of a new
pulpit power.[4]

We need greater variety of forms in our Sunday morning sermons.
Jensen's book *Telling the Story* has a good subtitle: "Variety and Imagination in Preaching." Jensen calls for a greater variety in preaching,
and he is right. We don't always need to have the standard, preacher-
get-up-and-then-sit-down sermon. We don't need to use the same homiletical cookie cutters for every sermon, routinely mash down on the
dough of the text and out pops another three-point sermon.[5] The Bible's
presentation of the gospel is much more diverse than that.

NONTRADITIONAL SERMONS

The remainder of this chapter will examine several nontraditional
sermon forms:
    group dialog;
    films/slides with commentary;
    overhead projections;
    dramatic impersonations;
    dramas;
    story sermons;
    dialog sermons.
Of course, the list of types of nontraditional sermons can be as limitless
as the human imagination.

Achtemeier is correct when she suggests that there is no replacement
for the well-crafted sermon:

Let it be said very clearly: There is no substitute for the traditional
preaching ministry of the church. Indeed, the church exists only
where the Word is truly preached and the sacraments are rightly

administered. There is, by the promise of God, no tool more effective for creating and sustaining the life of the people of God than a well-delivered, well-shaped, proclamation sermon from a well-exegeted Biblical text. Far too many preachers have turned to gimmickry in the pulpit because they are unwilling to expend the discipline, thought and labor necessary to master their craft.[6]

Achtemeier advises us well; there is no substitute for the solidly prepared and delivered sermon.

But I think she is wrong in suggesting that many pastors are turning to "gimmickry in the pulpit" because they aren't sufficiently disciplined in study and preparation. In the questionnaire I sent to pastors in the Pacific Northwest, very few were using nontraditional sermons. Only 10% of the pastors who responded were using any form of nontraditional sermon and, even then, such sermons occurred very rarely. She doesn't need to worry about pastors—at least in the Northwest—using too much "gimmickry." Gimmickry is not the problem, according to my survey.

Besides, to use a nontraditional form takes the same amount of work, exegesis, and preparation—in fact, sometimes much more so. Often the preacher invites more people than himself into the preparation of the sermon (drama, dialog); this in itself complicates the preaching process and takes more time. Nontraditional sermons usually take more time, energy, and imagination, not less.

It is interesting to me that Dr. Achtemeier, who titles her book *Creative Preaching* and who, along with Buechner, is most imaginative in her use of pictorial language, seems to resist nontraditional sermon forms. Commenting on preachers who are beginning to use overhead projections as a means of aiding the sermon, she writes: "If our purpose is to preach to the ear, let us learn to do it effectively, so that words create such images in the minds of your congregations that they do not need accompanying written words."[7] Of course, that's great advice if you have her poetic gifts. But, and this is more important, research has been done on the comparative effectiveness of the retention of data between talks with visual aids and talks without visual aids. In talks with visual aids, retention and impact was 80% higher than in those without.[8]

Just as past centuries were auditory generations, ours is a visual generation. With the advent of large pieces of paper, felt pens, overheads, slides, movies, and television, our culture is becoming increasingly visual. It is incredible that we don't use more of these visual means of communication in the pulpit—especially if the visual aid helps us to remember, especially if the visual aid contributes to imprinting powerful images in the mind and heart. I hope that we have by now been persuaded about the freedom of Jesus to be secular—to use the idioms and images of his day—and about our freedom to do the same. The following are examples of, and suggestions about nontraditional sermon forms.

GROUP DIALOG

Group dialog occurs when a group of people, usually five, individually study the pericope, then discuss the text together a few times, then recreate the most vivid and helpful parts of the discussion into a sermon. The sermon feels like the best parts of the discussions during the preparation phase.

There are several advantages to group dialogs: the preparatory discussions are personally helpful to each person as they clarify what God is saying to them in the text; five imaginations are better than one; five voices are more varied than one; the laity hear the laity; and the congregation is often touched by the quality of insight and struggle from people they know in the congregation. For further suggestions about creating group dialogs see the Appendix.

In our congregation we try to have one group dialog per year. The congregation loves the form. It's a good change of pace. "Stewardship" and "Christian parenting" are two natural, topical sermons for group dialogs. We did one group dialog on "Nicodemus and Being Born Again" (Holy Trinity, Series B), and it was beneficial to hear a group of laypersons struggle with what it means to be "born again." On Holy Cross Sunday, we had a group dialog entitled "Carrying the Cross in Suburbia." We attempted to apply the text "Whoever would be my disciple, let him deny himself, take up the cross, and follow me" to the situation of the rich young ruler, that is, to us living in suburbia.

There were no easy answers in that sermon, but plenty of struggle. The group discussions in preparation for that sermon were as beneficial as the sermon itself.

FILMS/SLIDES WITH COMMENTARY

Films are especially powerful vehicles of communication, and can be incorporated into a sermon. From my perspective, one of the most powerful of world hunger films is *Remember Me*. It is 15 minutes long and briefly shows the story of 10 children in 10 different parts of our hungry world. These 10 vignettes are utterly moving. Starvation is essentially a children's disease, with 12 of the 15 million who starve to death each year being under five years old. I wanted *everyone* in our congregation to see this film, not just those interested in the topic of world hunger who would come to a class. Everyone needs to see this film, including our children—especially our children, because hopefully they will be future hunger fighters. The film is tastefully done and is not a montage of bloated bellies. So on our annual World Hunger Sunday, we showed the film as the core of the sermon, followed by about five minutes of commentary about what we Christians can specifically do to help alleviate starvation in the world. The people won't forget those film images for a long, long time. The images from the film continue to work on the imagination of our hearts. Films can be powerful preaching and should not be confined to a teaching role.

Again, from my perspective, one short film, with or without the supplement of the spoken word, is healthy for a church, at least once a year. In 20th-century, visually oriented America, it doesn't seem appropriate to confine our forms of communication to the first century.

OVERHEAD PROJECTIONS

More and more, people are using overheads today; they are excellent teaching tools. After using chalkboards and felt pens for years, I find overheads even more effective in imprinting information on the mind. Overheads are also helpful in preaching, especially when the sermon is a "teaching" sermon. For example, in series B for the fifth Sunday of Easter, the epistle text is about Philip and the eunuch. The sermon I designed was too complex and it needed some visual aids. One overhead was of a map of Philip's trips in Palestine; another was an outline of some complex ideas. This sermon was an old-fashioned Bible study, and especially the unchurched or newly churched enjoyed the map and the outline. We forget how totally illiterate the unchurched are; and if you are aiming your message at them as well as church members, these visual teaching aids can be helpful in a teaching sermon.

DRAMATIC IMPERSONATIONS

These sermons are often used during Lent. In dramatic impersonations one individual impersonates a biblical character. My studies of pastors who use this form of preaching indicate that these mini-dramas are deeply appreciated by the congregation.

Here again is the opportunity to involve the laity in the preaching process. Laity can do the research for and write scripts. Often there is a creative author or two hidden out there in the congregation, waiting to be discovered. And there are enough published plays to stimulate the images of a budding new author in your parish. Still others in the parish may be willing to play the roles. Dramatic impersonations are often easy to produce because they involve only one character. Assign eight Old Testament personalities like Ruth, David, and Jeremiah to eight different laity. It's amazing what they can do.

DRAMAS

Chancel dramas have a fine history in the church. In fact, the medieval church was the place where drama received much of its impetus in the Christian community. The Bible itself is filled with many dramatic stories which lend themselves to drama.

In my research on pastors in the Northwest, those who were using nontraditional forms rated "drama" more effective than the children's sermon. That surprised me. I thought almost all pastors would say that the children's sermon is the most effective nontraditional preaching tool. But those preachers who are using drama rate it the "most effective" nontraditional form.

At that point we had not tried dramas in our parish. But based on the positive evaluations of other pastors, we decided to experiment with plays. My pastoral colleagues were right: dramatic presentations are the most powerful form of nontraditional preaching. For example, members of our congregation wrote a series of plays, *The Seven Deadly Sins*. They were a takeoff from C. S. Lewis' *Screwtape Letters* and were well received by the parish.

Unfortunately, dramas are often confined to Lenten midweek services. We need to have more dramas written, based on passages of Scripture. These dramas should not be exclusively a repetition of the biblical story, using biblical costumes, biblical beards, and biblical bathrobes. Rather, we need to create more 20th-century, American textual dramas for use on Sunday morning. Maybe you and your congregation could write a book of them.

STORY SERMONS

A story sermon is one in which the whole sermon is one story. Jensen has three fine examples of story preaching, and those sermons can be used almost word for word. One sermon is entitled, "The Lonely Lady of Blairstown Park," and is a modern re-creation of the story of the prodigal son.[9] The whole sermon is the story of Grace Simon who sits alone in the city park all day. Gradually, her story is unveiled: a dead son is not dead after all; he's been in prison and he fabricated a story of his death to cover up the fact that he was in prison. Now he's coming home; he is welcomed and loved by his mother. Next, the mother decides that her once-dead son should also have a part of the family business—and the sparks begin to fly between his brother and sister who are now co-owners of the business which they took over from their mother. Brother and sister collaborate to resolve the conflict legally and in the process, are able to eliminate their "crook" of a brother from the business. And where is poor Mother Grace? She is heartsick and alone in the park. It's a great story, a very clever re-creation of the dynamics of Jesus' story of the prodigal. When the Fourth Sunday of Lent, Series C, arrives, this story of Grace Simon needs to be retold.

Story sermons are a lot of work. They take brooding, simmering, imagination, creativity, and time. You just can't sit down and whip out a good story like "The Lonely Lady of Blairstown Park." To begin writing story sermons, I suggest that you preach one of Jensen's. By preaching one of Jensen's sermons, you get into the feel and flow of how to create them. Of course, it is not necessary to write re-creations of biblical stories. A person can create totally new stories that have no biblical parallels. That's what Jesus did.

And yet, agreeing with Achtemeier that there is no replacement for the well-exegeted, well-designed, and well-delivered textual sermon, I believe that a good sermon with vivid SAIs can often touch more deeply than story sermons. Within a normal sermon, the preacher may have 10 SAIs echoing the central message of the text. Perhaps one or two of these 10 SAIs will speak deeply to the listener. And this is the disadvantage of the story sermon, where you have only one long SAI. You are lessening the possibility of people being touched by one small part of the sermon. I remember well the preaching of Dr. Morris Wee of Bethel Lutheran Church, Madison, Wisconsin. His sermons were filled with innumerable SAIs. Perhaps in a sermon I heard only one SAI deeply, but that's all I needed, and then my mind began to refashion that SAI into the imagination of my heart. My people grab on to only one or two SAIs in a sermon. The whole sermon usually doesn't have an affect on them, but one or two "words" may penetrate.

Of course, the choice is not either-or. We need both: good story sermons and well-designed, textual, SAI sermons.

DIALOG SERMONS

I really enjoy dialog sermons, and in my congregation, we try to have one or two per year. I find it a pleasure to preach dialog sermons with the associate pastor, intern, or lay leader.

Why are they so pleasurable? Two heads are better than one. Two imaginations are better than one. Two points of view are better than one. In preparation for the sermon, after each of us has done our exegesis and contemplated the possible sermon directions, we begin our discussion. Those discussions spark creativity and imagination in each other. It's like bringing two sets of electrical impulses together that generate new energy, new insights, new dimensions. We also help each other clarify our thoughts so they aren't so muddied.

Another advantage of dialog sermons is that they are *conversational*. It is difficult to "read your part" to each other. The very nature of the dialogical conversation encourages the two preachers to talk with each other and the congregation, and thereby discourages "reading ideas off a page." The "living speech" dimension (Wilder) of the gospel is accentuated in a dialog sermon. I have worked with interns and associate pastors. Initially, all of them wanted to read their sermons, but when we got into a dialog sermon, they automatically began talking their sermons and not reading ideas off the page. They became more natural, more direct, more dialogical in those particular sermons, and it rubbed off on their other sermons as well. The very form of a dialog sermon enhances the quality of "living speech." The change of voice and pace helps the sermon come alive.

SUMMARY

Jensen is right: we need to have more variety and imagination in the pulpit. Achtemeier is also right: there is no replacement for the well-exegeted, well-shaped, and well-delivered textual sermon. Perhaps we can benefit from the best of each of these authors.

Appendix
Where Do We Go from Here?

A basic thesis of this book is that if any pastor works for 18 months specifically and intentionally to improve his or her preaching with the help of eight or nine perceptive members of the parish, the preaching of that congregation will improve. The key is to *create* the processes and then *use* those processes.

One way is for the preacher to work on preaching with the wise men and women of his or her congregation.

The basic idea is this. A pastor selects seven to nine people (there is no magic number) who are willing to work with his or her preaching. Each of these individuals has at least three important qualities: (1) They love and appreciate the pastor, and the pastor knows this. Risk is always more possible in a loving environment, where you trust the people and know that they are fundamentally supportive. (2) They understand and appreciate the gospel. They have experienced the grace of God through Christ, and therefore can intuitively recognize gracious words when they hear them from the pulpit. (3) They understand and appreciate the principles of oral communication. Just as some members have a natural gift of empathy and make good counselors within the congregation, so there are others who understand the dynamics of "living speech." This group of people is selected and meets for 18 months, intentionally working on several aspects of the preaching of that parish.

This partnership in preaching between the laity and pastor involves three assumptions: (1) Preaching is the crucial responsibility of the congregation and not just the pastor. (2) The laity need to assume a greater partnership in the preaching task. (3) The laity know something about good preaching and can enable pastors to become better preachers in a way that the seminary community and fellow pastors can not.

The following is the outline of the course.

Initial Preparation

1. Select a group of seven to nine laypersons who are insightful, compassionate, and articulate, and who intuitively understand both the gospel and the principles of oral communication.

2. Select a person who has skills as a group leader, who can create and facilitate group processes. This person will be one of the keys to the effectiveness of this enterprise, as he or she will be responsible for planning and leading the monthly meetings. This leader will work in close partnership with the pastor during all phases of this course.

3. Lay the groundwork for videotaping at least three of the preacher's Sunday sermons.

4. Transcribe from tape ten recent Sunday sermons. Don't edit these sermons, but leave them as pieces of "living oral communication." Make copies of these sermons for each participant.

5. Order this book, *Quest for Better Preaching,* for each participant.

Session 1: Setting the Goals

Preparation: Read *Quest for Better Preaching.*

Process: What can be done to improve the preaching within our congregation? Lay the groundwork for this two-year study. Overview of the sessions. Share initial reactions to *Quest for Better Preaching.*

Session 2: The Preacher as Person and Theologian

Preparation: Study *Quest for Better Preaching,* Chapters 3 and 4.

Process: Examination of pastor's personhood, prayer life, and theology as these qualities reflect themselves in the preaching.

Session 3: The Preacher as Textual Exegete and Interpreter

Preparation: Study *Quest for Better Preaching,* Chapter 5. Pastor gives samples of exegetical research which can be studied by the group.

Process: Pastor teaches in detail his process for exegeting text and preparing a sermon.

Session 4: Criticisms of the Preaching in Our Parish

Preparation: Study *Quest for Better Preaching,* Chapter 2. Examine carefully 10 recent sermons.

Process: Evaluation of the present preaching form and content in light of Chapter 2, the "Eleven Deadly Sins of Preaching."

Session 5: The Preacher's Use of a Central Message and Clear Outline

Preparation: Study *Quest for Better Preaching,* Chapter 2. Examination of 10 of the pastor's recent sermons for centrality of theme and clarity of outline.

Process: Discussion of the research done in preparation of this session.

Session 6: The Preacher's Use of SAIs

Preparation: Study *Quest for Better Preaching,* Chapters 8 and 9. Examination of 10 sermons for the preacher's use of stories, analogies, and images.

Process: Discussion of the research done in preparation for this session.

Session 7: The Preacher's Delivery and Language

Preparation: Study *Quest for Better Preaching,* Chapters 10 and 11. Study videotapes of the pastor's Sunday sermons.

Process: Reaction and discussion of the videotaped pastor's sermons.

Session 8: The Preacher's Reading

Process: Examine the pastor's reading styles and time given for it.

Homework: For summer reading, the pastor may want to read the recommended preaching textbooks which are listed in *Quest for Better Preaching.*

Session 9: The Preacher Listens to the Laity

Preparation: Pastors can benefit from "feedback" and "feed-in" groups. "Feedback" occurs when there is a discussion group that reacts to the sermon. "Feed-in" groups gather to study the biblical text for the sermon with the pastor in preparation for the sermon. Members of such a group study the text first individually and then together.

Process: Discussion of techniques for "feedback" and "feed-in" groups. If desirable, create such groups within the parish; after nine months, evaluate their effectiveness.

Session 10: The Preacher's Proclamation of the Gospel

Preparation: Study *Quest for Better Preaching,* Chapter 4. Examine several of the pastor's most recent sermons for the clarity of the gospel being proclaimed.

Process: Discussion of the research done in preparation for this section.

Session 11: The Preacher as Prophet

Preparation: Study *Quest for Better Preaching,* Chapter 6. Examine recent sermons that had social justice themes.

Process: Discussion of what it means for the pastor to preach and write about social issues.

Session 12: The Preacher's Source of Renewal—Seminars, Courses, Preaching Workshops, Third World Trips

Preparation: Examine possibilities for a pstor's educational leave.

Process: Discussion of more creative sources for renewal.

Homework: Plan more "exotic" educational encounters with preacher, especially a visit to the Third World.

Session 13: Variety of Forms—Storytelling

Preparation: Read examples of storytelling sermons from Jensen's *Telling the Story* (Minneapolis: Augsburg, 1980).

Process: Examination of the process of storytelling.

Homework: Do story sermons and evaluate them.

Session 14: Variety—Chancel Dramas

Preparation: Read a series of chancel dramas (e.g., *The Seven Deadly Sins* [Lima, Ohio: C. S. S. Publications, 1983]).

Process: Discussion of chancel dramas as a form for Sunday morning and Lenten services.

Homework: Plan a series of Lenten dramas or Sunday morning dramas.

Session 15: Variety—Group Dialogs

Preparation: Read samples of group dialog sermons and the section on group dialog in Chapter 12 of this book.

Process: Discussion of group dialog sermons.

Homework: Plan a group dialog sermon.

Session 16: Variety—Dialog Sermons

Preparation: Read samples of dialog sermons and the section on Dialog sermons in Chapter 12 of this book.

Process: Discussion of group dialog sermons.

Homework: Plan a dialog sermon.

Session 17: Variety—Films and Slides

Preparation: Read the section "Films/Slides with Commentary" in Chapter 12 of this book.

Process: Discussion of the use of films/slides in church.

Homework: Plan a sermon using films/slides.

Session 18: Variety—Children's Sermons

Preparation: Order books of children's sermons and examine them.

Process: Examination of children's sermons given in our church at the present time.

Session 19: Evaluation of This Two-year Process to attempt to make good preaching better in the life of the parish.

Such an outline is highly adaptable. All pastors will do it differently, picking and choosing what they want to use, or they will create their own course and design. The key is to retain maximum flexibility and creativity. (For additional resources and suggestions for group processes, contact Pastor Markquart, Grace Lutheran Church, 22975 24th Ave. So., Des Moines, WA 98188.)

I am convinced that any pastor who specifically and intentionally works on his or her preaching for 18 months with the help of honest and open laypersons who are willing to struggle with the pastor will discover that the preaching of that parish will grow in vitality. Some courage is required for a pastor to put his or her preaching on the line, but risk, courage, and exposure to honesty and faith are keys to growth and change. All of us can become better preachers of the gospel!

Notes

1. "Why Can't We Have Better Preaching?"

1. Helmut Thielicke, *The Trouble with the Church* (Grand Rapids: Baker, 1965), p. VII.
2. Cited by Elizabeth Achtemeier, *Creative Preaching* (Nashville: Abingdon, 1980), p. 9.
3. Edward F. Markquart, "Luther, the Preacher," unpublished manuscript, Grace Lutheran Church, Des Moines, Wash., 1980.
4. Reuel L. Howe, *Partners in Preaching* (New York: Seabury, 1967), p. 39 (emphasis added).
5. Paul E. Scherer, *For We Have This Treasure* (Grand Rapids: Baker, 1943), p. 22.
6. Phillips Brooks, *Lectures on Preaching* (Grand Rapids: Baker, 1969), pp. i, 159; also Arndt L. Halvorson, *Authentic Preaching* (Minneapolis: Augsburg, 1982), p. 102.

2. Criticisms of Preaching

1. Clyde E. Fant, *Preaching for Today* (New York: Harper and Row, 1975), pp. 1, 3.
2. Cited by Paul Harms, *Power from the Pulpit* (St. Louis: Concordia, 1980), p. 47.
3. Fred B. Craddock, *Overhearing the Gospel* (Nashville: Abingdon, 1978), p. 12.
4. Cited by Craddock, *Overhearing the Gospel,* p. 12.
5. Ibid., pp. 12-13, 19.
6. John Burke, O.P., ed., *A New Look at Preaching* (Wilmington, Del.: Michael Glazier, 1983), p. 17.
7. Walter J. Burghardt, S.J., "From Study to Proclamation," in *A New Look at Preaching,* p. 32.
8. Helmut Thielicke, *The Trouble with the Church* (Grand Rapids: Baker, 1965), p. 41.
9. Ibid., pp. 9-10.
10. Harms, *Power from the Pulpit,* p. 12.
11. Thielicke, *The Trouble with the Church,* p. 98.

12. John Stott, *Between Two Worlds* (Grand Rapids: Eerdmans, 1982), p. 83.

13. Charles L. Rice, "The Story of our Times," in Edmund A. Steimle, Morris J. Niedenthal, and Charles L. Rice, *Preaching the Story* (Philadelphia: Fortress, 1980), p. 58.

14. Harms, *Power from the Pulpit*, p. 47.

15. Fant, *Preaching for Today*, p. 3.

16. Ibid.

17. Cited by Harms, *Power from the Pulpit*, p. 30.

18. Fant, *Preaching for Today*, p. 6.

19. Ibid.

20. Edward F. Markquart, "Preaching Practices of American Lutheran Church Pastors," unpublished research, Grace Lutheran Church, Des Moines, Wash., 1979.

21. H. H. Farmer, *The Servant of the Word* (Philadelphia: Fortress, 1942), p. 71.

22. H. Grady Davis, *Design for Preaching* (Philadelphia: Fortress, 1958), p. 157.

23. Ibid., p. 158.

24. In *Preaching for Today*, p. 173.

25. Thielicke, *The Trouble with the Church*, pp. 65, 80.

26. Ibid., p. 67.

27. Ibid., p. 27.

28. Richard A. Jensen, *Telling the Story* (Minneapolis: Augsburg, 1982), p. 11.

29. Arndt L. Halvorson, *Authentic Preaching* (Minneapolis: Augsburg, 1982), p. 116.

30. Reuel L. Howe, *Partners in Preaching* (New York: Seabury, 1967), p. 28.

31. Lowell O. Erdahl, *Preaching for the People* (Nashville: Abingdon, 1976), p. 46.

32. Steimle, Niedenthal, and Rice, *Preaching the Story*, p. 10.

33. Phillips Brooks, *Lectures on Preaching* (Grand Rapids: Baker, 1969), p. 126.

34. H. Thielicke, *Encounter with Spurgeon* (Grand Rapids: Baker, 1977), p. 22.

35. Erdahl, *Preaching for the People*, pp. 48, 60.

36. *Luther's Works*, vol. 54: *Table Talk* (Philadelphia: Fortress, 1967), pp. 235-236.

37. Ibid., p. 383.
38. Ibid., pp. 383-384.
39. Fred W. Meuser, *Luther the Preacher* (Minneapolis: Augsburg, 1983), p. 53 (TR 3, 3421).
40. Martin Luther, "Treatise on Good Works," *Luther's Works*, vol. 44 (Philadelphia: Fortress, 1966), p. 22.
41. *Luther's Works*, vol. 54, p. 160.
42. Edward F. Markquart, "Luther, the Preacher," unpublished manuscript, Grace Lutheran Church, Des Moines, Wash., 1980.
43. Stott, *Between Two Worlds*, p. 147.
44. Fred B. Craddock, *Overhearing the Gospel*, p. 30.
45. Brooks, *Lectures on Preaching*, p. 6.
46. Fant, *Preaching for Today*, p. 162.
47. *Luther's Works*, vol. 54, p. 428.
48. In Thielicke, *Encounter with Spurgeon*, p. 193.
49. Fred B. Craddock, *As One without Authority* (Nashville: Abingdon, 1971), p. 100.
50. Thielicke, *The Trouble with the Church*, p. 52.
51. Howe, *Partners in Preaching*, p. 27.
52. Harms, *Power from the Pulpit*, p. 22.
53. Henry M. Mitchell, *The Recovery of Preaching* (San Francisco: Harper and Row, and Sevenoaks, Kent: Hodder & Stoughton, 1977), p. 40.
54. Ibid., p. 142.
55. Ibid., p. 41.
56. Ibid., p. 42.
57. Harms, *Power from the Pulpit*, p. 19.
58. William D. Thompson, "Editor's Foreword," in Justo L. Gonzalez and Catherine G. Gonzalez, *Liberation Preaching* (Nashville: Abingdon, 1980), p. 9.
59. Stott, *Between Two Worlds*, p. 315.
60. Elizabeth Achtemeier, *Creative Preaching* (Nashville: Abingdon, 1980), p. 58.
61. Brooks, *Lectures on Preaching*, p. 27.
62. Ibid., pp. 39, 46.
63. In Thielicke, *Encounter with Spurgeon*, p. 245.
64. Farmer, *The Servant of the Word*, p. 82.
65. Howe, *Partners in Preaching*, p. 29.
66. Karl Rahner, *The Renewal of Preaching* (New York: Paulist Press, 1968), p. 1.

67. Davis, *Design for Preaching*, p. 208.
68. Ibid., pp. 204-205.
69. Ibid., p. 208.
70. Fant, *Preaching for Today*, p. 29.
71. Howe, *Partners in Preaching*, p. 31.
72. Ibid., pp. 37-38.
73. Ibid., p. 27.
74. Steimle, Niedenthal, and Rice, *Preaching the Story*, p. 141.
75. Ibid., pp. 141-142.
76. Harms, *Power from the Pulpit*, p. 19.
77. Frederick Buechner, *Telling the Truth* (San Francisco: Harper and Row, 1977), p. 44.
78. Herman G. Stuempfle Jr., *Preaching Law and Gospel* (Philadelphia: Fortress, 1978), p. 34.
79. Davis, *Design for Preaching*, p. 239.
80. Mitchell, *The Recovery of Preaching*, p. 148.
81. Erdahl, *Preaching for the People*, p. 18.
82. Fant, *Preaching for Today*, p. 90.
83. Craddock, *Overhearing the Gospel*, pp. 28-29.
84. Fant, *Preaching for Today*, p. 8.
85. Craddock, *Overhearing the Gospel*, p. 93.
86. Leander E. Keck, *The Bible in the Pulpit* (Nashville: Abingdon, 1980), p. 100.
87. Cited by Davis, *Design for Preaching*, p. 106.
88. Keck, *The Bible in the Pulpit*, p. 102.
89. Ibid., 102-103.
90. Ibid., p. 104.
91. Stuempfle, *Preaching Law and Gospel*, p. 63.
92. Davis, *Design for Preaching*, pp. 133-134.
93. Keck, *The Bible in the Pulpit*, p. 105.
94. Cited by Achtemeier, *Creative Preaching*, p. 71.
95. Steimle, *Preaching the Story*, p. 172.
96. Davis, *Design for Preaching*, pp. 209-219.
97. Ibid., p. 217.
98. Keck, *The Bible in the Pulpit*, p. 15. (emphasis added)
99. Brooks, *Lectures on Preaching*, pp. 156-158.
100. Thielicke, *The Trouble with the Church*, p. 1.
101. Ibid., p. 81.
102. Thielicke, *Encounter with Spurgeon*, p. 7.

103. Howe, *Partners in Preaching*, pp. 37-38.
104. Stott, *Between Two Worlds*, p. 124.
105. Craddock, *Overhearing the Gospel*, p. 127.
106. Howe, *Partners in Preaching*, pp. 24, 37.
107. Brooks, *Lectures on Preaching*, p. 100.
108. Ibid., p. 159.
109. Ibid., pp. 100-101.
110. Ibid., p. 104.
111. Farmer, *The Servant of the Word*, p. 19.
112. Harms, *Power from the Pulpit*, p. 29.
113. Mitchell, *The Recovery of Preaching*, p. 50.
114. Howe, *Partners in Preaching*, p. 39.
115. Ibid., p. 36.

3. The Preacher as Person

1. Elizabeth Achtemeier, *Creative Preaching* (Nashville: Abingdon, 1980), p. 12.
2. Arndt L. Halvorson, *Authentic Preaching* (Minneapolis: Augsburg, 1982), p. 82.
3. Phillips Brooks, *Lectures on Preaching* (Grand Rapids: Baker, 1969), p. 5.
4. Clyde E. Fant, *Preaching for Today* (New York: Harper and Row, 1975), p. 59.
5. Both lists are cited by John W. Doberstein, *Minister's Prayer Book* (Philadelphia: Fortress, 1959), p. 422.
6. Brooks, *Lectures on Preaching* (Grand Rapids: Baker, 1969), p. 38.
7. Achtemeier, *Creative Preaching*, p. 38.
8. Ibid., p. 37.
9. Ibid., p. 36.
10. Ibid., p. 42.
11. Ibid., p. 43.
12. Halvorson, *Authentic Preaching*, p. 21.
13. Walter J. Burghardt, S.J., "From Study to Proclamation," in John Burke, O.P., ed., *A New Look at Preaching* (Wilmington: Michael Glazier, 1983), pp. 32-35.
14. Milo L. Brekke, Merton P. Strommen, and Dorothy L. Williams, *Ten Faces of Ministry* (Minneapolis: Augsburg, 1979), pp. 26ff.
15. Ibid., Appendix C.

16. Helmut Thielicke, *The Trouble with the Church* (Grand Rapids: Baker, 1965), p. 5.

17. Ibid., pp. 23-24.

18. John Stott, *Between Two Worlds* (Grand Rapids: Eerdmans, 1982), p. 268.

19. Thielicke, *The Trouble with the Church,* p. 18.

20. Stott, *Between Two Worlds,* p. 269.

21. Cited by Thielicke, *Encounter with Spurgeon* (Grand Rapids: Baker, 1977), pp. 102, 118, 95, 60.

22. Fred B. Craddock, *Overhearing the Gospel* (Nashville: Abingdon, 1978), pp. 51, 43, 28, 47, 43, 49.

23. Paul Harms, *Power in the Pulpit* (St. Louis: Concordia, 1980), pp. 8-9.

24. Stott, *Between Two Worlds,* p. 285.

25. Ibid., p. 283.

26. Paul E. Scherer, *For We Have This Treasure* (Grand Rapids: Baker, 1943), p. 205.

27. Brooks, *Lectures on Preaching,* p. 38.

28. Stott, *Between Two Worlds,* p. 286.

29. Ibid., p. 284.

30. Thielicke, *Encounter with Spurgeon,* pp. 80-82.

31. Acts 20:31; cf. vv. 19, 37. Cited by Stott, *Between Two Worlds,* p. 275.

32. Halvorson, *Authentic Preaching,* pp. 13ff.

33. Carol Ostrum, *Seattle Times,* 21 May 1983.

34. Scherer, *For We Have This Treasure,* p. 28.

35. Spurgeon, in Thielicke, *Encounter with Spurgeon,* p. 174.

36. Charles L. Rice in Edmund A. Steimle, Morris J. Niedenthal, and Charles L. Rice, *Preaching the Story* (Philadelphia: Fortress, 1980), pp. 23, 26.

37. Frederick Buechner, *Telling the Truth* (San Francisco: Harper and Row, 1977), p. 8.

38. Halvorson, *Authentic Preaching,* p. 33.

39. Fant, *Preaching for Today,* pp. 59-61.

40. Buechner, *Telling the Truth,* p. 40.

41. Fred Meuser, *Luther the Preacher* (Minneapolis: Augsburg, 1983), p. 40.

42. Stott, *Between Two Worlds,* p. 289.

43. P. 24.

44. Stott, *Between Two Worlds,* p. 287.
45. Ibid.
46. Ibid., pp. 287-289.
47. Fant, *Preaching for Today,* p. 72.
48. Ibid., p. 73.
49. Ibid., p. 74.
50. Brooks, *Lectures on Preaching,* pp. 41-42.
51. Ibid., p. 60.
52. Craddock, *Overhearing the Gospel,* p. 56.
53. Ibid., p. 128.
54. Achtemeier, *Creative Preaching,* p. 105.
55. H. H. Farmer, *The Servant of the Word* (Philadelphia: Fortress, 1942), p. 70.
56. Charles L. Rice, *Preaching the Story,* p. 62.
57. Craddock, *Overhearing the Gospel,* p. 55.
58. Lowell O. Erdahl, *Preaching for the People* (Nashville: Abingdon, 1976), p. 55.
59. Cited by Morris J. Niedenthal in *Preaching the Story,* p. 76.
60. Halvorson, *Authentic Preaching,* p. 33.
61. Harms, *Power from the Pulpit,* p. 10.
62. Brooks, *Lectures on Preaching,* pp. 51-52, 152.
63. Erdahl, *Preaching for the People,* p. 92.
64. Stott, *Between Two Worlds,* p. 328.

4. The Preacher as Theologian

1. Herman G. Stuempfle Jr., *Preaching Law and Gospel* (Philadelphia: Fortress, 1978), p. 12.
2. H. Thielicke, *Encounter with Spurgeon* (Grand Rapids: Baker, 1977), p. 190.
3. Leander E. Keck, *The Bible in the Pulpit* (Nashville: Abingdon, 1980), pp. 51, 53.
4. Arndt L. Halvorson, *Authentic Preaching* (Minneapolis: Augsburg, 1982), p. 142.
5. Paul Harms, *Power from the Pulpit* (St. Louis: Concordia, 1980), p. 10.
6. In *A Compend of Luther's Theology,* ed. Hugh T. Kerr (Philadelphia: Westminster, 1943), p. 147.
7. "Lectures on Galatians, 1535," *Luther's Works,* vol. 26 (St. Louis: Concordia, 1963), p. 6.

8. "The Twelfth Sunday after Trinity, 1531," *Luther's Works,* vol. 51 (Philadelphia: Fortress, 1959), p. 226.

9. Colin Morris, cited by John Stott, *Between Two Worlds* (Grand Rapids: Eerdmans, 1982), p. 312.

10. *Luther's Works,* vol. 51 (Philadelphia: Fortress, 1951), p. 227.

11. *Luther's Works,* vol. 36 (Philadelphia: Fortress, 1959), p. 116.

12. Frederick Buechner, *Telling the Truth* (San Francisco: Harper and Row, 1977), pp. 91-92.

13. Ibid.

14. Ibid., p. 92.

15. Ibid., p. 96.

16. Ibid., p. 97.

17. Ibid., p. 83.

18. Ibid., p. 7.

19. Ibid.

20. Stuempfle, *Preaching Law and Gospel,* pp. 40-41.

21. Fred W. Meuser, *Luther the Preacher* (Minneapolis: Augsburg, 1983), p. 16.

22. Cited by Thielicke, *Encounter with Spurgeon,* p. 50.

23. Ibid., p. 194.

24. Ibid., p. 189.

25. Paul E. Scherer, *For We Have This Treasure* (Grand Rapids: Baker, 1943), p. 18.

26. Clyde E. Fant, *Preaching for Today* (New York: Harper and Row, 1975), p. 14.

27. Phillips Brooks, *Lectures on Preaching* (Grand Rapids: Baker, 1969), p. 6.

28. H. Grady Davis, *Design for Preaching* (Philadelphia: Fortress, 1958), p. 108.

29. Stott, *Between Two Worlds,* p. 16.

30. H. H. Farmer, *The Servant of the Word* (Philadelphia: Fortress, 1942), p. 14.

31. Ibid., pp. 46-47.

32. Stott, *Between Two Worlds,* p. 17.

33. Ibid., pp. 124-125.

34. Stephen Ministries, 1325 Boland, St. Louis, MO 63117.

35. Stott, *Between Two Worlds,* pp. 123-124.

36. Meuser, *Luther the Preacher,* p. 25.

37. Fant, *Preaching for Today,* p. 14.

38. Stott, *Between Two Worlds,* pp. 16-17, 123-125.
39. Cited by Stott, p. 22.
40. Ibid.
41. Ibid.
42. Cited by Meuser, *Luther the Preacher,* p. 26 (see *Luther's Works,* vol. 39, p. 314).
43. Cited by Meuser, p. 39.
44. Cited by Meuser, p. 39.
45. Stott, *Between Two Worlds,* pp. 23-24.
46. Fant, *Preaching for Today,* p. 23.
47. Ibid.
48. Ibid.
49. Ibid., p. 22.
50. Farmer, *The Servant of the Word,* p. 3.
51. Halvorson, *Authentic Preaching,* p. 139.
52. Meuser, *Luther the Preacher,* p. 11.
53. Ibid., p. 12.
54. Gerhard Ebeling, *Luther: An Introduction to His Thought* (Philadelphia: Fortress, 1972), p. 65 (emphasis added).
55. Martin Luther, *Table Talk,* Luther's Works, vol. 54 (Philadelphia: Fortress, 1967), p. 213.
56. Martin Luther, "The Sacrament of the Body and Blood of Christ," in *Luther's Works,* vol. 36 (Philadelphia: Fortress, 1959), p. 340.
57. Martin Luther, "Psalm 51," *Luther's Works,* vol. 12 (St. Louis: Concordia), p. 363.
58. Clyde E. Fant, *Preaching for Today* (New York: Harper and Row, 1975), pp. 20-21.
59. Ibid., p. 22.
60. Farmer, *The Servant of the Word,* p. 15.
61. Cited by Fant, *Preaching for the People,* p. 21.
62. Stott, *Between Two Worlds,* p. 108.
63. Meuser, *Luther the Preacher,* p. 13.
64. Farmer, *The Servant of the Word,* pp. 15, 25, 38.
65. Ibid., pp. 38-39.
66. Fant, *Preaching for Today,* p. 29.
67. Brooks, *Lectures on Preaching,* p. 7.
68. Fred B. Craddock, *As One without Authority* (Nashville: Abingdon, 1971), p. 24.
69. Brooks, *Lectures on Preaching,* p. 14.

70. Ibid., p. 8.

71. Ibid., pp. 5, 6, 8, 14.

72. Halvorson, *Authentic Preaching,* p. 82.

73. Davis, *Design for Preaching,* pp. 203-304.

74. Fant, *Preaching for Today,* p. 107.

75. Elizabeth Achtemeier, *Creative Preaching* (Nashville: Abingdon, 1980), p. 12.

5. The Preacher as Textual Exegete and Interpreter

1. Cited from *Deutsche Messe* (1526) by H. Grady Davis, *Design for Preaching* (Philadelphia: Fortress, 1958), p. 120.

2. Ibid.

3. Leander E. Keck, *The Bible in the Pulpit* (Nashville: Abingdon, 1980), p. 120.

4. Cited by Keck, *The Bible in the Pulpit,* p. 19.

5. Ibid., pp. 32, 39.

6. Clyde E. Fant, *Preaching for Today* (New York: Harper and Row, 1975), p. 43.

7. Fred B. Craddock, *As One without Authority* (Nashville: Abingdon, 1971), p. 43.

8. Arndt L. Halvorson, *Authentic Preaching* (Minneapolis: Augsburg, 1982), pp. 49-50.

9. Paul Harms, *Power from the Pulpit* (St. Louis: Concordia, 1980), p. 17.

10. Elizabeth Achtemeier, *Creative Preaching* (Nashville: Abingdon, 1980), p. 18.

11. Keck, *The Bible in the Pulpit,* p. 61.

12. Craddock, *As One without Authority,* p. 129.

13. Reuel L. Howe, *Partners in Preaching* (New York: Seabury, 1967), p. 52.

14. Helmut Thielicke, *The Trouble with the Church* (Grand Rapids: Baker, 1965), p. 21.

15. Achtemeier, *Creative Preaching,* p. 58 (emphasis added).

16. Harms, *Power from the Pulpit,* p. 18.

17. Walter A. Burghardt, s.j. "From Study to Proclamation," in *A New Look at Preaching,* ed. John Burke, o.p. (Wilmington: Michael Glazier, 1983), p. 40.

18. Elisabeth Schussler Fiorenza, "Reponse," in *A New Look at Preaching* (Wilmington: Michael Glazier, 1983), pp. 54-55.

19. Ibid., p. 55.
20. Halvorson, *Authentic Preaching,* pp. 54, 56, 57.
21. Achtemeier, *Creative Preaching,* p. 38.
22. John Stott, *Between Two Worlds* (Grand Rapids: Eerdmans, 1982), p. 201.
23. *Faith and Ferment* (Minneapolis: Augsburg, 1983), p. 26.
24. Cited by Burghardt in *A New Look at Preaching,* p. 29.
25. Stott, *Between Two Worlds,* p. 184.
26. Ibid.
27. Ibid., p. 180.
28. Ibid., p. 213.
29. Keck, *The Bible in the Pulpit,* p. 107.
30. Ibid., pp. 54, 61.
31. Ronald J. Allen and Thomas J. Herin, "Moving from the Story to Our Story," in E. Steimle, M. Niedenthal, and C. Rice, *Preaching the Story* (Philadelphia: Fortress, 1980), p. 155.
32. Halvorson, *Authentic Preaching,* p. 48.
33. Ibid., p. 60.
34. Craddock, *As One without Authority,* p. 98.
35. Halvorson, *Authentic Preaching,* p. 52.
36. H. H. Farmer, *The Servant of the Word* (Philadelphia: Fortress, 1942), p. 61.
37. Fred W. Meuser, *Luther the Preacher* (Minneapolis: Augsburg, 1983), p. 47.
38. Achtemeier, *Creative Preaching,* p. 47.
39. Thielicke, *The Trouble with the Church,* pp. 63-65.
40. Allen and Herin in *Preaching the Story,* pp. 158-159.
41. Craddock, *As One without Authority,* p. 100.
42. Halvorson, *Authentic Preaching,* p. 70.
43. Jowett, cited by Davis, *Design for Preaching,* p. 37.
44. Ibid., pp. 46-47.
45. Achtemeier, *Creative Preaching,* pp. 61-63.
46. Fant, *Preaching for Today,* p. 103.
47. Ibid., p. 100.
48. Ibid., pp. 99, 106.
49. Stott, *Between Two Worlds,* p. 126.
50. Cited by Meuser, *Luther the Preacher,* p. 42.
51. Davis, *Design for Preaching,* p. 162.
52. Fant, *Preaching for Today,* p. 19.

53. Ibid.
54. Meuser, *Luther the Preacher*, p. 35.
55. Charles R. Brown, cited by Fant, *Preaching for Today*, p. 158.
56. Thielicke, *The Trouble with the Church*, p. 50.
57. Halvorson, *Authentic Preaching*, p. 179.
58. Davis, *Design for Preaching*, p. 204.
59. Thielicke, *The Trouble with the Church*, p. x.
60. Lowell O. Erdahl, *Preaching for the People* (Nashville: Abingdon, 1976), p. 71 (emphasis added).
61. Cited by Stott, *Between Two Worlds*, p. 220.
62. Ibid.
63. Cited by Thielicke, *Encounter with Spurgeon* (Grand Rapids: Baker, 1977), p. 116.
64. Cited by Stott, *Between Two Worlds*, p. 220.
65. Fant, *Preaching for Today*, p. 29.
66. Stott, *Between Two Worlds*, p. 150.
67. Craddock, *As One without Authority*, pp. 120-121.
68. Davis, *Design for Preaching*, pp. 204, 208.
69. Amos N. Wilder, *Early Christian Rhetoric* (Cambridge: Harvard University, 1974), p. 122.
70. Thielicke, *The Trouble with the Church*, p. 40.
71. Ibid., p. 41.
72. Keck, *The Bible in the Pulpit*, p. 122.
73. John Burke, O.P., "Introduction," in *A New Look at Preaching* (Wilmington: Michael Glazier, 1983), p. 13.
74. Farmer, *The Servant of the Word*, p. 85; emphasis added.
75. Ibid., p. 90.
76. Craddock, *As One without Authority*, p. 115.

6. The Preacher as Prophet

1. Charles L. Rice, in Edmund A. Steimle, Morris J. Niedenthal, and Charles L. Rice, *Preaching the Story* (Philadelphia: Fortress, 1980), p. 56.
2. Ibid.
3. Ibid., pp. 58, 70.
4. Steimle, in *Preaching the Story*, p. 136.
5. Ibid.
6. Rice, in *Preaching the Story*, p. 61.

7. Fred B. Craddock, *Overhearing the Gospel* (Nashville: Abingdon, 1978), p. 33.

8. Ibid., pp. 28, 33.

9. Ibid., p. 34.

10. Ibid., p. 36.

11. H. H. Farmer, *The Servant of the Word* (Philadelphia: Fortress, 1942), p. 84.

12. Ibid., p. 96.

13. Ibid., p. 98.

14. Robert Schuller, *Self-Esteem: The New Reformation* (Waco, Texas: Word Books, 1982).

15. Ibid.

16. Cited by Charles L. Rice in *Preaching the Story,* p. 69.

17. Dean R. Hoge, *Converts, Dropouts, Returnees* (New York: Pilgrim Press, 1981).

18. Farmer, *The Servant of the Word,* p. 101.

19. Jacobo Timerman, *Prisoner without a Name, Cell without a Number* (New York: Vintage Books, 1982), pp. 140-141.

20. Helmut Thielicke, *The Trouble with the Church* (Grand Rapids: Baker, 1965), p. 12.

21. Phillips Brooks, *Lectures on Preaching* (Grand Rapids: Baker, 1969), p. 136.

22. Ibid., pp. 141-142.

23. Clyde E. Fant, *Preaching for Today* (New York: Harper and Row, 1975), p. 104.

24. Steimle, in *Preaching the Story,* p. 168.

25. Brooks, *Lectures on Preaching,* p. 188.

26. *Luther's Works,* vol. 21 (St. Louis: Concordia, 1956), p. 57.

27. John W. Doberstein, *Minister's Prayer Book* (Philadelphia: Fortress, 1959), p. 422.

28. Brooks, *Lectures on Preaching,* p. 56.

29. Thielicke, *The Trouble with the Church,* p. 111.

30. Brooks, *Lectures on Preaching,* p. 56.

31. Lowell O. Erdahl, *Preaching for the People* (Nashville: Abingdon, 1976), p. 65.

32. Leander E. Keck, *The Bible in the Pulpit* (Nashville: Abingdon, 1980), pp. 199-200.

33. Henry W. Mitchell, *The Recovery of Preaching* (San Francisco: Harper and Row and Sevenoaks, Kent: Hodder & Stoughton, 1977), p. 26.

34. Herman G. Stuempfle Jr., *Preaching Law and Gospel* (Philadelphia: Fortress, 1978), p. 28.

35. Steimle, in *Preaching the Story,* p. 41.

36. Norman Neaves, in *Preaching the Story,* p. 113.

37. Erdahl, *Preaching for the People,* p. 65.

38. Elizabeth Achtemeier, *Creative Preaching* (Nashville: Abingdon, 1980), p. 108.

39. Phillips Brooks, *Lectures on Preaching,* pp. 195-196.

40. Stuempfle, *Preaching Law and Gospel,* p. 73.

41. Justo L. Gonzalez and Catherine Gonzalez, *Liberation Preaching* (Nashville: Abingdon, 1980), p. 38.

42. Ibid., p. 69.

43. Ibid., p. 102.

7. The Preacher as Storyteller

1. Fred B. Craddock, *Overhearing the Gospel* (Nashville: Abingdon, 1978), p. 19.

2. H. Grady Davis, *Design for Preaching* (Philadelphia: Fortress, 1958), p. 1.

3. Ibid., p. 5.

4. Craddock, *Overhearing the Gospel,* p. 139.

5. Davis, *Design for Preaching,* p. 2.

6. Ibid., pp. 10-11.

7. Craddock, *Overhearing the Gospel,* pp. 10, 16.

8. Fred B. Craddock, *As One without Authority* (Nashville: Abingdon, 1971), p. 52.

9. Davis, *Design for Preaching,* p. 12.

10. Clyde E. Fant, *Preaching for Today* (New York: Harper and Row, 1975), p. 111.

11. Amos N. Wilder, *Early Christian Rhetoric* (Cambridge: Harvard University Press, 1974), p. 71.

12. Craddock, *Overhearing the Gospel,* p. 139.

13. Davis, *Design for Preaching,* p. 157.

14. Elizabeth Achtemeier, *Creative Preaching* (Nashville: Abingdon, 1980), p. 45.

15. Henry M. Mitchell, *The Recovery of Preaching* (San Francisco: Harper and Row and Sevenoaks, Kent: Hodder & Stoughton, 1977), p. 155.

16. Frederick Buechner, *Telling the Truth* (San Francisco: Harper and Row, 1977), p. 62.
17. Craddock, *Overhearing the Gospel,* p. 134.
18. Wilder, *Early Christian Rhetoric,* p. 73.
19. Ibid., p. 86.
20. Ibid., p. 74.
21. Edmund A. Steimle, in Steimle, Morris J. Niedenthal, and Charles L. Rice, *Preaching the Story* (Philadelphia: Fortress, 1980), p. 166.
22. Reuel L. Howe, *Partners in Preaching* (New York: Seabury, 1967), p. 77.
23. Paul Harms, *Power from the Pulpit* (St. Louis: Concordia, 1980), p. 16.
24. Niedenthal, in *Preaching the Story,* p. 108.
25. Mitchell, *The Recovery of Preaching,* p. 150.
26. Wilder, *Early Christian Rhetoric,* p. 55.
27. Ibid., p. 73.
28. Steimle, in *Preaching the Story,* pp. 13-15, 80.
29. Buechner, *Telling the Truth,* p. 9.
30. Cited by Mitchell, *Recovery of Preaching,* pp. 93-95.
31. Ibid., p. 156.
32. Wilder, *Early Christian Rhetoric,* p. 55.
33. Compare the story of Sister Ingeborg in Mary R. Schramm, *Gifts of Grace* (Minneapolis: Augsburg, 1982), p. 30.

8. The Importance of Stories, Analogies, and Images (SAIs)

1. John Stott, *Between Two Worlds* (Grand Rapids: Eerdmans, 1982), p. 241.
2. H. Grady Davis, *Design for Preaching* (Philadelphia: Fortress, 1958), p. 5.
3. Fred B. Craddock, *Overhearing the Gospel* (Nashville: Abingdon, 1978), p. 133.
4. Elizabeth Achtemeier, *Creative Preaching* (Nashville: Abingdon, 1980), p. 46.
5. Phillips Brooks, *Lectures on Preaching* (Grand Rapids: Baker, 1969), p. 110.
6. Henry M. Mitchell, *The Recovery of Preaching* (San Francisco: Harper and Row and Sevenoaks, Kent: Hodder & Stoughton, 1977), pp. 145-158.

7. Helmut Thielicke, *The Trouble with the Church* (Grand Rapids: Baker, 1965), p. 22.
8. Fred B. Craddock, *As One without Authority* (Nashville: Abingdon, 1971), p. 85.
9. Richard A. Jensen, *Telling the Story* (Minneapolis: Augsburg, 1980), p. 119.
10. Adapted from the citation in Paul Harms, *Power from the Pulpit* (St. Louis: Concordia, 1980), p. 31.
11. Arndt L. Halvorson, *Authentic Preaching* (Minneapolis: Augsburg, 1982), p. 116.
12. Cited by Craddock, *Overhearing the Gospel,* p. 143.
13. Ibid., pp. 104ff., 143.
14. Cited by Edmund A. Steimle, in Steimle, M. J. Niedenthal, and Charles L. Rice, *Preaching the Story* (Philadelphia: Fortress, 1980), p. 173.
15. Martin Luther, "Eight Sermons at Wittenberg," *Luther's Works,* vol. 51 (Philadelphia: Fortress, 1959), p. 76.
16. Cited by Paul Althaus, *The Theology of Martin Luther* (Philadelphia: Fortress, 1966), p. 39, from WA 10/III, p. 260.
17. Reuel L. Howe, *Partners in Preaching* (New York: Seabury, 1967), pp. 32-33.

9. Characteristics of Good SAIs

1. Amos N. Wilder, *Early Christian Rhetoric* (Cambridge: Harvard University Press, 1974), p. 84.
2. Frederick Buechner, *Telling the Truth* (San Francisco: Harper and Row, 1977), pp. 63, 69.
3. Wilder, *Early Christian Rhetoric* (1974), p. 85.
4. Elizabeth Achtemeier, *Creative Preaching* (Nashville: Abingdon, 1980), p. 99.
5. Ibid.
6. Achtemeier, *Creative Preaching,* p. 107.
7. Fred B. Craddock, *As One without Authority* (Nashville: Abingdon, 1971), pp. 58ff.
8. John Stott, *Between Two Worlds* (Grand Rapids: Eerdmans, 1982), pp. 70, 76.
9. Ibid., p. 292.

10. Cited by Niedenthal in E. Steimle, M. Niedenthal, and C. Rice, *Preaching the Story* (Philadelphia: Fortress, 1980), p. 76.

11. See Fred B. Craddock, *Overhearing the Gospel* (Nashville: Abingdon, 1978), p. 136.

12. Ibid., p. 137.

13. Stott, *Between Two Worlds*, p. 239.

14. Arndt L. Halvorson, *Authentic Preaching* (Minneapolis: Augsburg, 1982), p. 119.

15. Ibid., p. 51.

16. Craddock, *As One without Authority*, pp. 80, 86, 90.

17. Ernest Campbell, lectures at Pacific Lutheran University, Tacoma, Washington, July 1984.

18. Ibid.

19. Halvorson, *Authentic Preaching*, p. 51.

20. Achtemeier, *Creative Preaching*, p. 30.

21. Cited by H. Thielicke, *Encounter with Spurgeon* (Grand Rapids: Baker, 1977), p. 242.

22. H. H. Farmer, *The Servant of the Word* (Philadelphia: Fortress, 1942), pp. 66-67; emphasis added.

23. Lowell O. Erdahl, *Preaching for the People* (Nashville: Abingdon, 1976), pp. 72-73.

24. Neaves, in *Preaching for the People*, p. 111.

25. Phillips Brooks, *Lectures on Preaching* (Grand Rapids: Baker, 1969), pp. 75-77.

26. Craddock, *As One without Authority*, p. 59.

27. Ibid., p. 92.

28. Reuel L. Howe, *Partners in Preaching* (New York: Seabury, 1967), p. 82.

29. Ibid., p. 38.

30. Halvorson, *Authentic Preaching*, p. 116.

31. Craddock, *As One without Authority*, p. 59.

32. Cited by Halvorson, *Authentic Preaching*, p. 119.

33. Ibid.

34. Edward F. Markquart, "Preaching Practices of American Lutheran Church Pastors," unpublished manuscript, 1979, Grace Lutheran Church, Des Moines, Washington.

35. Stott, *Between Two Worlds*, pp. 194ff.

36. Paul E. Scherer, *For We Have This Treasure* (Grand Rapids: Baker, 1943), p. 147.

37. Brooks, *Lectures on Preaching,* p. 104.
38. Neaves, in *Preaching the Story,* pp. 110-111.
39. H. Thielicke, *The Trouble with the Church* (Grand Rapids: Baker, 1965), p. 22.
40. Walter J. Burghardt, s.j., "From Study to Proclamation," in *A New Look at Preaching* (Wilmington: Michael Glazier, 1983), p. 41.
41. Craddock, *As One without Authority,* p. 79.

10. The Importance of Language

1. Cited by Gerhard Ebeling, *Luther: An Introduction to His Thought* (Philadelphia: Fortress, 1972), p. 30.
2. H. H. Farmer, *The Servant of the Word* (Philadelphia: Fortress, 1942), p. 29.
3. Elizabeth Achtemeier, *Creative Preaching* (Nashville: Abingdon, 1980), p. 22.
4. Frederick Buechner, *Telling the Truth* (San Francisco: Harper and Row, 1977), pp. 19-23.
5. Ibid., p. 40.
6. Cited by H. Thielicke, *Encounter with Spurgeon* (Grand Rapids: Baker, 1977), p. 182.
7. Amos N. Wilder, *Early Christian Rhetoric* (Cambridge: Harvard University Press, 1974), pp. 5, 17-20.
8. Robert Goeser, Pacific Lutheran Theological Seminary, unpublished class lectures on Luther, July 1980.
9. John T. Waterman, *A History of the German Language* (Seattle: University of Washington Press, 1966), p. 136.
10. Ebeling, *Luther: An Introduction to His Thought,* pp. 28-29.
11. Martin Luther, "Against Latamus," *Luther's Works,* vol. 32 (Philadelphia: Fortress, 1958), pp. 165, 167, 195-201.
12. Martin Luther, "On Translating: An Open Letter," *Luther's Works,* vol. 5 (St. Louis: Concordia, 1968), p. 15.
13. Edward F. Markquart, "Luther, the Preacher," unpublished manuscript, 1980, Grace Lutheran Church, Des Moines, Washington.
14. Clyde E. Fant, *Preaching for Today* (New York: Harper and Row, 1975), p. 171.
15. Henry M. Mitchell, *The Recovery of Preaching* (San Francisco: Harper and Row and Sevenoaks, Kent: Hodder & Stoughton, 1977), pp. 96ff.
16. Ibid., p. 100.

17. Edmund A. Steimle, in Steimle, Morris J. Niedenthal, and Charles L. Rice, *Preaching the Story* (Philadelphia: Fortress, 1980), pp. 166-167.
18. Thielicke, *The Trouble with the Church* (Grand Rapids: Baker, 1965), pp. 39-40, 95.
19. Paul Harms, *Power from the Pulpit* (St. Louis: Concordia, 1980), p. 20.
20. Buechner, *Telling the Truth*, p. 24.
21. Edward F. Markquart, "Luther, the Preacher."
22. Phillips Brooks, *Lectures on Preaching* (Grand Rapids: Baker, 1969), p. 23.
23. Ibid., pp. 111-112.
24. Achtemeier, *Creative Preaching*, p. 104.
25. *Table Talk, Luther's Works*, vol. 54 (Philadelphia: Fortress, 1967), pp. 157-158.
26. Fred B. Craddock, *As One without Authority* (Nashville: Abingdon, 1971), p. 93.
27. Ibid., p. 60.
28. Harms, *Power from the Pulpit*, p. 23.
29. Brooks, *Lectures on Preaching*, p. 57.
30. Buechner, *Telling the Truth*, p. 60.
31. Achtemeier, *Creative Preaching*, p. 17.
32. Ibid., pp. 30-31.
33. Ibid., p. 22.
34. Ibid., p. 33.
35. Niedenthal, in *Preaching the Story*, p. 84.
36. Achtemeier, *Creative Preaching*, pp. 22, 24, 26.
37. Craddock, *As One without Authority*, p. 78.
38. Cited by Harms, *Power from the Pulpit*, p. 26.

11. The Importance of "Living Speech"

1. Amos N. Wilder, *Early Christian Rhetoric* (Cambridge: Harvard University, 1974), p. 13, citing John 8:8.
2. Ibid.
3. Ibid., p. 14.
4. Ibid., pp. 40, 42.
5. Ibid., p. 40.
6. Cited by Fred W. Meuser, *Luther the Preacher* (Minneapolis: Augsburg, 1983), p. 41.

7. Cited by Richard A. Jensen, *Telling the Story* (Minneapolis: Augsburg, 1982), pp. 73f.

8. Herman G. Stuempfle Jr., *Preaching Law and Gospel* (Philadelphia: Fortress, 1978), p. 17.

9. John W. Doberstein, "Preface," *Luther's Works: Sermons I,* vol. 51 (Philadelphia: Fortress, 1959), p. XVI.

10. Clyde E. Fant, *Preaching for Today* (New York: Harper and Row, 1975), p. 112.

11. Phillips Brooks, *Lectures on Preaching* (Grand Rapids: Baker, 1969, p. 12.

12. Ibid., p. 108.

13. Lowell O. Erdahl, *Preaching for the People* (Nashville: Abingdon, 1978), p. 57.

14. Fant, *Preaching for Today,* pp. 114-115.

15. Jensen, *Telling the Story,* p. 73.

16. H. Grady Davis, *Design for Preaching* (Philadelphia: Fortress, 1958), pp. 165ff.

17. Henry M. Mitchell, *The Recovery of Preaching* (San Francisco: Harper and Row and Sevenoaks, Kent: Hodder & Stoughton, 1977), pp. 1, 8.

18. H. H. Farmer, *The Servant of the Word* (Philadelphia: Fortress, 1942), p. 19.

19. *Table Talk, Luther's Works,* vol. 54 (Philadelphia: Fortress, 1967), p. 383.

20. Davis, *Design for Preaching,* p. 36.

21. Ibid., p. 168.

22. "Martin Luther King Jr.: The Legacy of a Dream."

23. Elizabeth Achtemeier, *Creative Preaching* (Nashville: Abingdon, 1980), p. 17.

24. Paul Harms, *Power from the Pulpit* (St. Louis: Concordia, 1980), p. 34.

25. Ibid., p. 32.

26. Fant, *Preaching for Today,* p. 68.

27. Harms, *Power from the Pulpit,* p. 37.

28. Cited by Mitchell, *The Recovery of Preaching,* pp. 22-23.

29. Ibid., p. 156.

30. Wilder, *Early Christian Rhetoric,* p. 89.

12. The Importance of Variety of Forms

1. Amos N. Wilder, *Early Christian Rhetoric* (Cambridge: Harvard University Press, 1974), p. 120.
2. Leander E. Keck, *The Bible in the Pulpit* (Nashville: Abingdon, 1980), pp. 65-66.
3. H. Grady Davis, *Design for Preaching* (Philadelphia: Fortress, 1958), p. 9.
4. Fred B. Craddock, *As One without Authority* (Nashville: Abingdon, 1971), p. 45.
5. Clyde E. Fant, *Preaching for Today* (New York: Harper and Row, 1975), p. 110.
6. Elizabeth Achtemeier, *Creative Preaching* (Nashville: Abingdon, 1980), p. 76.
7. Ibid., p. 85.
8. Keith Sanderson, Management Consultant, Chevron Corporation, member of Grace Lutheran Church, Des Moines, Washington.
9. Richard A. Jensen, *Telling the Story* (Minneapolis: Augsburg, 1980), pp. 162ff.